TAKE
CONTROL

TAKE
CONTROL

Michael Janke

MADISON BOOKS

Lanham • New York • Oxford

Published by Madison Books
4720 Boston Way
Lanham, Maryland 20706

12 Hid's Copse Road
Cumnor Hill, Oxford OX2 9JJ, England

Distributed by National Book Network

Illustrations by Lynne Morgan based on original drawings
by Melissa Edgerly-Shultz

Library of Congress Cataloging-in-Publication Data

Janke, Michael A., 1968–
    Take control : master the art of self-discipline and change your life
    forever / Michael A. Janke.
        p.   cm.
    Includes index.
    ISBN 1-57833-172-X (hardcover : alk. paper)
    1. Self-control. 2. Self-management (Psychology). I. Title

BF632.J36 2000
158.1—dc21   00-058223

⊗™ The paper used in this publication meets the minimum requirements of
American National Standard for Information Sciences—Permanence of
Paper for Printed Library Materials, ANSI/NISO Z39.48—1992.
Manufactured in the United States of America.

CONTENTS

PREFACE

Every human being has the potential to take control of their life. We all have the power to achieve great things and live a life full of pleasure, accomplishment, and purpose. For most people, this power is sleeping deep inside, waiting to be discovered and unleashed. This book is the result of my burning desire to understand what makes some people experience all of the achievement, success, health, and happiness that life has to offer, while others simply undergo the average life. As a Navy SEAL, consultant, and speaker, I have traveled to the most remote corners of the world to learn the information and techniques found here in these pages. Most of the information found in this book comes from elite commando units, ancient cultures and philosophy, and modern performance strategies.

I have designed this book to help anyone—from the stay-at-home parent to the corporate business manager to the college student—anyone who would like to gain control of their lives, improve their efficiency, and break free from the prison of average living. This book is a practical guide designed to dramatically improve your performance and is based upon years of study, training, and practical application, instead of just theory and talk. You will find useful exercises, tips, and illustrations to help guide you through the process of taking control. Although we live in an incredible age of prosperity and technological wonder, our lives have become so hectic, stressful, and out of balance that, to most people, control seems like a distant dream. It is imperative to understand that the first step to gaining control of your life is to have the desire to change. My intent is to take you on a journey of self-discovery and to give you the tools to dramatically improve your performance in areas of life.

I am going to walk side-by-side with you in this journey through the process of mastering discipline and achieving a life of control. Each chapter is a small step in the journey to a life of success, happiness, and control. My role as your personal coach is to help you discover the hidden path that allows you to control the circumstances in your life and take charge of your destiny. Each of our paths is different in length and direction. It is up to you to determine the start and finish lines. Make today your starting line by using this book to break out of your comfort zone and take control of your life.

1

THE POWER OF CONTROL

Man is still responsible. He must turn the alloy of modern experience into the steel of mastery and character. His success lies not with the stars, but with himself. He must carry on the fight of self-correction and discipline.
—Frank Curtis Williams

In today's world, having a stress-filled daily schedule is normal to most people. It seems that we have a million things to do and only a short time in which to do them. Most people want to improve their health, relationship, financial state, and quality of life, but fail to realize that the answer lies within. The only answer to gaining control of our lives in this day and age is harnessing the power of self-discipline, building your self-esteem, and realizing you have the power of choice.

To see this ability in ourselves and live by these means is very difficult for many people. It is so easy, so enticing, so utterly pleasurable to let our minds toil and hide in everyday tasks. We decide to shut our eyes to the possibility of having more or leading a higher quality life, and we settle on the reality of our day-to-day conditions and circumstances. It is the plight of the everyday lamb, who fails to notice that inside lurks a predator of success. For some people, it takes nothing more than reading and understanding this concept, and for others it takes much more.

Thus begins your first step in a long journey. Throughout this book you will learn many powerful techniques to help you understand and develop the discipline and control that is fast asleep inside you, waiting to be unleashed and experienced. You must understand that simply wanting something is not enough—you must define, plan, focus, and schedule specific actions that you will take to have what you desire. The amazing power of control can alter your life. By simply understanding the process and forces at work in the human body and mind, you will have the greatest chance of success in your quest for self-discipline. Use the powerful techniques that you will learn in this book to prepare a personal battle plan for achieving your desires, wants, and goals.

A NEED FOR PERSONAL DISCIPLINE

Many times throughout my career as a Navy SEAL, I have come across circumstances where personal discipline meant life or death. One of those times was deep in the Amazon jungles of Peru. As a SEAL Team sniper, I found myself living in a small native Indian fishing village on the banks of the Amazon River. I was there working with a handful of Peruvian Special Forces snipers on advanced jungle-warfare tactics. We had set up our small camp in the confines of the fishing village and were warmly received by the local people. These people give new meaning to the terms resourcefulness and resolve. I have always believed that if every American teenager had the opportunity to spend just a few days with these people, they would have such a great sense of appreciation for the comforts we enjoy that they would never look at life the same way again.

One morning I accompanied a hunting party on a three-day trip to bring back food. We loaded into tiny hand-hewed canoes called "cuyukas" and began the 12-hour paddle up the Amazon to camp in the heart of their fishing and hunting grounds. After we set up our primitive camp, the older men slowly waded waist-deep into the shaded part of the inlet and the younger men moved out into the sun-drenched area. The younger men, who had to deal with the strong current, were immediately surrounded by hordes of mosquitoes, flies, and bees. I watched the older men spear fish after fish and the younger men struggle to stay still in the current and deal with the massive amount of flying insects. As I grabbed my spear and headed toward the older men, who obviously had the better deal, one of the elders looked up and waved for me to join the younger men. To the amusement of the older men, I immediately began swatting the thousands of flying bugs now making a meal out of me while floundering around in the strong current.

Since I considered myself somewhat of a logical man, I quickly made my way to the comfort of the shaded area and let out a big sigh of relief. After the laughter had died down, one of the Peruvian Special Forces soldiers told me that the younger men were made to fish this way in order to build their discipline and concentration. This ancient tradition was in fact a training exercise for the younger men. Later that evening, I noticed that the younger men slept on the ground while the elders slept comfortably in hammocks strung from the trees. Finally, after several days of observing what seemed to be useless torture, I asked one of the elders to explain the purpose behind these ancient ways. He told me that the entire village depended upon the men's hunting and fishing skills and without the ability to stay disciplined no matter the distraction, the village would go hungry. He went on to explain that if a man could stand still and spear fish in a current with thousands of bugs eating him, then he had mastered his weaknesses and would be a good provider during lean times.

To most people, this way of life may sound brutal or inhuman, but to these people personal discipline and self-control is the difference between life and death. I have come to understand that, in our society, the ability of a person to take control of their actions, thoughts, and words is the difference between success and failure, happiness and depression, and health and sickness. The good news is that we don't have to endure hordes of biting bugs or meditate for hours on end to build self-discipline and take control of our lives. The bad news is that we live in a society where instant gratification, comfort, and overindulgence reign supreme. It's not easy to gain control of our lives when our senses are so bombarded with images, words, and ideas about having everything all the time. It's not easy to control our health when fast-food restaurants occupy every street corner or control our behavior in a society that lives for entertainment.

Today, everybody seems perplexed as to why young children are gunning down their classmates in school, when 75% of the television shows they watch and video games they play are filled with murder, sex, violence, drugs, and fantasy. They grow up in a society where seven out of ten marriages end in divorce and where concepts like honor, integrity, and discipline have been replaced by money, freedom of expression, and overindulgence. Each year we continue to build new prisons to accommodate the overwhelming number of people who have lost the battle of personal control. We have become so inundated by the concept of wealth that our low-income families are spending more money on the lottery than on educating their children. Don't get me wrong; we live in the greatest society this planet has ever seen and it is an absolutely exciting time to be alive, but now more than ever, we need to develop a sense of control.

DEFINING SELF-DISCIPLINE

Throughout history, successful people have had one obvious thing in common: self-discipline. High achievers are always willing to do things that average humans are unwilling to do. But how does one define self-discipline? According to *Webster's Dictionary,* discipline is defined as:

> Training that corrects, molds or perfects; Control gained by obedience or training; To train or develop by the exercise of self-control; A system of rules governing conduct.

From this we can gather that self-discipline is:

> A personal system of rules that govern our individual words, thoughts, and actions. A personal system of training that establishes self-control and corrects, molds, and perfects our daily performance.

Self-discipline is the ability to regulate your conduct by principle, persistence, and sound judgment rather than by desire or social acceptance. The achievement of anything of value requires such discipline. The disciplined person sets goals. He or she is living a life of self-discipline and control for the purpose of reaching his or her daily, monthly, yearly, and lifelong goals. Many people don't set daily goals, they just live from day to day and complain about how unfair life is. The self-disciplined person moves deliberately each day toward something specific. What are your everyday and lifelong goals?

Self-discipline is not related to punishment. It is pure, sustained self-control. From recorded history, self-discipline has been responsible for the improvement of all mankind. Self-discipline has enabled scholars to discover breakthroughs in medicine, chemistry, physics, computers, and all other fields. Self-discipline has empowered warriors with the ability to fight against oppression and for freedom. It has blessed artists, writers, composers, and musicians with the persistence to complete beautiful works of art. It has elevated athletes to the top of their sports. It has allowed average men and women to overcome tremendous obstacles in their personal journeys to happiness, wealth, and success. It builds character, self-esteem, morals, courage, and honor in everyday people.

We cannot expect success and true happiness without building each aspect of our lives with self-discipline, control, and integrity. No one can have anything of lasting value without personal discipline. Self-discipline is the backbone of a successful, happy, and long life. Personal discipline brings prosperity, strong character, and freedom into our lives.

It is through self-discipline that we set an example for our children, spouses, coworkers, and all others to see and admire. It is the essence of our character and the result of our thoughts, actions, and words. Learning effective discipline can set you free and reward you beyond your wildest dreams. At one time or another in your life, you have probably experienced the freedom and pride that comes from self-discipline. When you inject discipline, self-control, and persistence into your daily life, you open the door to a realm of limitless achievement and power.

THE SEVEN DRIVING FORCES

The fact remains that unless you are a Buddhist monk or from another planet, you probably think, talk, and act in a certain way because you are affected by certain human desires, wants, and needs. The problems begin when we have no system of controlling and directing these driving forces. The power of self-discipline is the ability we all have that is capable of guiding these driving forces in the direction of our goals. These powerful driving forces can become overwhelming when they are left to chance or uncontrolled.

The Seven Driving Forces

Problems	Desires
1. "I am overworked and underpaid!"	"I want more MONEY!"
2. "I am fat and out of shape!"	"I want to be ATTRACTIVE!"
3. "My life is so hectic and stressful!"	"I want more CONTROL!"
4. "I hate my job!"	"I want a satisfying CAREER!"
5. "My personal life is a nightmare!"	"I want to be LOVED!"
6. "Nobody listens to me!"	"I want to be RESPECTED!"
7. "I just can't seem to get anywhere!"	"I want SATISFACTION!"

With the advent of increasing technological wonders, the need for a personal system of checks and balances has become even more critical. The pace of life has increased so dramatically that our lives can spin out of control before we even realize it. In order to better understand the consequences of living without self-discipline, let's take a look at some of today's human performance statistics related to these driving forces.

Money

81% of all American families live in debt.

One in every 200 Americans files for bankruptcy.

Today's midlevel drug dealer makes $120,000, and a teacher $30,000.

Today's porn star makes around $200,000, and a policeman $35,000.

°°Source: Federal Reserve System Annual Report/American Bankruptcy Institute.

Health

The average American consumes over 22 pounds of sugar, 24 gallons of alcohol, 52 gallons of soft drinks, and 261 pounds of meat each year.

A shocking 52% of Americans are medically overweight.

The top three items purchased at supermarkets in 1994 were Marlboro cigarettes, Coca-Cola Classic, and Kraft Processed Cheese.

The average American consumes approximately 3,600 calories a day. A healthy adult requires only 2,500 to 2,700 calories a day.

According to the National Institute of Mental Health, 28.1% of adults over 18 years of age have mental disorders.

In 1999, there were over 32 million reported cases of AIDS.

°°Source: U.S. Department of Health and Human Services/National Center for Health and Statistics/1999 *Wall Street Journal Almanac*.

Work

In 1998, theft, employee error, and fraud cost $43 million to the retail industry alone.

There were 600 workplace-related murders last year.

21% of all violent assaults occurred on the job.

°°Source: U.S. Bureau of Labor Statistics.

Control

Every four seconds a violent crime is committed, and every nine seconds a murder is committed.

The average American household watches 50.1 hours of television per week or approximately 7.2 hours of television each day.

According to a 1997 University of Michigan study, 22.1% of all eighth-graders and 42.4% of all high school seniors used illicit drugs regularly.

°°Source: U.S. Justice Department/Nielsen Media Research/University of Michigan.

Love

In the United States today, seven out of ten marriages will end in divorce.

Marital violence and rape are at epidemic proportions.

In 1998, 32.4% of all children in the United States were born to unmarried women.

°°Source: National Center for Health and Statistics/The Joint United Nations Programme on AIDS.

These statistics are not meant to leave you with the impression that everything is hopeless and beyond help. In fact, there is more good in the world than bad. However, the fact remains that we are quickly spinning out of control and need to rediscover the power of discipline before things really get crazy. Along with all of the new freedoms and wonders that technology brings into our lives, it also provides us with many more choices. It is a universal law of human nature that with more choices come more mistakes, and with more mistakes come greater problems in our lives.

TAKE CONTROL TIP

Become Organized

A good place to start in the journey to taking control can be found in your home. Set aside one day this week to clear out the clutter and organize your possessions. Brew the coffee, roll up your sleeves, and get busy with the task of organizing and cleaning every room in your house.

THE POWER OF CHOICE

Everything in life is a matter of choice. There are only two things in life in which we have no choice. We cannot change these two facts of life no matter how hard we try. The first unchangeable fact is that we must die. Death is an absolute fact. The second fact is that we must live a certain number of years before we die. Now understand this—everything else in your life is the result of your power to choose. Everything that you say, think, wear, drive, eat, read, watch, and do is a personal choice made by you. We live in the confines of what we call "our life" because we have created this existence through our individual ability to make choices.

Examine where you are in your life. Where you are is where you have chosen to be. Consciously or unconsciously, you have made this your life by choice. Understand that certain universal laws of human nature are at play in your life. Throughout my experiences as a Navy SEAL, consultant, and corporate speaker, I have been blessed with the opportunity to help people improve the quality of their life by understanding two basic laws of human performance. These two basic laws, the law of effort and the law of choices, must be understood and acknowledged before any real changes can be made in a person's overall performance in life.

The Law of Effort

The law of effort simply states that anything worth having in life requires effort, and the greater the goal, the greater the required effort. The difference between those who achieve their goals and those who don't usually comes down to effort. Achievement comes only to those who continually give maximum effort and persist through every adversity. Is your life working out the way you dreamed it would? Do you have the things you would like to have? Are you where you would like to be? Do you have the house, body, job, checking account, relationship, or character that you always wanted? If the answer to any of these questions is no, then let's take a look at the second universal law of nature.

The Law of Choices

The law of choices states that our lives are what we choose them to be and that every circumstance is a product of these decisions. Most of us are trying to become successful, trying to become happy, or wealthy, or loved, or to gain something from life that is presently not there. These can be summed up as dreams, and the choices we make each day are either a step toward our dreams or a step away from them. This is the power of choice. The ability to know what you want in life, and then make correct choices based upon these wants, is called goal setting. Goal setting is simply making choices based upon a desired result. It is knowing where you want to go. If you are not achieving what you are capable of achieving, it is because your goals are not clearly defined. Having goals is one thing, but having a plan to achieve them is another. Your success in any project will be determined largely by your individual plan of action.

The power of choice is the one control mechanism we possess that advertising, television, music, and outside influence try to wrestle from us. When you see people wearing a certain popular style of clothing, or listening to a certain type of music, or eating a certain type of food, you can see the influence that society has over their power of choice. When we lack self-disci-

along the way we get caught up in the schedule of life. As life becomes a routine occurrence instead of a journey of self-discovery, we tend to lose our personal set of rules and regulations little by little. This technique of understanding our built-in tendency to choose the path of least resistance, instead of the path of greater value, allows us to gain clarity during the decision-making process.

The ability to choose what is better for us, instead of what is easier on us, comes from the process of building up our self-discipline or willpower one step at a time. This technique is the foundation of powerful concepts that are implanted into our mind and used when the decision-making process is begun. The object of this technique is to provide a thought pattern that first, and foremost, begins by controlling the human tendency to take the path of least resistance. When we have the ability to look at our choices in life and make our decisions based upon our own personal guidelines and rules, instead of instant satisfaction and immediate pleasure, we have begun to master discipline.

THE SIX ELEMENTS OF CONTROL

Before I began teaching individuals and corporations how to dramatically improve their performance, I was blessed with the opportunity to spend more than a decade working with many of the world's most dominant organizations. Throughout my years in the world of special operations, I have studied and practiced techniques from cultures on every continent that are designed to elevate the performance of human beings in all types of environments, including life-and-death situations. I have come to understand that human performance is in no way related to race, religion, gender, or education, but is simply a product of personal control. The level of control that a person has over their mind, body, and behavior is directly responsible for their success and quality of life. Don't get me wrong; there are many factors and situations that happen every day beyond our ability to control, but everything else is what we choose to make it.

There are six main elements of control that must be addressed, studied, and practiced in order to harness this amazing power in our lives. It makes no difference whether you are a secretary, plumber, or CEO of the world's largest corporation, as we all possess the ability to control our performance in ... The problem is that most people have never been taught how to do this ...rectly. Here are the six elements of control that you will learn in this book:

pline, our ability to make correct decisions based upon *our* needs and wants, and not those of society, becomes very weak. It is essential to our personal success and happiness that we continue this chain of self-discipline, correct decision-making, and self-esteem.

YOUR SELF-ESTEEM

There is a direct connection between the power of choice and our self-worth. As we develop self-discipline and condition ourselves to make correct choices, we in turn increase our self-esteem. Self-discipline enables us to win small victories each day over our habits, urges, and compulsive behavior. The more good choices we make, the more positive our self-esteem becomes. As our self-esteem builds, we begin to develop powerful momentum in the direction of our goals.

Just as the chain reaction of good choices leads to increased self-esteem and self-discipline, the momentum of poor choices leads to depression, obesity, and poor daily performance. Have you ever had a bad day where you woke up and didn't feel on top of the world? You decide to skip your morning exercise session, trade a healthy breakfast for coffee and donuts, and eat fast food for lunch. By the time dinner rolls around, you feel so depressed and lethargic from your poor decisions that you decide to plop in front of the television instead of working on your goals. The next morning you wake up feeling even more depressed and continue with this cycle of poor choices.

I don't believe there is a person alive who has not experienced this cycle of poor decision-making at some point in their life. The development of self-discipline is the only weapon we possess to combat this inevitable fact of life. The natural human tendency to justify the circumstances in our lives by placing the blame on chance, other people, or lack of time is the direct result of low self-discipline. You must find the inner strength to identify your own weaknesses and accept the challenge of changing them. In order to change your cycle of poor choices, you must begin admitting that you have made poor choices and not justify or sidestep the blame. For most people, this is a very difficult admission, but it is the necessary starting point of lasting change. If you wish to develop self-discipline and break the cycle of poor choices, you must embrace this concept. This is the only way to generate the power to accomplish what you want, reach your goals, and continue improving the quality of your life.

If you wish to make lasting changes in your life, instead of bouncing from one diet to another, low self-esteem to high self-confidence, and high stress

pline, our ability to make correct decisions based upon *our* needs and wants, and not those of society, becomes very weak. It is essential to our personal success and happiness that we continue this chain of self-discipline, correct decision-making, and self-esteem.

YOUR SELF-ESTEEM

There is a direct connection between the power of choice and our self-worth. As we develop self-discipline and condition ourselves to make correct choices, we in turn increase our self-esteem. Self-discipline enables us to win small victories each day over our habits, urges, and compulsive behavior. The more good choices we make, the more positive our self-esteem becomes. As our self-esteem builds, we begin to develop powerful momentum in the direction of our goals.

Just as the chain reaction of good choices leads to increased self-esteem and self-discipline, the momentum of poor choices leads to depression, obesity, and poor daily performance. Have you ever had a bad day where you woke up and didn't feel on top of the world? You decide to skip your morning exercise session, trade a healthy breakfast for coffee and donuts, and eat fast food for lunch. By the time dinner rolls around, you feel so depressed and lethargic from your poor decisions that you decide to plop in front of the television instead of working on your goals. The next morning you wake up feeling even more depressed and continue with this cycle of poor choices.

I don't believe there is a person alive who has not experienced this cycle of poor decision-making at some point in their life. The development of self-discipline is the only weapon we possess to combat this inevitable fact of life. The natural human tendency to justify the circumstances in our lives by placing the blame on chance, other people, or lack of time is the direct result of low self-discipline. You must find the inner strength to identify your own weaknesses and accept the challenge of changing them. In order to change your cycle of poor choices, you must begin admitting that you have made poor choices and not justify or sidestep the blame. For most people, this is a very difficult admission, but it is the necessary starting point of lasting change. If you wish to develop self-discipline and break the cycle of poor choices, you must embrace this concept. This is the only way to generate the power to accomplish what you want, reach your goals, and continue improving the quality of your life.

If you wish to make lasting changes in your life, instead of bouncing from one diet to another, low self-esteem to high self-confidence, and high stress to a feeling of control, you must be ready and willing to change. The power of choice must become a conscious area of focus throughout the day. It is very important to understand the impact that our daily choices have upon our lives. There is no doubt about it: you are what you choose to be. Life is made up of thousands of choices, choices made in each second of every day of your life. This, in essence, is how you create your life—by the choices you make.

THE PATH LEAST TRAVELED

The life of a Navy SEAL may sound like a Hollywood movie or an excerpt from a Tom Clancy novel, but in reality, SEAL teams represent the modern version of the samurai warriors of ancient times and stand as the ultimate consequence against undisciplined decision-making. Possibly the most powerful weapon we wield is the power of personal discipline, both mentally and physically. Self-discipline is responsible for turning around countries, economies, wars, and personal lives virtually overnight.

In the SEAL teams, we use many tactics and techniques that are based upon human behavior and human nature to control our actions. One technique or tactic that is responsible for a lot of our success in combat is simply referred to as "the path least traveled." This technique is based upon the human tendency to go the easy route, or take the path of least resistance to make situations more pleasant for oneself. When we plan a route through a country or city, we find the most horrible, difficult, thickest, nastiest, and unpleasant location in and around our area of operation. We find the steepest cliff, the thickest swamp, the most run-down area of a city, or the most impassable terrain available and use it to our advantage.

This concept appears in everyday life of the majority of people today. The overweight person that knows he should not eat high-fat and high-cholesterol foods chooses the path of least resistance by eating at a fast food restaurant instead of making a light and healthy lunch the night before. The person who would rather sit on the couch all day than do maintenance on his house or vehicles, or use his time wisely to better his life, is an example of this concept.

The technique of choosing the path least traveled is not one of self-martyrdom, or a decision to do things the hard way. Rather, it is one of identifying and correcting personal actions and thoughts to improve our performance in all aspects of daily life. This is accomplished by programming our minds to use discipline during decision-making to help ensure the choices we make in everyday life are of the greatest benefit and not necessarily the easy way out.

By taking control of our lives through discipline, our thoughts and behaviors will maximize the amount of success, health, and vitality we experience in our short life span. Self-discipline can be further defined as a measure of one's willpower and conscious effort to better one's body, mind, and spirit. We have a saying in the SEAL teams for when the environment is at its worst, and we use this saying to remind us of our need to apply personal discipline when we need it the most. This simple saying of "Get what you need!" is said to remind each other of our inherent human tendency to take the path of least resistance in a time of decision-making.

When we decide to conduct our operations in the harshest of environment and location, we understand that this decision actually saves our lives and the lives of the people we are there to rescue. The consequences of operating without discipline are a known and proven fact, therefore we implement self-discipline in our lives to ensure our success and survival. By sacrificing in one small area of our personal comfort, we benefit in all other areas of our lives.

This simple technique can be used in every aspect of a person's life to increase the overall quality of their existence. For example, let's say you decide to take control of your life by budgeting a little more time and money for your appearance and clothing for work. You have sacrificed in one small area, but gain a respectful, clean, competent, and disciplined look and attitude. Another example of this technique can be used for your personal management skills. If you have a job that requires you to work in an office setting with a 9 to 5 schedule, chances are that you probably go with your coworkers out to lunch everyday. When you discipline yourself to make a healthy, balanced, and fat-free meal the night before, you not only save about $75 a week, but give yourself more personal quiet time to work on your future goals or to exercise. This small, yet simple, change has not really caused you to sacrifice a whole lot but has created a substantial benefit to your health, finances, and knowledge. When you add self-discipline to your life, you not only change *your* life, but the lives of everyone around you.

The changes you make in your life to improve your overall personal health, appearance, diet, and energy levels are accomplished by simply adding small amounts of discipline over a scheduled length of time. These moderate changes elevate your work performance, family life, financial stability, and general mental and physical health to powerful new levels. Most of us understand this concept by the time we reach adulthood, but somewhere along the way we get caught up in the schedule of life. As life becomes a routine occurrence instead of a journey of self-discovery, we tend to lose our personal set of rules and regulations little by little. This technique of understanding our built-in tendency to choose the path of least resistance, instead of the path of greater value, allows us to gain clarity during the decision-making process.

The ability to choose what is better for us, instead of what is easier on us, comes from the process of building up our self-discipline or willpower one step at a time. This technique is the foundation of powerful concepts that are implanted into our mind and used when the decision-making process is begun. The object of this technique is to provide a thought pattern that first, and foremost, begins by controlling the human tendency to take the path of least resistance. When we have the ability to look at our choices in life and make our decisions based upon our own personal guidelines and rules, instead of instant satisfaction and immediate pleasure, we have begun to master discipline.

THE SIX ELEMENTS OF CONTROL

Before I began teaching individuals and corporations how to dramatically improve their performance, I was blessed with the opportunity to spend more than a decade working with many of the world's most dominant organizations. Throughout my years in the world of special operations, I have studied and practiced techniques from cultures on every continent that are designed to elevate the performance of human beings in all types of environments, including life-and-death situations. I have come to understand that human performance is in no way related to race, religion, gender, or education, but is simply a product of personal control. The level of control that a person has over their mind, body, and behavior is directly responsible for their success and quality of life. Don't get me wrong; there are many factors and situations that happen every day beyond our ability to control, but everything else is what we choose to make it.

There are six main elements of control that must be addressed, studied, and practiced in order to harness this amazing power in our lives. It makes no difference whether you are a secretary, plumber, or CEO of the world's largest corporation, as we all possess the ability to control our performance in life. The problem is that most people have never been taught how to do this correctly. Here are the six elements of control that you will learn in this book:

- Goal management
- Personal management
- Thought control
- Physical discipline
- Nutritional control
- Professional discipline

Each of these elements encompasses a variety of skills, techniques, and information that will enable you to make the necessary changes to your life and develop the limitless power of personal control. Remember that the road to improving your performance is not traveled in one day and there are no instant-success formulas, quick-fix solutions, or magic fat pills that will make you a new person overnight. If you are hoping to read this book and wake up tomorrow a superhuman, then you have missed out on the true message. Understand that all of the techniques, information, and time-proven performance methods in the world will do you no good unless you decide to take action now.

TAKE CONTROL TIP

Becoming Superhuman
What traits do you most admire? How would you like to look? Take the time to write out a description of the person you would like to be. Write out how this person would look, act, and talk. This is the first step to creating a personal goal.

A BALANCED LIFE

One underlying factor in controlling your life is to carefully balance the six elements. Without having balance, you start to create deficiencies. It is just as important to improve upon the things you are doing right as it is to destroy the things that you are doing wrong. Self-discipline is the tool that must be used to enhance the positive aspects of your life and talents, or they too will wither and die. In my life, I must continually find a balance between my spiritual side, my family side, and my professional side, or my overall performance in life begins to decline.

Balance can be a deceptive word. Balance does not mean the equal application of time and energy to all tasks, but a division of time and energy that equals success in each task. In everyday life it is not so easy to detect imbalance or inefficiencies in our daily schedule. In other words, don't spend all of your time and effort on fixing your problem areas, or your strengths and attributes will be deficient. Once you are able to control the application of self-discipline in all areas of your life, noticing an imbalance is very easy.

POSITIVE POWER AND OPTIMISM

The amazing power of the human mind should never be underestimated. If you stop and listen to your inner voice from time to time, you will discover the answer to most of your problems. The problem lies in the negative statements we make to ourselves that bring about negative circumstances. The old adage "you are what you think" is one of the basic laws of human nature. Take the time to investigate your own beliefs and thought patterns. Begin to eliminate the constant barrage of negative programming by focusing on positive thoughts of accomplishment. Use the power of discipline to program your mind for success and happiness. Think positive and optimistic thoughts, and good things will happen.

SELF-ANALYSIS

At some point in time, it becomes necessary to clear away all of the nice-to-know information and get down to the heart of the matter. This is such a time. It makes no difference what your background is, where you went to college, how much you earn, what job title you have, or even how old you are. What matters most is that we are all members of a certain species that share certain things in common. The human species of today has very similar needs, wants, problems, and desires that create the circumstances in our lives. In order for us to use the power of self-discipline to bring our desires into reality, we must learn more about ourselves.

The majority of people today get so caught up in the daily grind that they soon forget why they are working so fast and furiously. When was the last time you took a hard look at yourself and thought about why you go to work every morning? Have you ever thought about why you dress the way you do or why you work in the field of industry that you do? Why do you feel depressed or stressed out? When was the last time you analyzed your words, thoughts, and actions to determine why you behave or think a certain way? All of these questions point to your basic wants and problems.

FINDING YOUR PATH

In today's age of incredible technology and scientific wonders, there exist so many opportunities, lifestyles, and directions for a person to choose from that our chances of making wrong decisions are dramatically increased. As with anything in life, there is good and bad in all things. Without an organized set of clear-cut goals, needs, desires, and aspirations, it becomes very hard to determine exactly what options in life you have to choose from. To simplify this subject further, we must first determine what it is we want in life, and exactly what outcome we desire.

To give you a simple example, imagine that your spouse or significant other sends you to a huge multiproduct store like Wal-Mart or Super Kmart. However, upon arrival you cannot remember what it is you were supposed to buy. In this superstore you have millions of items and products to choose from, so you walk around endlessly trying to figure out what you want. By the end of the day, you have seen only a tenth of what this superstore has to offer, but still have not found what you are looking for. This is much like most people in life, who have a thousand different choices each day of their lives and seemingly spend all day frantically doing nothing. This is because they have not yet found what it is they want, or what it takes to get it.

When I made the decision that I wanted to become a SEAL, I found out that there was a set order of tasks, accomplishments, guidelines, and steps that I needed to follow in order to reach my goal. The human mind needs to have a set task and schedule to follow in order to focus its power. Without a clear direction to follow, it starts to download glitches. The computer in your head is much like the computer you have at home or at work. In order to work efficiently and correctly, it needs a program or set order of guidelines to follow. Without this program of guidelines, it becomes nothing more than a useless box of information that continuously spins its circuits and chips while accomplishing nothing.

The first step to mastering discipline is a basic and simple one, but for most people it is the hardest to pin down. The first step is to determine what it is we want in life, or what we want to become. I am not saying you need to determine that you want to be an astronaut or any other type of professional. Rather, we need to dig through our brain and come up with a general idea of the way we want things to be. All of this information is in there just waiting to be discovered.

Everyday we think, see, dream, and desire things in life. The problem is, we are unable to consciously focus and organize our efforts toward attaining them. The first and most crucial step to bringing discipline into our lives is accomplished by determining exactly what we want in our short existence. In today's world, there are so many experts and therapists telling us to get in touch with our feelings and to just let things happen that people get even more confused about what actions to take. The truth is that you do not need to repeat a special chant or pay thousands of dollars for a therapist to find clarity in your life. By discovering what your goals in life are, and focusing your time and energy toward them, your life takes on clarity and purpose.

PERSONAL RESPONSIBILITY

What areas of your life are missing self-discipline? How often do you choose the easy way out? What habits and traits do you possess that have more control over you than you have over them? Do you remember the age-old saying that "nobody's perfect"? All humans have faults, bad habits, and character flaws, but you can use self-discipline to reduce your flaws and stand above the average human. Developing self-discipline is not the act of punishment, total restriction, self-inflicted pain, or behaving like a robot. It is your responsibility to take control of your life. Self-discipline is a tool that each of us possesses to exact control over how we act, think, speak, and live, but the less we use it, the more out of control our lives become.

How do you develop self-discipline? In the SEAL teams, each and every SEAL is personally responsible for his everyday performance and actions. By giving highly motivated and intelligent people the necessary information and environment to better themselves, you create a chain reaction of superior performance through self-discipline. If you place people who do not want to change in this environment, you get chaos, defiance, and poor performance. The two components that are found among highly successful people are superior effort and personal discipline. How can you begin exerting control over your life if you aren't willing to put forth the effort?

In today's fast-paced world of technology, stress, and two-job households, life can seem like a ride on a burning Ferris wheel. Sometimes we can become so caught up in the schedule of everyday life that we fail to notice the impression we leave behind. If you stop and think about it, everything we do and say leaves an impression on the people around us. Whether it's our coworkers, family, or friends with whom we interact, our commitment to personal discipline is the foundation of our perceived character.

Although we might not realize it, each day we leave an indelible impression of our personal self-worth, beliefs, work ethic, and character with every person with whom we come in contact. Over a period of days, weeks, and years these little impressions begin to build a picture or "advertisement" of our character for others to see. It is human nature to make mistakes, but it is also human nature to not overlook the legacy of daily impressions we leave behind.

Generational discipline is the legacy that each of us leaves behind for our friends, spouses, and children to remember us by. It is also the legacy of our work ethic that our coworkers, employers, and customers remember us by. Each day that we show up to work, interact, and perform a task, we are building our own "advertisement" for others to see. The little things that we do might not seem like a big deal at the time, but over the course of our lifetime they amount to nothing less than our character image. Words like "reliable," "selfless," or "exuding commitment and integrity" describe a person that cares about his or her daily performance.

Have you ever thought about how your actions affect the lives of your children, spouse, and family? As an example of generational discipline, let's take a look at the lives of two men: Max Jukes and Jonathan Edwards. Max Jukes believed in the abolition of laws and rules. Mr. Jukes believed in and preached about a lifestyle of free sex, no laws, no formal education, and no responsibilities. Jonathan Edwards was known by all as the "disciplinarian." Not because he disciplined his children harshly, but because he was a self-disciplined man. He became a preacher that believed in leading by example. He authored two books on the subjects of responsibility and integrity. Mr. Edwards became known for teaching people from all walks of life how to be responsible for their actions. Both of these men came from very similar backgrounds, but they developed opposing lifestyles and beliefs. The only common ground these men shared was that they both fathered 13 children. Here are the legacies they left behind:

Max Jukes
1,026 descendants

Legacy
300 convicts
190 prostitutes
536 alcoholics and drug addicts

Jonathan Edwards
929 descendants

Legacy
430 ministers
86 college professors
75 authors
13 university presidents
7 congressmen
3 governors
1 vice president of the United States

There is no question that developing self-discipline will change your life for the better, but real results can only be seen in the legacy of performance we leave behind. When we begin to use self-discipline to control our emotional highs and lows, our appearance, our work ethic, and our commitment to physical exercise, we are doing much more than improving our own lives. Our ability to begin focusing on our daily performance is directly proportional to the success our descendants will experience. Remember that personal achievement is not only about you, your job, your bank account, or even your own personal satisfaction. Developing self-discipline for a lifetime of above-average performance and prosperity is about the legacy you leave behind.

TAKE CONTROL TIP

Create Personal Space
Take a long drive or a quiet walk through the park. Lock yourself in the bathroom or go out to the garage. Make it a point to spend some quiet time alone with your thoughts. Use this time to relax and think about how to improve your quality of life.

MISSION DE-BRIEF
★ ★ ★ ★

At this point, I hope that you are still not looking for that instant success formula or million-dollar phrase that will bring the power of self-discipline into your life. You have already taken the first step to learning how to master self-discipline by reading and taking the responsibility of doing a little soul-searching.

In the SEAL teams, the process of developing strategies to attain goals is a neverending necessity. This goal development process is what creates self-discipline, and self-discipline, in turn, creates goal development and personal management. You must understand that the ability to master self-discipline is gained by winning one small battle at a time. Remember that every human being has the ability to control their environment, life, and destiny. In order to start making things right, you must first learn exactly what is wrong. Once you have read and completed this book, you will possess an instruction manual for how to take control of your life.

2

CONTROLLING DESTINY

The Mastery of Goal Management

If you don't know where you are going, you might wind up someplace else.
—Yogi Berra

The world's most successful people, from leaders of countries to parents who have a healthy, happy, and loving family, all share a single powerful habit: the ability to set goals. Without a solid life plan and precisely defined goals, your life becomes the daily grind that has neither meaning nor purpose.

The mastery of goal management is nothing more than knowing where we want to go, creating a map to get there, and using personal management skills to navigate safely. By mastering self-discipline we are able to keep afloat when we hit some rocks or need to weather the storms of life. A life without goals is one that leads to little productivity and personal effectiveness, but also provides little happiness and even less fulfillment.

In this chapter, you will find methods for determining your goals, writing out your mission statement, outlining your objectives and purposes, developing means to reach your goals, and testing and redefining your life plan.

SEAL TEAM MISSION GOALS

As the sweat rolling off their foreheads and eyebrows falls noiselessly to the deck of the C-141 aircraft, large, well-muscled Navy SEALs quickly climb into their wetsuits and prepare to parachute into the North Atlantic. Their goal is to successfully neutralize a group of terrorists who have over-taken a Pakistani freight ship loaded with dangerous chemicals. The quiet, easygoing demeanor of this unit almost conceals the glowing confidence and cold determination that shows in their eyes. After nearly 13 hours of monotony, a voice booms out "15 minutes!" and the SEALs suddenly come to life.

Oxygen cylinders are checked, free-fall parachutes donned, and fins taped to their legs in preparation. Each SEAL has a partner to whom he gives all of his attention—checking straps, ripcords, weapons, night-vision goggles, and small waterproof rucksacks. Eventually the plane ramp is lowered to reveal the beautiful loneliness of space. The dark and cold quickly engulf the inside of the aircraft as the −40 degrees Fahrenheit rushes in to meet the SEALs as they leap in unison. The wind violently pushes them around the sky until they settle into a small 12-man circle as they reach terminal velocity. Quick glances at the altimeters on their wrists tell the tale of gravity, as they descend at the rate of one thousand feet every five seconds, moving closer and closer to Mother Earth.

Finally ripcords are pulled and the 12 SEALs maneuver in the night sky. While under canopies, they don their fins and activate the oxygen cylinders. Immediately upon entering the water, they slip out of their parachutes and dive under the surface to gather in a small group where signals are passed, timers are set, and the electronic compass is activated.

Several hours later, a single head slowly breaks the surface of the calm bay waters 500 yards behind the large and rusting Pakistani freight ship, and quickly disappears again below the surface. As the SEALs make their way along the bottom of the ship, they stop at the huge 45-foot rudder. Each man quickly takes off his pure-oxygen rebreather, dive belt, and fins, and hooks them onto a line suspended from the ship's hull by powerful magnets. Their MP-5 Heckler and Koch miniature machine guns are unfastened and read-ied for use in the dark shadows behind the vessel. Slowly and methodically, with guns pointed outward in a 360-degree circle, the men extend a re-tractable pole outfitted with a rubber-coated titanium hook. As the hook qui-etly grabs hold of a railing, the pole is retracted and slowly sunk to the bottom. The men patiently wait for the water to drain off of their bodies be-fore climbing higher onto the back of the ship by means of a lightweight, wire ladder.

The first couple of men reach the top of the ship's railing and flip down their night-vision goggles to scan the shadows of the ship's deck for terror-ists. As the last man reaches the cover of the shadows, a faint, almost inaudible sound is heard, followed by the faint smell of gunpowder drifting from the barrel of a silencer. A terrorist quietly crumbles to the deck of the ship. Then the 12 shadows spring into action on cue, flowing over the ship like a violent and powerful wave. Surprise, speed, and disciplined violence are the tools these 12 SEALs use to bring justice to the unsuspecting soldiers of terrorism.

In minutes, the threat of terrorism no longer exists and the sounds of sirens can be heard off in the distance. Quickly, the SEALs gather on the aft deck of the ship. A small satellite beacon is activated as they climb back into the cold bay waters. Twenty minutes later, the extraction is completed as the last man climbs down the bridge ladder of the U.S. nuclear submarine.

SELF-DISCIPLINE GOALS AND LIFE MISSIONS

In the SEAL teams, our overall mission is to reach certain goals that are set by our country. These goals can be rather simple or extremely difficult, and every American feels results of our failures and successes. Like the example above, our goals come in the form of missions, and our ability to master goal management directly determines whether we fail or succeed. Our success depends on self-discipline.

This same concept can be applied to your self-discipline goals and life mission, but the only way that you will succeed in accomplishing your life mission is to first know exactly what your mission is. To have any lasting control, you must plan your mission in advance. Plan for the attainment of your dreams and prepare yourself to deal with the obstacles that life puts in your path. It is imperative that you take the time to carefully think about what it is you want in life and conduct a thorough inventory of what you now have.

Highly successful individuals, world leaders, great artists, and history's most influential people all have one thing in common: they use self-discipline on a daily basis to achieve their goals. Clear and specific goals are the essential foundation of not only self-discipline but also a lifetime of health, wealth, and longevity. Self-discipline goals are somewhat different than success-oriented goals, in that self-discipline goals are defined by personal improvement. Once you identify areas of your life that you wish to gain total control over, you have now defined specific areas of improvement.

Self-discipline goals are essential to generating self-control, motivation, and persistence, the other three key ingredients needed for self-discipline. Here are examples of self-discipline goals:

- I want to have total control over when, how, and what I eat for the next 30 days.
- I am going to gain control of my finances by sticking to my scheduled budget each and every day for the next 90 days.
- I want my fellow coworkers to look up to me as a leader and example of discipline by the way I speak, act, and dress in 60 days.
- I will gain control of my emotions by disciplining my anger, depression, and attitude around my family, friends, and coworkers.
- I am going to set aside one hour every day to work on my goal of being self-employed in one year.
- I will set aside one hour each day to organizing, maintaining, and cleaning my household, my clothing, and my possessions.
- I want to dedicate one evening each week to my spouse and use this evening to improve our relationship and show my love and appreciation.
- I will set a disciplined example for my children by becoming more involved in their lives and showing them how I have gained control over my life.
- I will discipline my body to quit smoking by gradually reducing the amount of cigarettes I smoke each week, until I have completely quit in 30 days.
- I want to reduce the amount of television I watch to 45 minutes per day, by disciplining myself to use this time for constructive efforts.

You must understand that simply wanting something is not enough—you must define, refine, focus, and schedule specific actions that you will take to have what you desire. The amazing power of self-discipline can alter your life if you simply understand the process and forces at work in the human body and mind. Think of your life as a ship upon the sea, and the habit of goal management a complete navigation system. The early years of your life are like the building of a great ship. This great ship is carefully and meticulously pieced together over time with the information and experiences of your childhood. How seaworthy your vessel is depends upon a great many factors and situations, but it is never too late to rebuild your ship. During our teenage years we began to prepare our ship for its launch, and for most of us there was no planned destination, just the intense desire to get away. The point we are at now in our lives is a direct result of how much useless cargo we have picked up along the way and our ability to set goals or navigate. The process of mastering self-discipline is like that of rebuilding our ship, we throw out all the harmful and useless junk, fix the leaking holes, and install a new and powerful navigation system that will take us swiftly to meeting our goals.

DETERMINING YOUR GOALS

Obtaining self-mastery and happiness will only come about when you set precise objectives for every area of your life. Successful people and top performers know exactly where they are going emotionally, mentally, physically, and financially. If you cannot see what it is you want, how can you find the path to get there?

Begin by thinking and imagining the achievements, toys, job, home, career, family life, and anything else that you desire, and begin to write these down. Take the time to think about your personal improvement desires and clearly write them down as well. Here is an example of a clearly defined life-mission and self-discipline goal:

> **Life-Mission:** I will save $5,000 each year for the next five years. I will use this money to buy a three-acre parcel of land by Lake Lookout on which I will build a log cabin.
>
> **Self-Discipline Goal:** I will turn off the television each night at 8:00 P.M. and spend one hour preparing my clothing, packing a lunch, and completing a To Do List for work each of the next 30 days in a row.

The greatest advice ever given to me was this: Discover in life what it is you like to do, and then figure out how to get paid doing it. Begin to focus your concentration on thinking deeply about where you want to be in 1, 5, 10, 15, and 30 years from now. You are now defining your dreams and your life.

Take Control Exercise

> To successfully accomplish the first mission, I need you to take your time in thinking about each question that you are asked. I want you to use a pencil and notebook to answer these questions. I urge you to keep a personal journal of all the information you will gather from reading this book. Once you are satisfied that you have answered honestly, thoughtfully, and without external motivators, you can move on. For this mission I don't want you to talk with your spouse or friends

about the questions, and I don't want you to talk to anyone about the results.

This is a personal mission that only you can accomplish. Once you have answered all of the questions in your notebook, I want you to sit down and take a look at your life from this perspective. This mission is based upon a technique we use in the SEAL teams to discipline ourselves and determine our exact goals by taking a serious, yet objective, look at our strengths and weaknesses.

1. Are you overweight?
2. What is your age?
3. What skill or subject would you like to learn?
4. Rate the stress your job puts on you from 1 to 10.
5. How much money would make you secure to retire?
6. What is your dream home like and where would you like to live?
7. How many minutes or hours do you exercise per week?
8. Do you smoke of drink? How much per week?
9. What is your favorite hobby?
10. How much personal quiet time do you have per day?
11. Are your house possessions, office, vehicles, and finances well-organized?
12. How would you rank your marriage or relationship from 1 to 10?
13. What would you like your gravestone to read?
14. Are you happy with your body?
15. How many hours per week do you watch television?
16. What is your number one fault? Number two?
17. At what age would you like to retire?
18. What occupation have you always dreamed of?

WHERE DO YOU WANT TO BE?

Where do you want to be 5, 10, or 20 years from now? This is not so much a question of location as it is a question of your position in life. How often have you sat down and made an honest attempt to answer this question? Going through life without a set of clearly defined goals is like driving down a street in a large city without directions or any real idea of where you want to go. Now that you have completed the exercise, it is time to put this information to use.

It is very important to understand that your goals can and will change over time, but without a clearly defined idea of what you want in life, success and achievement will always be just words. In order to refine the information that you have gathered from the exercise, you must take the time to think about what goals you would like to have achieved in these five areas of your life.

1. Money: How much? Salary, savings, personal worth?
2. Health: What state of physical fitness? Appearance?
3. Work: Your job title? Self-employed? Retired?
4. Love: Your marriage? Children? Milestones?
5. Personal: Character goals? Spiritual goals? Possessions?

Congratulations! By answering these questions, you have begun to define your life goals. This is something that 99% of the world's population has never and will never do. Can you imagine a SEAL team being sent into a foreign country with no clear idea of what to do, where to go, or how to get there? Sounds pretty ludicrous and careless, doesn't it? Well, that is exactly how most people spend every minute of every day. The difference between those who have and those who have not, those who succeed and those who don't, and those who are in control and those who aren't is simply a clearly defined set of goals followed by a mission statement on how to achieve them.

MISSION STATEMENT

Although it is crucial to have clearly defined goals in life, they must become more than just words on a piece of paper—they must become your battle cry and personal vision quest. The ability to take your goals and form them into a personal mission statement is vital to staying focused over the long run. A mission statement is a term we use in the world of special operations to define all of our goals for a particular mission with one short statement. For example, we have many different goals that we must achieve throughout a mission, such as infiltrating without being noticed, successfully communicating with headquarters, executing the mission, and getting extracted without being noticed. These are just a few of the goals that we must achieve for a particular mission, but we use a mission statement to stay focused on the overall objective. Here is an example of how goals can be defined into a personal mission statement.

As you can see from the above mission statement, I have created a personal battle cry that incorporates most of my goals. Once you have written a

Goals

1. **MONEY:** Save enough money to pay off our house, buy a vacation home, and retire with $500,000 in the bank.
2. **HEALTH:** Work out four times a week and keep my weight at 200 pounds. Run a marathon. Quit smoking and drinking. Eat more fruits and vegetables.
3. **WORK:** Double my sales in the next year. Advance to vice president. Win Salesman of the Year award. Be recognized as the top employee.
4. **LOVE:** Improve my marriage and celebrate our 30th anniversary. Help with more of the household chores. Teach my children better values through my example. Tell my spouse I love her every day.
5. **PERSONAL:** Learn all that I can about investing, stocks, and finances. Learn to speak and write French. Visit a new country each year. Learn how to sail. Finish my master's degree. Improve my organizational skills. Write a novel.

Mission Statement

I am going to dedicate my time, energy, and resources to reaching my goals. I am going to exercise more, eat healthier, and lose weight. I am going to become the best salesman and vice president at my company. I will become a great husband and father and provide for a great future. Nothing will stop me or slow me down and failure is not an option.

Signed: _____ Date: _____

mission statement, you must memorize it. Post it in your home, office, vehicle, and any place that you spend time. Think of your mission statement as a personal challenge—a challenge that you must focus on every day and will become the basis for every decision, action, and task that you undertake. A mission statement is not limited to just your personal goals. You can develop a family, company, and marriage mission statement for other areas of your life, or in conjunction with friends, coworkers, and family.

TAKE CONTROL TIP

Failure Is Not an Option!
Too often in life we treat failure as a part of the equation. Don't plan for the achievement of your goals with an acceptable loss in mind. Instead, take control of your attitude and know that you will succeed no matter what.

Take Control Exercise

For this exercise, I want you to formulate your personal mission statement. It is important to understand that self-discipline is about doing the things we know that we must do, even if we don't feel like doing them. Think of your mission statement as an address to the place you want to be in life. Use the example above as a guide. Record your goals and personal mission statement in your notebook.

DEVELOPING A BATTLE PLAN

Now that you know what you want from life and you have clearly stated your mission, you must begin to develop a strategy. A technique we use in the special operations world to help us reach our goals is called mission planning. This critical step to achieving our goals is about developing a specific and written plan of action. Think about the small details involved and outline a plan that incorporates time lines, actions, and possible roadblocks to achieving your goals. This is a time-proven format we use to organize, delegate, and prepare ourselves for the process of attaining our goal, or accomplishing our mission. Mission planning is the technique we use to empower ourselves with the knowledge and tools needed to accomplish set goals. This technique can be used in everyday life to help us organize and begin the journey of reaching our life's dreams.

The very first step to developing a personal plan of action toward achieving your goals is to list all of the possible ways in which a particular goal might be achieved. One of the most amazing facts of human performance is that 90% of all failures can be attributed to a lack of proper planning. Many people and businesses have goals and work very hard toward achieving them, but fail to put any time into selecting and developing an organized step by step strategy. The simple act of sitting down and formulating a battle plan based upon all of your options, resources, and contingencies is the most important aspect of achieving any goal. In the SEAL teams we use a very simple planning tool called a course-of-action (COA) grid. The COA grid is crucial to our ability to plan, organize, and execute a successful mission. By using a COA grid we are able to eliminate all biases and dramatically speed up the planning process.

The COA grid is completed in a five-step process. Here are the five steps to creating a COA grid:

1. Write your desired goal at the top of a piece of paper or notebook.
2. List all of your available resources, options, and ideas.
3. Draw your COA grid and fill in the appropriate information.
4. Grade the value of each option from 1 to 4. The number 4 has the highest value and the number 1 the least value.
5. Add up all of the numbers for each column and circle the highest score.

The box on page 29 shows what the COA will look like for a goal of learning a new language.

To begin a COA grid, you first must first have a clear picture of your desired outcome or final goal. Next, you need to list all of the resources and options available to you on a sheet of paper or in your personal notebook. Once you have written down all of this information, you will need to draw the framework for your grid and begin filling in the appropriate information.

When was the last time you actually thought about, developed, and executed a plan for reaching a goal or objective in your life? If you are like most people, probably never. Almost everybody who lives on this planet has goals they would like to achieve in life, but often believe that fate, destiny, or just plain luck is why a select few actually succeed and they don't. Regardless of what excuse we use to validate our lack of action, there is no escaping the fact that action without planning is the number one cause of failure in business and life.

The ability to take control of your life is within your grasp. Nothing worth having in life is going to fall into your lap or be given to you on a silver platter, but with proper planning and discipline you can increase your chances a thousandfold. Now is the time for you to develop a personal battle plan, a course of action. Use the information and examples that you have learned in this chapter to help guide you through the mission-planning process and develop a personal strategy for achieving your goals.

Goal: Learn to speak Spanish.

Options:
1. Begin a self-study program by spending $200 on books and tapes.
2. Enroll in a 90-day class at local college. $800 from savings. Evening classes.
3. Hire a personal tutor for two months. $1,200 from savings.
4. Travel to Mexico for three-week study program. $2,000 from savings.

Resources/Obstacles:

Savings: $2,000	°Saving for retirement and emergencies.
Time: 2 hours in evening	°Spending time with family.

Resources/Obstacles:

Local College	°30 minute driving distance.
Personal Tutor	°Available only Monday through Thursday.

OPTIONS	COST	FLEXIBILITY	FAMILY	TIME	TRAVEL	SCORE
Self-study	4	4	3	1	4	(16)
College	3	2	2	3	1	11
Tutor	2	3	3	3	4	15
Mexico	1	2	2	4	1	10

Course of Action: Take $200 out of savings. Purchase books and tapes. Schedule time to study each day. Inform family of goal and schedule important functions. Talk to tutor for cost of possible one-day-per-week visit. Develop mission statement for achieving the goal of learning a new language.

It is important to be as specific as possible by including deadlines and contingencies. Remember that anything worth achieving in life comes not from luck but through hard work, proper planning, and the attitude that "failure is not an option."

THOUGHT DOMINATION

In order to take control of your life you must allow your goals and strategies to dominate your thoughts and actions. Spend 90% of your time and energy working toward your goals by utilizing mental self-discipline (chapter 4), physical activities (chapter 5), proper diet (chapter 6), and knowledge acqui-

Evaluate Your Brain Food!
Take the time to evaluate the information, pictures, words,
and thoughts that you allow to enter your mind each day.
Remember that your brain is like a computer's hard drive and
what you put in is what you will get out.

TAKE CONTROL TIP

sition (chapter 7) to help develop ideas and strategies for achievement. By thinking nonstop of the realization of your dreams, you develop a remarkable belief and determination that will truly amaze you. The self-disciplined person expects success. Every morning begin by thinking of how you will look, feel, and act when all of your dreams become reality. Dress successful, think successful, and act like an achiever. Picture the happiness and joy you will feel at the end of your life, knowing that you have mastered personal success and reached your goals.

Another technique to try is this: Make photocopies of your self-discipline goals, paste them all over your office, put them in your car, stick them to your bathroom mirror, and visualize yourself achieving total control. It is one thing to say that you want to lose weight, but it is another to clearly define the amount, how, and when you are going to lose the weight. Begin pasting your course of action worksheets beside pictures of what you are trying to achieve. Start filling your mind with information that is pertinent to your strategies and goals instead of negativity, television, and instant gratification.

TESTING AND REDEFINING YOUR MISSION

The act of using self-discipline to set and regularly review your life's goals will allow your mind to see opportunities that will fulfill your desires. The mastery of goal management gives you the ability to live your dreams and pack far more enjoyment into your life. When you are developing your mission plan, clearly state deadlines and guideposts for the attainment of goals. Include methods for testing your achievement toward those goals. It is very important to continually test your goals and strategies to determine if they need to be redefined or altered to meet new changes in your life. Take the time to think about your personal mission statement and its relevance to your priorities. The ability to discipline your actions toward a specific goal, regardless of life's little stumbling blocks, is the key to developing good habits and controlling bad ones.

Remember that if you can do anything for 14 days, you have begun to develop a life-changing habit. When things go wrong or not as you have planned, stick with it and fight through the battle with persistence. Through the process of programming yourself to master self-discipline, you begin building the foundation of persistence, and with this you wield the power of flexibility. Condition yourself to pick up the pieces when things fall apart— failure is nothing except the process of brushing yourself off and learning from mistakes. Persistence is what separates the successful people from the almost-successful people.

MISSION DE-BRIEF
★★★★

Once you begin to clearly see the path that you wish to travel, your days and their activities take on a whole new meaning. Your life now becomes filled with focus, passion, and purpose, but you must develop a plan, attach deadlines, and apply self-discipline techniques in order to gain clarity. Your goals must be broken down into smaller and smaller bits to become manageable and to gain confidence. Start using course-of-action grids to organize and develop a strategy, which begins with small steps and ends with your supreme goals.

Don't forget to treat yourself to the sweet rewards of everyday life, and stop along the journey to success to truly enjoy the gift of breathing. It is the small victories in life that generate the power to win the large victories. Master self-discipline by reflecting on what you did right and wrong. Be hard on yourself and life will be easy on you. Remember that it is peace of mind that you are searching for, but do not get so caught up in the process of achieving your goals that you forget the small pleasures in life. Reward yourself for attaining the small goals. Learn from errors and practice self-discipline to make sure they do not happen again. Enjoy feeling productive, focused, and truly happy. Learn to become the creator of your destiny, to gain control, and navigate your ship to your promise—life with self-discipline.

3

THE ART OF PERSONAL MANAGEMENT

You can't wake a person who is pretending to be asleep.—Navajo proverb

Taking control of your life does not mean you must set out on a journey of sacrifice or deprivation. The power to manage, understand, and control your physical and mental talents toward a certain lifestyle will not restrict or deprive you of pleasure and fun, but rather enhance these experiences and assist you in accomplishing your goals.

Now that you have a plan, just how do you accomplish your dreams, meet your goals, and fulfill your life mission? How do you turn that raw desire into focused determination? How can you master self-control? Is there a way to defeat procrastination and poor time management skills? The power of self-discipline is the answer. Self-discipline is a combination of willpower, self-control, and personal organization that is focused toward self-mastery. The great philosopher Aristotle once stated that "the greatest victory is over the inner self." Do you really need to be convinced that this is true? All that you need to do is open up your daily newspaper, turn on the television, or watch the nightly news to see the effects of living without self-discipline.

In my travels as a professional speaker and consultant, I can tell you that beyond a shadow of a doubt the lack of personal management skills is the number one problem facing all people, companies, and teams. The control of our time management, organizational, and personal communications skills is the greatest battle we must win in order to become successful. Ef-

fective personal management, as used by the Navy SEALs in the special operations world, elevates ordinary men and women, with blind determination,
to the top of the performance food chain. Personal management is the key to
taking control of your life. In the SEAL teams, we know that self-discipline
and personal management skills are what separate professional operators
from regular military personnel. This fact holds true in today's business arena
as well. The difference between those who rise to the top of corporations, experiencing professional achievement, and those who simply move with the
9 to 5 sheep herd is the misunderstood skill of personal management.

Self-discipline, combined with personal management skills, is the golden
key that opens the door to your potential. Of course we all want to have certain things in life, but before you begin to see improvements in your outside
world, you must first raise the standards in your inner world. This is accomplished by effective personal management, which means honing your time
management skills and decision-making ability, mastering your moods, and
building a foundation of character strength. Personal management is a very
powerful tool that can be developed for achieving almost anything that you
can dream. In the SEAL teams, each and every SEAL is personally responsible for his everyday performance and actions. We have learned that by giving highly motivated and intelligent people the necessary skills to better
themselves, you create a chain reaction of superior performance through
personal management.

Become a Gladiator

TAKE CONTROL TIP
Achieving your goals in life is more than a journey—it is a battle! Work on reducing the chinks in your armor by defeating
your bad habits and controlling your urges. Remember to
build upon your strengths and gain control of your weaknesses by developing self-discipline.

JACK OF ALL TRADES

Check the e-mail, return voice mail messages, check your beeper, prepare a
healthy dinner, coach the little league team, grade the math homework, and
prepare tomorrow's sales report. In today's age of wonderful technology, we
have become the wearer of many hats, the jack of all trades. As the list of our
various tasks and responsibilities grows year by year, so must our ability to
make decisions and manage our lives. Nothing can raise your stress level and

destroy a good attitude faster than being caught behind the proverbial power curve.

In the SEAL teams we consider ourselves jacks of all trades for good reason. We treat personal management as a life-and-death skill—because it is! Imagine being in a hostile third-world country and forgetting your gun, or showing up five minutes late for your extraction helicopter, or even jumping out of a plane from 25,000 feet at night only to find that you have forgotten your altimeter. Luckily, in everyday life the consequences for poor personal management skills are less severe—or are they? Thousands of companies go under each month because of poor decision-making, hundreds of thousands of employees lose their jobs each year because of poor time management, and many talented people fail to achieve their goals each day due to poor organizational skills. In the age of the jack of all trades, effective personal management is the difference between those who succeed and those who continue to try.

Before you can begin to manage your life, you must get a grasp on what needs to be managed. When was the last time you sat down with a notebook and took an inventory of your responsibilities, daily tasks, and possessions? If you are like most people, probably not in the last five years. An effective personal management system is made up of three key elements, which you must learn. These are time discipline, self-control, and character construction.

TIME DISCIPLINE

What a fascinating time to be part of the workforce in this era of incredible technology! Have you ever taken the time to notice the plethora of electronic gizmos that today's working warrior carries on an average day? We have cellular phones and beepers to stay in touch, laptop computers for mobile office work, watches that display calendars, and pocket computers that manage our time and even keep track of the stock market. Yet, with all of this management technology covering us from head to toe, the average person considers time management to be the hardest skill to master. How can this be? To put it simply, if you lack the personal ability to discipline your time, all of the gizmos in the world aren't going to help you.

Technology and computers are designed to enhance your efficiency, but if you lack the basic skills of time discipline to begin with, they only serve to create more confusion. As a speaker and consultant to many of today's Fortune 500 companies, lack of efficient time management skills ranks in the top two of the complaints I hear most about today's employee. Corporations spend literally billions of dollars a year in training, computers, and software to improve their workers' efficiency. This is as smart as putting a $5,000 stereo system into a car at the junkyard. Your ability to gain control of your life is a direct result of the time, effort, and methods you use to organize. Through organization we find clarity of purpose. Thirty years ago, a person might have had a chance to become successful without good personal management skills, but in today's rat-race world, we must master time discipline if we wish to succeed.

The time discipline system is a combination of time management basics and self-discipline-building techniques. The five key components of the time discipline system are:

- The book
- Daily tasks
- Course of action
- Priority scale
- Weekly grid

The Book

A simple black ledger with lined, white pages is the foundation of this simple, yet extremely effective, system. Many people are under the false impression that you need to purchase a fancy leather-bound organizer to become organized. I have found that these briefcase-size organizers have so many features and add-ons that the average person needs a master's degree to use one. The fact remains that no two people organize the exact same way and a personal management system must be individualized for maximum efficiency. A time discipline system must be focused on effectively managing your time and not centered around logging receipts, cataloging business cards, planning a wedding, or calculating the sun's rotation. In the SEAL teams we live and die by one simple rule—keep it simple, stupid.

A properly designed time discipline book should include an area at the beginning of the book for your contact list. I believe that it is vitally important to hand-write each name, phone number, and e-mail address, as this helps ingrain the information into the subconscious mind. In the back of the book, I paste miniaturized monthly schedules along with hotel, airline, area code, and whatever information I need to access the most. Since my profession requires a tremendous amount of coordinated travel arrangements, I have individualized my book to focus on this time-sensitive task.

The next step in the setup process involves cutting out pictures that best represent the goals you are striving to achieve in life. In my book, I have pasted pictures of the house I would like to someday own, the body I wish to create, and various other goals I wish to achieve. I also include a page for my mission statements and detailed courses of action for how I am going to attain my goals. Remember that the whole idea for developing a personal management system is to help you achieve your goals in life. Once you have individualized the book to focus on contacts, goals, and schedule-related information, you are now ready to begin learning the basics of the time discipline system.

Daily Tasks

There is a distinct difference between a goal and a task. A goal is something that you wish to achieve and a task is something that you must accomplish. To organize my tasks, every day I start a list. At the top of the first page, I write the day, month, and year in small letters. Underneath this, I write in large bold letters the words "To Do." This is simply my personalized method of recording the date and daily tasks that I must accomplish. At the beginning of each line under the heading "To Do," I draw a small square box. (This box is my status report for each of the daily tasks that I must accomplish for this day. Once a task has been accomplished, I will clearly mark an X in the box.) Next, I write out the task I must achieve on the line beside the box. The daily tasks that must be accomplished are stated in simple two- or three-word statements like "Call Harry," "Finish Sales Report," or "Morning Exercise." Each is a task that must be completed for the given day and should be written out the evening before.

The power of the subconscious mind is amazing. The act of preparing your daily tasks the evening before your day begins helps ingrain this information in your subconscious mind. As you sleep or go about your business before bed, your subconscious mind is busy at work preparing answers and data that relate to your specific tasks for the following day. Another advantage to writing down your tasks the evening before is that you can now begin to prepare yourself for the day ahead. Such tasks as packing a healthy lunch, preparing your clothing, and making sure you have the necessary paperwork and tools that you will need to accomplish the tasks can all be taken care of now that you see what is ahead of you.

Course of Action

Action without proper planning is the number one cause of failure in business and life. Now that you have prepared your list of tasks, the next step in the time discipline system is to write out a detailed course of action statement beside each task. As we discussed in the previous chapter, a course of action is the strategy you will employ to accomplish a goal. Having a course of action statement written beside each task helps you foresee problems; details the who, when, and where; and streamlines the decision-making process. Going through a day without a prepared plan is like sending a SEAL team into a foreign country with no objective, equipment, or game plan. A written course of action statement helps you discover what needs to be done, how close you are to finishing, and what steps need to be taken next with a simple glance into your time discipline book.

Your brain operates much like a computer. It needs a focused program of directions to attack a project. Working without a course of action is like trying to operate a computer without an operating system such as Windows or Mac OS. Here is an example of a course of action statement written beside a specific task:

Monday, August 21, 2000: TO DO

> Morning Exercise. Set alarm for 5:00 A.M. Lay out shoes, socks, and shorts. Program coffee maker for 5:05 A.M. Run nature trail at east end of park—5.5 miles long. Return by 6:00 A.M. Shower and eat healthy breakfast.

Priority Scale

Now that you have successfully established the tasks you must accomplish tomorrow, along with a course of action to clearly define your plan, you must find out which ones have a higher priority than others. Creating a priority scale is simply the act of finding out which tasks are relevant to your overall goals and which are irrelevant. The ability to see what needs to be done and prioritize accordingly is a learned skill. In order to help you determine the priority level of a specific task, you should ask yourself, "What impact does this task have on my job, my productivity, and my life-goals?" Throughout the course of a day, our urges for instant gratification, procrastination, and entertainment seem to creep into the prioritizing process and hamper our productivity. By establishing a list of tasks to complete, preparing a plan for their accomplishment, and attacking them from a priority-based system, we can increase our overall efficiency 50%, 100%, and even 300%.

A priority scale is designed to help you focus on the most important tasks first and then move on to the second, third, and fourth most important individual tasks that you must accomplish. It is important to work on one task at a time and stay with it until completion. The priority scale is graded by using A, B, C, D, and E. Once you have completed your list of daily tasks and prepared a course of action for each, you must now focus on which ones are the most important. Here is a description of the priority scale.

- A: First priority—the most important tasks to be completed.
- B: Second priority—important, but less a priority than the A's.
- C: Third priority—nice to accomplish, but not critical.
- D: Delay or delegate—these can be put off or passed on to others.
- E: Eliminate—these have no relevance and are a waste of time.

Weekly Grid

Now that we have developed a time discipline system that clearly defines our daily tasks, a course of action for their accomplishment, and a priority scale to identify the tasks of critical importance, we need to coordinate our activities on a weekly scale. A weekly grid is nothing more than a spyglass that allows us to plan on a week by week basis. Most of us are confronted with tasks that require more than one or two days to accomplish or projects that are scheduled many weeks and months in advance. A weekly grid allows us to stay ahead of constant changes in our schedule and balance time between work, home, and personal affairs. This forward-planning tool is placed every seven pages in our time discipline book and is filled out as our schedule begins to fill up.

In today's workforce, most people use a commercial planner or electronic organizer to stay on top of their work-related schedule, but very few people develop a system for balancing their time and tasks at home and in their personal lives. It is important to understand that an effective time discipline system must be able to manage our schedule in other areas of our lives instead of solely focusing on our tasks at work. A weekly grid is divided into four separate blocks that cover the entire spectrum of our lives. The

---

Time Discipline Sample Page

Monday, August 21, 2000
TO DO

A ☐ Morning Exercise: Set alarm for 5:00 A.M. Lay out shoes, socks, and shorts. Program coffee maker for 5:05 A.M. Run nature trail at east end of park—5.5 miles long. Return by 6:00 A.M. Shower and eat healthy breakfast.

B ☐ Schedule Meeting with Harry: Call Harry Doe at (100) 555-0000. Schedule sales meeting for Thursday. Ask about his wife, Claire. Call him at 9:30 A.M.

E ☐ Call Harvey: Call Harvey at (100) 111-5555. Talk about golf tournament this weekend. Ask about possibly meeting for bowling this weekend.

D ☐ Prepare Monthly Sales Report: Type in last quarter numbers. Forward to sales staff. Double check final calculations. Print three copies for management. Save onto floppy disk.

A ☐ Buy Flowers for Anniversary: Call Jane's Flowers (100) 555-3333. Order two dozen red roses for 4:00 P.M. pickup. Buy nice card and chocolates. Ask for special wrapping and box.

C ☐ Study Spanish Book at Lunch: Pack book in briefcase. Pack white note cards. Close office door and read book while eating lunch. Finish workbook exercises 7 and 8.

---

four areas of our lives that a weekly grid manages are work, home, personal, and life-missions.

In a time where two-income families, soccer games, school plays, and fast food dinners are the norm, keeping a balance in how you spend your time can feel like a daunting task. A major reason that we experience a high level of stress today is because we fail to recognize the importance of creating priorities and balance in our lives. Nothing will destroy your productivity and efficiency at work faster than an unbalanced personal life. Our minds have been programmed to believe that in order to be successful in life, we must have a certain type of car, style of clothes, job title, or luxury home.

Living in the world's most prosperous nation has developed a style of living that directly relates our self-worth to our bank account, which forces us to place a high priority on making money. The fact remains that this unbalanced way of life actually reduces our overall productivity and increases our level of stress. This cycle of reduced performance and increased stress is a direct result of unbalanced time management and priorities. It is through self-discipline and personal management that we are able to stay ahead of the power curve and create a balanced use of our time. A weekly grid is designed to do just that.

Sample Weekly Grid System
WEEK OF: August 21 – August 26, 2000

WORK	HOME
△ Sales report for first quarter	△ Repair garage gutters
△ Performance reviews	△ Review Billy's homework
△ Call new leads	△ Organize book shelves
△ Friday managers meeting	△ Fix wife's car
△ Backup work files	△ Mow lawn on Saturday
△ Clean office	△ Prepare daily lunches

PERSONAL	LIFE-GOALS
△ Work out four days	△ Study investment strategies
△ Special dinner for wife	△ Work on future business
△ Buy wife flowers	△ Study Spanish book
△ Attend church meetings	△ Assess promotion chances

Once you have prepared a weekly grid system on Sunday, it is simple to fill in the tasks for the appropriate days you will work on them. Remember that these tasks can be completed anytime throughout the week. I distinguish these weekly tasks by including the triangle and place an X through them once completed.

As I complete my list of tasks for the day, I fold the top corner of the page over to mark my place in the time discipline book and to identify that this particular day is completed. I fold only the To Do pages and not the weekly grid pages, as this provides a very efficient means of referring back to unfinished tasks. It is important to remember that an effective time discipline system must be individualized to meet your specific likes, needs, and style of organization. The simple act of handwriting your daily tasks and weekly grids into your time discipline book will not only help you stay focused on prioritizing your time, but also simplify your management needs.

Throughout my career as a SEAL, corporate speaker, and consultant, I have come to understand the basic rule of modern human performance that I call the 10% law. This law states that 10% of the tasks we work on throughout the day are actually of vital importance to our life-goals and the other 90% of the things we do are either reactions to problems we encounter or low-priority tasks. One of the hardest things to do on any given day is to avoid distractions and stay focused on our top-priority daily tasks. Without a pre-planned list of prioritized tasks to focus on, we begin to react to distractions and use our time for less important tasks. This is a normal human work characteristic that contributes to our belief that there is not enough time in the day or that we are overloaded with responsibilities.

When I teach the time discipline system to people around the country, invariably one or two people will tell me, "I need to manage my time better, but I don't like to be so strict with my time. I like to be more flexible and take things as they come." This is one of the major excuses that people use to validate their lack of self-discipline and focus. Being flexible and taking things as they come has nothing to do with being organized or managing your time better, but has everything to do with justifying our lack of control. Nothing great in this world has ever been achieved without the ability to focus. Think about how focused and determined we become when we are having fun or seeking pleasure. The ability to focus on one task at a time and put off distractions is one of the fastest ways I know to increase your efficiency and productivity. As a SEAL sniper, the ability to focus was the greatest weapon I carried and the difference between success and failure.

TAKE CONTROL TIP

No Complaining Zone
Improve your character by mentally stating your complaints, instead of verbally stating them. Nobody likes to be around a complainer. If you feel things are unjust, step out of the complaining zone and take action. Complaining does nothing except tarnish your character.

SELF-CONTROL

Self-control is simply the act of controlling our emotions, actions, thoughts, and words in every situation. Sounds simple, but it takes incredible mental discipline to maintain self-control and focus on your life-mission. Everyone has been exposed to discipline as a child—perhaps by too much discipline, too little discipline, unbalanced discipline, or the wrong kind of discipline. Now is the time to assess our personal discipline and management and work on our self-control. Practice thinking about your self-control by recognizing your dominant moods, words, attitude, and habits throughout the course of an average day.

Our failure to recognize that our level of self-control is directly related to our character and that our character is a huge billboard upon which we advertise our competence, self-worth, and work ethic is the first mistake that many of us make in the quest for self-mastery. You must understand that it is useless to learn new time management techniques, go on a diet, or become a solid decision-maker without first developing a strong level of self-control. The first step to gaining self-control is one of identifying the areas in our lives that are out of control. We have to take a close look at the food we eat, the bad habits we have, the character traits we possess, and the overall direction of our lives. Once we identify those things we need more control over, we can start small by gaining little victories each day. You must begin denying yourself one cigarette a day, the extra snack, that extra beer after work, or the satisfaction of indulging your emotional out-bursts. If you try to go "cold turkey" on all of your cravings, habits, and behaviors, you will likely fail.

Nothing brings more perspective to our lives than writing down a list of possessions, habits, cravings, and behaviors. As a consultant who works with many of today's high-powered CEOs and high achievers, I am always amazed at how much this simple exercise can change a person's perspective on their daily performance. It can be a real eye-opening experience to see an inventory of your life written out before your eyes. One of the main reasons that people often fail at losing weight, stopping procrastination, or sticking to a schedule is because they fail to understand that these are only results of a lack of control in certain areas of our life. We must focus on the cause and not the result, but before we can do this we must take an inventory. When you take an inventory of your life, you are actually creating a detailed dossier or personal profile from which you can see areas that need to be controlled.

Take Control Exercise

A technique for gaining self-control over our cravings and habits involves a self-inspection of our daily lives. By performing an inventory of our bad behaviors and habits, we can focus our efforts on controlling them. For this take control exercise, you are going to take an inventory of your life to determine exactly what areas need more self-control. Here is a step by step description of this self-control technique:

1. Personal Inventory: Find a quiet and private place to sit down with a paper and pen. Begin taking an overall inventory of your bad habits, destructive cravings, and uncontrolled behaviors. Create a list for work, home, relationship, and character traits.
2. Start Small: Begin reducing each habit or craving a little each day. Keep a journal of your progress and talk to yourself about the benefits of eliminating destructive behaviors.
3. Daily Denial: Start by denying yourself a certain pleasure each day. Target a daily activity like excessive eating, angry outbursts, or watching television.
4. Remind Yourself: Create small note cards with the words "Self-Control" at the top and a list of specific things you wish to control at the bottom. Place these cards on your mirror, desk, car dash, or wherever else you will see them often.

There are three key areas of our lives that we must focus on closely to begin developing self-control. These three key areas are the hardest to exercise control over, but are crucial to developing a strong foundation of self-discipline. These are attitude, communications, and habits.

Control Your Moods

Our moods are in fact the various attitudes we adopt toward circumstances in our lives. When someone is said to have severe mood swings, they are actually changing their mental attitude in accordance with emotions. The mood or attitude that you adopt in good times as well as bad times is the outward expression of your emotions. Most of the problems that occur in our personal life, occupation, and overall performance result from our inability to master our moods. It is important to understand that the answer is not suppressing your emotions, but rather controlling them when they begin to take over our actions, words, and behaviors.

Feelings of depression, anger, and lethargy are normal for every person throughout the day, but our ability to wield control over them is the foundation behind a positive attitude. Think about how your emotions changed your mood today. Did they decrease your productivity at work? Did they cause friction in your marriage? Have they decreased your communication skills? In order to gain insight into how our moods affect our lives, we must closely inspect our physical and mental reactions to them. Understand that you do have the ability to control the impact that your moods have upon your life. In order to develop self-discipline you must first learn to master your moods. Disciplined people live by their commitments and goals, and not by their emotions and habits. Controlling how you act and react is the result of emotional discipline.

Master Your Mouth

Disciplined people understand that what comes out of their mouths is a direct reflection of who they are and what they are. Think about what you want to say before you say it. This is the mastery of verbal discipline. Our words, just like our moods, can reflect an adverse picture to our friends, family, and coworkers when we fail to exercise self-control.

Nothing can alter our perception of a person faster than the words that come out of their mouth. I have known extremely talented individuals that have experienced more setbacks in their lives due to their inability to develop verbal discipline. Throughout history, a lack of verbal self-control has caused countries to go to war, companies to crumble, and marriages to break apart. In today's highly competitive business world, an employee who lacks verbal self-control can cause a company to lose hundreds of customers and tens of thousands of dollars a day.

Take the time to hear your words in your mind before you say them. The simple act of consciously thinking about your words in advance will help develop you ability to control them. Make a detailed list of how many times you swore, spoke out from emotion, or caused conflict for a 24-hour period. Take the time to think about the image you are portraying to everyone around you when you speak.

Deny Your Habits

Learn to say NO to your destructive urges, uncontrolled cravings, and selfish desires. Our primal and self-satisfying desires constantly demand appropriate control, and if we continue to satisfy our urges, we weaken our self-control. The narcotic of having everything all the time can dominate every action of our lives. When we begin to discriminate between what is actually needed and what is truly unnecessary, we develop a powerful sense of personal management.

Oftentimes, our bad habits become such a common part of our lives that we fail to even recognize them as destructive. The road to achievement first begins with self-mastery. This is not to say that simply because you have a few bad habits you will fail in life, but rather that they act as a set of brakes that slow down our progress. Nothing will kill your self-esteem faster than allowing your cravings to control your life. Most of the executives that I have worked with complain that they overeat to reduce stress, relieve depression, or to take their mind off of problems. As this cycle continues, they begin to build a craving that turns into a learned habit of overeating.

The development of a habit, good or bad, takes roughly 18 days to become ingrained into our lives. The fact remains that we are more vulnerable to developing bad habits today than at any other time in human history. We live in an age of instant gratification and tremendous prosperity. The ability to meet our every desire, whim, and craving is just a button-push away. The battle to win control over our habits has become the Waterloo for every person attempting to create a better life.

The incredible power of self-discipline is first developed by consciously attacking our bad habits. Take the time to carefully list your perceived bad habits and then ask a loved one to include their views. Begin controlling them a tiny fraction each day and never try to go cold turkey on them all at once. You erase a bad habit by overwriting it with a good habit for 18 to 21 days. This is a personal battle that must not be taken lightly, as your life will depend upon it.

Another very effective technique is called the power band. This method involves wearing a piece of colored string or rubber band around your wrist to constantly remind yourself of the habit or craving you are going to control today. Take a large rubber band and write the bad habit or behavior that you wish to focus on for this particular day and wear it around your wrist to constantly remind you of your control. I have personally seen this method change the lives of many people. Visualize in your mind that this rubber band empowers you with self-control that flows through your whole body. Every time you are faced with a certain thought, action, or environment that stimulates this craving or bad behavior, look to the power band for help. Remember that the power of your mind is the most important ally you have in the battle for self-control.

TAKE CONTROL TIP

Break the Comfort Zone
We are capable of ten times more than we realize. Build your resolve and strengthen your character by breaking out of your daily routine. Run a mile farther than usual, wake up earlier, or put forth more effort at work to break your comfort zone. Begin to expect more of yourself.

CHARACTER CONSTRUCTION

Disciplined people are always looking to improve their character and personality by exploiting their strong character traits and demolishing their weak habits. Start noticing what is weak in you and begin enhancing what is strong. Your character is the sum of all your strengths and the image you project from you actions, words, appearance, and work ethic. Think about the people in your life that you consider to be strong of character. What traits do they possess that portray this image to you? What actions, ethics, or behaviors do they display that command respect? You will begin to understand that character is not a function of beauty, money, or social standing, but that character is defined by our words, actions, and commitments.

Although our character is formed at a young age by our parents, positive influences, and early-life experiences, it can be continually changed by our beliefs, commitments, and experiences. Yes, you can build your character strengths and control your level of integrity. This is called the power of choice—possibly the most powerful and potentially dangerous freedom we possess as Americans. This is true regardless of your skin color, what language you speak, or what gender you are—our lives are what we choose them to be. Likewise, we have the ability to become the person we want to be, simply by working on our character traits.

Words like integrity, compassion, discipline, honesty, and commitment describe traits that we choose to display, or not to. When you begin to understand that our character is directly affected by our level of self-control, personal management begins to become more than just fancy words. Take the time to list the character traits you admire in individuals. Write words like honor, integrity, and discipline on little notes to yourself. Begin forming a picture of the person you want others to see in your mind and develop personal criteria for each of these traits.

The ability to control our emotions, actions, words, and character can be a difficult task. Once we stop succumbing to every whim, craving, and desire we have, our self-control begins to strengthen and creates a chain reaction. We become more alert and vigilant toward managing that which is good, and that which is unnecessary or bad. The power of self-control becomes strong enough to regulate our mental and physical cravings, society-induced desires, and influenced behaviors.

In order to build our character and become the person we want to be, it takes more than just reading a book or talking about integrity. It takes a constant awareness of our present character flaws and a burning desire to be a better person today than we were yesterday. Every time I walk into a bookstore I see hundreds of books on leadership, but very few of them address the real foundation of leadership—a strong character. The most basic foundation of leadership is respect, and how can you become a leader if people do not respect you? Leadership is not a right of passage simply because you have been promoted, and all the leadership books in the world will not help if you do not first have a strong character. If you want people to look up to you, respect you, and help you achieve your goals in life, then you must begin building a strong foundation of character traits.

The process of building stronger character traits is simply the process of imitating the strong traits of great people. We cannot all have the courage of Dr. Martin Luther King Jr., the compassion of Mahatma Gandhi, or the work ethic of Thomas Edison, but we can develop strong levels of these traits simply by making the conscious effort to evaluate our daily performance. Successful imitation is the process of becoming a better human being. Imagine that a genie has appeared in front of you and granted you the ability to have the characteristic traits of the ten most influential and successful men and women since the beginning of recorded history. All that you have to do is tell the genie what you want and from whom you want it. This is how we begin to create a strong character.

There are three key steps in the process of creating a strong character. It is important to understand that all great achievements in life are reached by those who learned from others that took a similar journey through life. Use these three steps to build your character and become the person you wish to be:

1. Imitate the successful journey of great people.
2. Educate yourself from their knowledge.
3. Initiate your own journey.

The following is a list of areas to expand your study of character traits. Use this resource to begin educating yourself on the journey that others have taken and learn all that you can about the traits you would like to build upon.

- Health and wisdom—Far Eastern philosophy, diet, medicine
- Wealth and power—American business, politics, investments
- Spirituality—Native Americans, Far Eastern philosophy
- Physical achievement—Olympic athletes, martial arts, Yoga
- Art and literature—European art, American classics
- Human nature—American psychology, Indian philosophy
- Courage and valor—Wars and combat, American Indians
- Self-discipline—Special operations units, Far Eastern philosophy

Take Control Exercise

In order to develop your character, you need a path and a plan. The ability to formulate a plan and choose the proper path is through knowledge and experience. In order to attain both, we must study and imitate the successful journeys of those who have gone before us. Below, I want you to think about each character trait and the person whom you feel best exemplifies that trait, and then begin to study everything you can about their failures and successes.

Characteristic	Master
1. Financial Wealth	
2. Courage	
3. Honor	
4. Discipline	
5. Spirituality	
6. Love and Devotion	
7. Humility	
8. Physical Greatness	
9. Health and Longevity	
10. Mental Greatness	

MAINTAINING YOUR MOTIVATION

The "fire inside" that fuels your efforts and makes accomplishments worth achieving is your motivation. Motivation is a group of reasons that develop a desire to accomplish, have, act, and perform in a manner that will satisfy a certain desire. Strong motivation is the underlying power behind some of the world's greatest achievements. Motivation is responsible for creating actions, thoughts, and situations that are directed toward a specific accomplishment. There is no use in trying to master self-discipline if you lack the motivation to have it. Every human being has been motivated by something at some point in their lives. The fact that you are reading this book shows that you have a certain degree of motivation to succeed at something.

Many people encounter obstacles when they try to motivate themselves to achieve a certain goal, and these obstacles are often false motivators. A false motivator is something that elicits a temporary emotion to have something and not a long-term desire to accomplish a goal. False motivation is the main problem behind most humans' poor daily performance. For example, the person who wakes up each and every day to go to work because he *has* to, and not because he *wants* to, is falsely motivated. The person who goes on a diet because their spouse wants them to is falsely motivated. The employee who performs a certain task because their boss told them to is falsely motivated. These are all examples of why people perform poorly or experience lackluster results.

True motivation is the result of a strong personal desire that focuses a person's thoughts, words, and actions in such a way as to elicit 100% effort. Imagine if you could muster the same motivation for performing at work as you do for personal gain. How strong would your motivation be if you were promised a million dollars for showing up to work every day this week? The reason that successful, self-disciplined individuals live a life of greatness and success is because they are truly motivated to accomplish their goals. How many people achieve a life of greatness or success in a job that they hate? How financially disciplined is a person who works simply to pay off daily bills and not for the attainment of goals? How many A's did you receive in classes that you were completely uninterested in? When we stop and think about our daily lives, we can easily distinguish false and true motivators simply by looking at our performance in certain areas.

When you truly desire to control certain habits, cravings, and behaviors in your life, you already have one of the key ingredients to self-discipline. Most people know that they want control over certain aspects of their lives, but lack the motivation to bring about true change. One of the easiest methods for strengthening motivation is through pressure. By telling your family, friends, and coworkers of your commitment to control an aspect of your life, you establish the presence of external pressure. Now, the motivation for achieving discipline is embarrassment, self-esteem, and challenge. Peer pressure is a very powerful motivator for most people. Tell your family and friends of the commitment you have made to losing weight and exercising. Tell all of your coworkers of your personal challenge, and let everyone at lunch and dinner know of your low-fat diet and see how strong your motivation becomes. Always be aware of your level of motivation. Use different techniques and situations to strengthen your motivation in specific areas. Only by focusing on self-control and motivation first can you expect to open the doors to a life of self-discipline.

TAKE CONTROL TIP

The Fire Inside
Learn to cultivate your desire to achieve. Paste pictures of your goals and mission statements in places that you frequent. Develop a burning desire inside to attain your goals. Keep yourself motivated by spending one hour each day working on your goals.

PERSISTENCE

Persistence is the ability to continue through adversity—the ability to brush off failure and stay focused on our goals. Persistence is continued action and effort toward an objective, even in the face of multiple failures. Success does not come without experiencing failure, and the only way to defeat failure is through persistence and perseverance. All highly motivated and successful people have found success and happiness with a never-say-die attitude. One of our country's most successful presidents was also one of history's most persistent failures. Here is his story:

Abraham Lincoln
1831 Failed in business—declared bankruptcy.
1832 Defeated for State Legislature.
1834 Again failed in business—declared bankruptcy.
1835 Fiancée died.
1836 Had a nervous breakdown.

1837 Defeated in election.

1843 Defeated in bid for U.S. Congress.

1846 Again defeated for U.S. Congress.

1847 Failed for a third time in bid for U.S. Congress.

1855 Defeated for U.S. Senate.

1856 Defeated for office of vice president.

1858 Again defeated for U.S. Senate.

1859 Elected president of the United States.

History books are filled with stories of persistent people who gained control of their destinies. The great prime minister of Great Britain Winston Churchill once said, "Success is going from failure to failure without a loss of enthusiasm." This is the most common reason for people's lack of self-control and personal management. It is because they failed once or twice at controlling their life that they become afraid to try again. There is no magic formula or ancient technique for becoming persistent. All the perseverance and persistence you will ever need is deep inside you, waiting to be exercised.

Of the ingredients required for self-discipline, persistence is probably the most powerful, because without persistence you will never experience success. You must plan to never give up, even before you begin. If you mentally motivate yourself to keep trying no matter what, you will subconsciously program yourself for persistence. If you are motivated, have self-control, and build strong character traits, but give up at the first sign of failure, you will never experience self-discipline or success.

THE EXCUSE VIRUS

Creating a strong character, keeping motivated, and staying persistent are keys to a life of accomplishment. However, we must constantly be on guard against our natural tendency to make excuses. We make excuses to justify our poor level of performance and to avoid looking at our own weaknesses. Nothing will destroy your character faster than the "excuse virus." Our natural tendency to make excuses can be likened to a virus because it slowly degrades our ability to accept responsibility.

Problem	Excuse
1. Overweight	"I don't have time to eat right!"
2. Procrastination	"I can only do so much in a day!"
3. Always in debt	"They don't pay me enough!"

4. Stressed out	"I never have time to relax!"
5. Marital conflict	"He/she is just too demanding!"
6. Work performance	"If they paid me more, I'd do more!"
7. Smoking	"I need it for stress relief!"
8. Drinking	"One drink never hurt anybody!"
9. Diet	"Who has time to prepare a meal?"
10. No daily exercise	"I just can't find the time!"
11. Anger	"They had it coming to them!"
12. Depression	"Nothing ever goes right for me!"
13. Poor appearance	"It's the newest fashion!"
14. Divorce	"We just couldn't work it out!"
15. Lack of self-discipline	"I have enough things to worry about!"

This list of problems and excuses is simply an example of our tendency to justify our words, actions, and behaviors. The problems we face and the methods we use to deal with them vary from individual to individual, but the underlying solution will always remain consistent. Before you can inject discipline into your personal operating system, you must take the action of personal responsibility. Get in the habit of identifying the real reason behind the circumstances in your life and defeat the excuse virus.

TAKE CONTROL TIP

Take Responsibility
Nothing is more admired than firmness of character. Learn to accept responsibility for your failures as well as your successes, with equal conviction. Make a conscious effort to identify the excuses you make throughout the day and reap the benefits of a strong character.

The power and influence of personal discipline is wonderfully expressed in a simple story, first told to me by a fisherman in the tiny Amazon village of Iquitos, Peru. In ancient times, a farmer tried year after year to grow crops on a little spit of land in the fertile jungle. Every year he would plant his crops and return to find them eaten and withered away. The farmer was very depressed because without a good crop, he would never be able to get married and have children. One day the farmer went up to the monastery on the hill to seek advice from the wise old monks. After hearing his tale of sorrow, a wise old monk agreed to help him grow the most prized crop of all—self-discipline. The monk took the farmer out into the vast desert, where he placed a small seed in his hand and told the farmer he must water it three times a day. The monk told him that this was the seed of self-discipline, and only by watering it three times a day would he see the fruit of self-discipline.

Day after day, year after year, the farmer traveled a great distance, three times a day, to water the small seed. Eventually, the small seed grew into a large tree that bore sweet figs and provided lots of shade for other crops. The farmer was able to build a small house in the shade of this tree and sell his crops, eventually enabling him to afford a wife and children. Each year the farmer would bring a handful of figs to the monk and ask him if this was the fruit of self-discipline, and each year the monk would shake his head and reply "No."

Finally, after years of frustration, the farmer yelled at the monk in anger and told him that no such fruit existed and that he had deceived him. The wise old monk replied, "You have successfully farmed the fruit of self-discipline, my son. You have become healthy, wealthy, and wise from this fruit, but you can never sell it or give it away. All you have desired has come true by planting the priceless seed of self-discipline in the rich soil of desire and motivation."

Perhaps you can identify with this story. You continually work day after day in the rich fields of life, but without real control and focus. Your efforts may not be toward a specific goal, and you might not realize the priceless seed of self-discipline we keep in our pockets. The good news is that most of us have desire and motivation, but just need a little push in the right direction. That push comes from personal control and self-discipline.

The SEALs have a saying that pretty much sums up our desire for perfection: "To be a perfect animal is one thing, but to be a perfect predator is the highest of callings." This simple saying is a constant reminder of the desire to want more, strive harder, accept no limits, and always continue to improve. Every successful person, corporation, and country has one underlying factor that ties them all together, and that is personal management. The mastery of personal management is accomplished by self-control, organization, motivation, and persistence. Organization of thoughts, actions, ideas, schedules, possessions, goals, and time is the task of personal management. It is through organization that the power of clarity is released, which in turn greatly increases our ability to focus on what we need to do every day to reach our goals and maintain self-control. The guiding principle of mastering personal management is to always put your life-goals first, be highly motivated, and be persistent.

MISSION DE-BRIEF
★★★★

What areas of your life are missing self-discipline? How often do you choose the easy way out? What habits and traits do you possess that have more control over you than you have over them? The disciplines you establish today will determine your health, wealth, and success tomorrow. Do you remember the age-old saying that "nobody's perfect"? All humans have faults, bad habits, and character flaws, but the superhuman uses self-discipline to reduce his or her flaws and stand above the average human. Developing self-discipline is not the act of punishment, total restriction, self-inflicted pain, or behaving like a robot. Self-discipline is a tool that each of us possesses to exact control over how we act, think, speak, and live, but the less we use of it, the more out of control our lives become.

4

THE BATTLE OF THE BRAIN

To enjoy good health, to bring true happiness to one's family, to bring peace to all, one must first discipline and control one's mind. If a man can control his mind he can find the way to enlightenment, and all wisdom and virtue will naturally come to him.—Buddha (568–488 B.C.)

I remember the time well. It was 2:20 in the morning on a freezing night in the middle of February. I had just returned from Jungle Training in Central America and couldn't sleep very well, so I decided to go to the SEAL Team Four gym. As I walked closer to the rear of the building, I noticed a series of strange thumping sounds and a soft, oriental style of music. When I turned the corner, I saw a fellow SEAL and friend of mine by the name of "Goat," who was kneeling on the cold pavement wearing only a pair of shorts. Goat was rhythmically striking a makawara board—a thick wooden post bolted to the pavement and covered with rice straw and thin ropes. His concentration was so complete that he was unaware of my presence. Blood was trickling from his knuckles onto the board, but he kept smashing it smoothly and powerfully over and over for several minutes before looking up. He then rose to greet me. I reached out and shook his powerful hand, and again noticed the blood trickling off his knuckles.

Since it is a common occurrence to see other SEALs in the gym at any hour of the night, I hadn't really given it a second thought when I first saw him. I had walked very quickly to the door of the gym, due to the fact that it was early February and very cold outside. As I stared at his raw meat-like hand, I asked him if that hurt very much. Goat said that he had not felt the pain until just this moment when he thought about it. "That's really going to hurt in the morning, Goat; you might want to stop beating the crap out of your hands," I said. Goat just looked at me and grinned a strange smile and told me the following story.

"When I was in Vietnam, I befriended an old man who taught Tai Chi Chuan to the local village children. When I wasn't out on SEAL operations, I would spend as much time with him as I could. One day I came back from several days of chasing down V.C. in the jungle and went to visit the old man, only to find him walking around with a large bandage around his stomach. He proceeded to tell me that he had been accidentally stabbed with a bamboo stick and that it had become severely infected. He told me that in the morning he was going to the Army medical tent to let the American doctors cut it out, and asked if I would accompany him to help translate.

"I agreed and met him the following morning at the Army's medical tent. The doctors told me that he would have to be operated on, and then tried to give him an anesthetic to put him out. When he immediately refused, the doctors told me that if he did not accept the anesthetic, they could not perform the operation, but the old man was insistent. After some discussion, the doctors finally agreed and asked me to help hold him down. The old man asked to be given a couple of minutes to prepare himself, and lay down on the table and closed his eyes. When he opened them, he said that it was okay to begin and that it was unnecessary for me to hold him down.

"The doctors looked at each other in amazement and began to cut out this large infection from his stomach. The surgery lasted about an hour and a half, and the old man never moved, spoke, or flinched even once. When the surgery was over he got up quickly from the table and began to get dressed, and we all looked at each other in stunned amazement. As we were walking out of the tent I asked the old man how he had done such a feat. He replied that he was in fact not even there for the surgery, but in a very special place. Later, he taught me to focus my eyes and mind on a tiny spot on the ceiling or floor and to regulate my breathing into a slow and steady rhythm.

"He told me that by focusing on that spot, he was able to take his mind away to a pleasant time and location he had created in his imagination. In this place he had a great banquet of food, and he had concentrated on feeling, tasting, smelling, and enjoying the incredible tastes it had to offer. The pain that the doctors spoke of could not reach him if he was not present."

Goat later went on to tell me that he was practicing the mental exercise of removing himself from his conscious mind and was in the process of being physically adored by 12 beautiful women when I had interrupted. In the SEAL teams, we control or diminish the immediate effects of pain, fear, sorrow, complacency, selfishness, and anger with mental techniques and training such as the one Goat was practicing. With such training, we develop amazing mental discipline that ultimately provides clarity not only during moments of intense physical and mental overload but in our day-to-day life as well. These techniques can be used for every mental emotion, feeling, and thought that is bad or harmful to our peace of mind and success.

In this chapter I will give you techniques taken from Far East philosophies, the Navy SEAL teams, and cutting-edge human performance training to help you harness and cultivate the power of the mind. The process of taking control of your life involves winning the battle of the brain by developing the skills to train your intuition, build your concentration, control your subconscious thoughts, and bring the power of mental discipline to your life. Again, as Aristotle said, "The greatest victory is over the inner self." The battle of the brain is about winning the struggle over our inner self, taking control of our life, and developing mental discipline to achieve our goals.

YOUR MIND—THE WEAPON OF CHOICE

The human brain has over 100 billion nerve cells, called neurons. Each of these has a number of branches that connect to other neurons. Most experts estimate that we have close to 1,000 trillion brain connections, and probably more. If you were able to string out all of your brain connections in a straight line, they would circle the Earth approximately ten times. During a fetus's nine-month gestation period in the womb, brain cells form connections at the rate of 250,000 cells per minute. Even more amazing is the fact that all of these connections are pre-wired in the genes of a fertilized egg, which is smaller than the point of a needle. The mathematician John von Neumann once calculated that the human mind can store up to 280 quintillion bits of memory—that's 280,000,000,000,000,000,000. A computer's speed is measured in flops, and the world's fastest supercomputer can process information at 100 billion flops. Experts estimate that the human brain can process information at the speed of 100,000 teraflops (a teraflop is 1 trillion flops). What this means is that your brain is more powerful than one million supercomputers.

In spite of all this magnificent computing power that we possess, most humans are hard pressed to remember names and numbers, let alone what they had for lunch last Monday. Some of the world's most famous superhumans, such as Albert Einstein, Leonardo da Vinci, and Stephen Hawking, only tapped into a tiny fraction of their brainpower. These individuals seem so amazing and talented that we label them as geniuses and hold them up as examples of superintelligence. What is the hidden secret to the immense talents of these superhumans? Einstein's brain has been studied by thousands of researchers for over 40 years and the one notable fact that was found from all of these studies was that Einstein had an increased number of glial cells (they help transfer signals between neurons) in his left parietal lobe. Glial cells increase as we learn more and challenge our brain more often. Likewise, these connections can shrivel and disappear when we cease to learn or challenge our minds. The ability to increase our intelligence and mental performance is directly related to how much time and effort we spend challenging our minds and learning new information.

Wise people since the dawn of time have been telling us what we accomplish or fail to accomplish in life is a direct result of how we think about our talents, abilities, and potential. Buddha put it very clearly: "All that we are is the result of what we have thought. The mind is everything. What we think, we become." The great Roman thinker Marcus Aurelius stated that our life is what our thoughts make it. Good or bad. Triumphant or hopeless. Miserable or joyous. In order to begin taking control of your life, you must understand that if you fail to believe in your talents and God-given abilities, then you are truly doomed to failure. If you believe that your background, childhood, or genetic abilities are limited to your present existence, then the world will go along with your evaluation and treat you as you treat yourself.

Most experts agree that we use only between 5% and 20% of our minds. What about the other 80% to 95% of our brains? In the mountains of India, devout Yogis have the ability to control their heartbeat, breathing, digestion, and nervous functions. These wise men have been practicing and learning about the wonders of the human mind for over 5,000 years and have taken human mental powers to a new level of existence. By utilizing breathing and meditation techniques, these wise men are able to withstand extreme climates without clothing, endure enormous amounts of pain, and go for extended periods of time without sleep or food. I am sure you have heard the tale of the old woman that lifts the heavy car off of her grandchild, or the amazing feats of people that move and bend objects with their minds. The American and Soviet governments have spent millions of dollars and well over 60 years studying and learning about these rare mental abilities. But before we get into the techniques used to train our mind for success and achievement, a brief discussion of cognition and the mental process is warranted. Specifically, let's talk about your conscious, your subconscious mind, and your mind's eye.

Never Stop Learning

TAKE CONTROL TIP

Take courses that pertain to your goals. Go back to school or read books. Become the expert by getting advanced training and learning new skills in your profession, or acquire a mentor. Think about how much time you spend improving your job knowledge. Become known as the go-to person in your field of expertise.

HOW WE THINK

Our minds have three totally separate and distinct entities. In the SEALs, we commonly call these the conscious mind, the subconscious mind, and the mind's eye. To be sure, there is an enormous amount of information and ideas for you to study and dissect about the workings of the brain. For the seeker of self-discipline, I encourage you to learn more about how, when, and why our brains function. You will be in a sense giving yourself an endless supply of mental ammunition to combat opposition and control your life by understanding the inner working of your most powerful ally. (See the suggested reading and source list at the end of the book for more information.)

The Conscious Mind

Part of your brain's main function is the preservation and survival of your body; it wants to save your life. This is your conscious mind. It is your basic animal instincts and reactions. It guides you in your struggles in the material environment. It also gathers information about your surrounding and records experiences of pain and pleasure, through your five physical senses: touch, taste, sound, sight, and smell. The conscious mind is the decision-maker. It calls upon the subconscious mind for data, assesses your best interests, and formulates a decision.

The Subconscious Mind

Behind your conscious mind is an entity that manages your conscious reactions and instincts. This part of you is called the subconscious mind. Its main function is the storage of information gathered by your conscious mind. Your subconscious has a set method of cataloging and associating information for retrieval when the conscious mind calls for it. This is where we interpret and decode our conscious thoughts in our own unique way as well as build up an arsenal of learned actions like riding a bicycle, playing the guitar, or dancing a polka.

When you perform tasks that you really don't remember consciously thinking about, your subconscious mind has taken over. For example, you get in your car after a long and hard day of work and the next thing you know you are sitting in your driveway wondering how you got there. Think of the many actions necessary to get you home, from unlocking the car door to merging into traffic to pulling into your driveway. This feat comes about through the subconscious mind.

This "second mind" is able to perform tasks twice as fast as the conscious mind, because it is preprogrammed to perform a certain task without conscious thought. It is known that the fastest you can draw a pistol from your holster while thinking through the whole process is around 1.5 seconds, but with a preprogrammed muscle memory, you can draw your pistol in around 0.3 to 0.6 seconds. This same subconscious process is found in sports. For instance, a basketball player dribbles the basketball while running and thinking about the tactics of the game. A batter is up at the plate timing his or her swing to intersect a 95 mph pitch, while processing the tactical situation of the runners on base, the number of strikes and balls he has, and the location and spin of the ball.

The subconscious mind is a powerful ally as you strive for mental discipline. We can achieve enhanced performance, organization, happiness, and instant action. Our subconscious responds to suggestion and reprogramming much like a computer. Through mental discipline, we can control the information and sensory input through our conscious mind. Just as your behavior and actions have once been learned and stored, you can reprogram and reorganize this process and thereby take control of your subconscious mind. To be successful at this endeavor, certain tasks must be committed to the subconscious mind by the techniques discussed in the next section.

Many people block the door to success by failing to fully comprehend the workings of their subconscious mind. When you know how to reprogram your subconscious, you gain the powerful weapon of mental discipline. You must remember that when your subconscious mind accepts an idea, it immediately begins to execute it. It uses all of its mighty resources to that end. This holds true for both good and bad ideas. Consequently, if you flood your mind with negative thoughts and statements, it brings trouble, failure, and confusion. When you begin thinking to enhance your present performance in life, your subconscious brings guidance, freedom, and peace of mind. The right answer and proper action are inevitable when your thoughts are positive, constructive, and loving. From this, it is perfectly clear that the one thing you must do to take control of your life is to accept this mission and train your subconscious mind.

The Mind's Eye

The third and most underestimated entity of the mind is called the mind's eye. The mind's eye is the picture, movie, or video screen that is present in our thoughts. The mind's eye is the television we use in our brain to view all of the images we formulate from the past, present, and desired future. It's our imagination, our fantasies, and our dreams. When we close our eyes and view certain images that we induce through thought, we are using the mind's eye. Your mind's eye is much more powerful than the two we have beside our nose. It possesses the ability to elicit pain, pleasure, power, riches, happiness, sadness, and just about every emotion we can feel or express. We use our mind's eye to reprogram our subconscious mind and thereby alter moods, feelings, thoughts, and actions by means of internal visual stimulation.

MENTAL DISCIPLINE

With the dawning of the digital age, we find as many pleasures and influences for the mind as we do for the body. There is so much information today that it is extremely hard to separate the useful from the useless. We may find ourselves having more mental habits than we do physical habits, and these mental habits can destroy our bodies just as quickly as do our physical habits. A mental habit is a continued destructive thinking pattern that triggers a destructive physical reaction. The bad mental habit of thinking you will never succeed or achieve your goals results in a poor attitude at work and poor performance. The mental habit of seeing yourself as ugly, unattractive, or overweight results in low self-esteem, perhaps followed by overeating. When we continually ingrain negative thinking patterns into our subconscious mind, we begin to lay the foundation for a negative mental habit.

Just as you can train your body for strength and power, you can train mental processing and your mind as well. Your brain requires proper and clean fuel, exercise, stimulation, and rest in order to function at optimal levels, just as your body does. The brain or computer you carry in your head is just as unique to you as your body and can be sculpted, strengthened, and enhanced in a similar fashion. However, it can be slowly poisoned, neglected, malnourished, and misunderstood to the point that it begins to break down and ultimately die.

Your mind and body can perform amazing miracles if properly used and conditioned for success and performance. The disciplined mind is constantly being reinforced, challenged, and bombarded with powerful positive thoughts and information directly related to enhanced performance and elevated happiness. The uncontrolled mind allows negative thoughts to guide physical behaviors and is constantly focused on pleasure and instant gratification. In order to break free from this prison, you must begin destroying your limited thinking patterns and start developing the tremendous power of mental discipline. You must comprehend the fact that your thoughts design your life and you cannot afford the damage created by even one negative thought. The mind must be conditioned to direct every thought to be one that will elevate your performance for the pursuit of your goals and dreams.

Mental discipline is the foundation for mastering all aspects of self-discipline and is crucial to taking control of your life. Mental discipline is the process of controlling your mind for achievement, increased performance, and a better quality of life, while physical discipline is the act of continually exerting control over your body, words, actions, appearance, and work performance.

Most of us know and admire people who stay cool under pressure. They handle criticism and anger with equal ease. When problems begin to mount during stressful situations, they are at their best and can be counted on to keep a level head. These people quickly rise to the top of companies, build successful relationships, and rebound from setbacks without slowing down. This is not magic or genetics. This is the learned skill of mental discipline.

Become a Risk-Taker

TAKE
CONTROL
TIP

Sitting on your butt accomplishes nothing. Wallowing in comfort and fearing change is the quickest way to an ordinary average life. Take a calculated chance and learn to move past your fear of failure. Remember that nothing great was ever accomplished without great risk.

STATE OF FOCUS

Have you ever been in such great pain or extreme anger that you could not control your reaction? How about when you smashed your thumb with a hammer, or slammed a door on your fingers? Your mind experienced such a rush of impulses that you probably yelled obscenities, jumped up and down, cried, and basically your body did things you weren't telling it to do. Navy SEAL teams refer to this as overload. Overload applies to any condition that shocks the body through external physical or mental experiences and elicits a set response. In other words, you react without thinking or planning your action. Your subconscious is in control.

To combat overload, you can train your subconscious mind to respond in ways you dictate, into a state of focus. When we are able to align our conscious, subconscious, and mind's eye into a single train of thought, we form "one" mind that works toward a common objective. This is the state of focus. Think of a magnifying glass. It takes scattered beams of light and focuses them into a single, powerful beam. A state of focus exists when the working parts of the mind come together for a single purpose and close off external distractions. We call this technique muscle memory because we are actually suggesting a programmed response to occur when a certain type of overload shocks our brain. It's your first step toward mental discipline.

Just as we use repetition to condition ourselves to perform a certain physical task, we can likewise use muscle memory to perform a mental task without conscious thought. To have muscle memory, we train our subconscious mind to accomplish certain thoughts and actions, through the mental or physical use of repetition. In most people, the ability to retain a certain muscle memory function usually occurs after 3,000 to 3,200 repetitions of that action. However, some smaller tasks only require 100 to 500 repetitions, like tying a new knot or typing on a keyboard. Muscle memory can be brought about by four reprogramming methods: visualization, positive reprogramming, word association and mental suggestion, and substitute thinking.

Visualization

Visualization simply involves actually thinking and imagining the results that you desire. By picturing the body you want to have, viewing the house and place you wish to own, or writing a statement of personal improvement, you are reprogramming your subconscious mind. Bombarding your mind with positive pictures and statements is much like the medical application of radiation to bombard and destroy cancer cells. You annihilate old thought patterns and reactions, allowing new ones to flourish. The technique of visualization is one of the greatest reasons for the sheer success, precision, ferociousness, and control that the Navy SEAL teams have experienced.

Visualization can also provide a springboard for our financial and job-related success. By picturing and imagining yourself giving a perfect presentation, getting a promotion, or closing the big deal, you are in effect living a desired outcome before it even happens. Before I go on a mission or training exercise at work, I visualize every step, word, action, and possible scenario that I will be asked to perform. This process helps me catch and eliminate any possible wrong move, thought, or reaction I may have, and by doing this over and over again I begin building up muscle memory for success.

Every person who ever was or ever will be successful uses visualization. The human mind is extremely powerful, but as the owners of this great tool, we use only about 15% of it. Surely all of you have heard the amazing stories of people lifting vehicles off of people, or the mental ability of some people to move objects and foresee events from the past and future. My intent is not to get sidetracked into subjects of the paranormal, but to simply reaffirm what you probably already know. If researchers were correct in calculating the 15% total usage of the brain, then logic would dictate that we have the capacity to perform those amazing mental feats somewhere in the other 85% of our brains.

Start by taping pictures and statements to your mirrors, car dash, home and work walls, and anyplace where you spend a lot of time. Take pictures from magazines, books, and whatever else you can find that best represent your desired goals. Go out and buy a yellow sticky pad and begin writing down positive statements like "I will run one mile today to burn away my disgusting fat" or "I will better manage my time to improve my job performance." Once you know what the desired outcomes are in your life, it is very simple to begin having them by utilizing visualization to gain control of your thoughts and reality.

Take Control Exercise

Many of today's top athletes, musicians, and scientists use visualization techniques to improve their performance and reach new heights in their professions. Visualization brings your mind into a state of focus and concentrates all of your mental powers toward accomplishing a single goal. For this exercise, we are going to use the power of visualization to prepare for a sales presentation at work. Once we have walked through the visualization process, I want you to practice this technique for a specific task that you need to accomplish in the future. Keep in mind that visualization can be used to improve your performance in any area of your life and is a powerful tool for reducing stress. Many of today's top performers use a visualization sheet to help them coordinate and focus through each phase of the task to accomplish. Here is a step-by-step visualization sheet for accomplishing a sales presentation.

Task: 45-minute sales presentation to upper management.
Time: 9:30 A.M.–10:15 A.M. Tuesday, August 22.
Action: Standing in front of 25 people. Speaking and using slide projector.
Dress: Black suit with red tie.
Environment: Conference room with white walls and blue chairs.
Outcome: My desired outcome is to have presented a flawless presentation of our sales material and to have the audience interested, educated, and ready to buy our product.
Visualization: Close your eyes and picture yourself standing in front of the audience feeling confident, secure, and in control. See the bright white walls and the dark blue chairs filled with people hanging on your every word. Listen to yourself talk about the specifics and watch the audience react with interest. Picture yourself discussing each slide and flowing easily into every segment of the presentation. See a picture in your mind of the decision-makers shaking their head in agreement and smiling with approval. Imagine yourself looking sharp, competent, and disciplined. Continue to visualize every portion of your presentation, including answering any questions that may be asked and the loud applause at the end.

Once you have completely visualized this exercise in your mind, prepare a similar visualization sheet for a task or skill you need to perform. Remember that you must find a quiet and relaxing place to visualize. For some people, speaking out loud during the visualization process helps create a more realistic environment. It is very important to completely avoid distractions and keep your mind in a state of focus.

Positive Reprogramming

From the moment of your birth, your first emotional experiences establish your subconscious perceptions of the world. There is not a moment of the day or night that you are not affected by your emotions. More often than not it is your programmed emotional states, not logic, that control your everyday behavior. Your subconscious mind flawlessly records everything you have ever done, seen, felt, heard, smelled, or tasted. It takes the information it accumulates, and divides and organizes it into separate programs that determine how you will respond to recurring circumstances and experiences in your daily life.

Experts estimate that your subconscious mind generates over 60,000 thoughts per day, and your inner voice speaks to you at a rate of 1,200 words per minute. However, you can only speak about 250 words per minute. You can now see just how active and powerful your subconscious mind is and that by controlling it, you control your life.

Once a program is formed by the subconscious mind, it will focus considerable effort to the continuation of the preprogrammed behavior or action, regardless of the consequences to your life. There are two subconscious actions that activate an emotional state, which results in a program of thoughts and actions. Think of these two different subconscious components as switches on a recording system. When these switches are pulled, the subconscious mind begins to power-up and create a response. This response is an emotional state, which in return creates a mental and physical reaction causing you to think or act out a preprogrammed response. The two trigger components of the subconscious mind are (1) asking yourself a question and (2) self-talk.

A good example of this process is when people constantly ask themselves negative questions or statements like "Why can't I make more money?" "Why am I so fat?" "I would do that if I had more time," or "I am too stressed to think about that now!" By asking these questions or thinking these negative statements, your subconscious mind automatically answers with negative responses such as "You won't make more money because you are in a nowhere job and you don't budget correctly," or "You are fat because you eat too much bad food because you are lazy and stressed." For each of these negative answers, the subconscious mind will produce a movie or picture in your mind's eye that shows you fat, overworked, underpaid, and stressed out. The mind now solidifies these pictures of negative situations and focuses incredible power toward maintaining this work and body situation. So basically, what you think and say mentally becomes reality.

In order to gain control of your reality, gain control of your thoughts. Begin by consciously replacing negative thoughts with positive ones. Instead of "I am never going make more money," think "I am going to dominate my job, get promoted, and work my way to the top money position." How many times have you told yourself, "I hate Mondays—I have so much work to do and I don't want to be here"? Replace this negative thinking habit with "This is a perfect opportunity for me to make more money, outperform my coworkers, and display my leadership ability."

Word Association and Mental Suggestion

Another application for muscle memory exists in the association of words. The power of visualization is an extension of suggestion. Suggestion is the process of applying visualization, thought repetition, and substitute thinking to override negative thinking patterns. By understanding and applying the technique of suggestion, we are actually practicing the power of self-discipline. When you see the runner who is up bright and early every day no matter what the weather, do you say to yourself, "Wow, that person has a lot of self-discipline?" How about the coworker who shows up early every day with a sharp, crisp, and well-groomed appearance to go along with his tireless energy and pleasant attitude? These are both examples of self-discipline manifesting itself in different ways, and I will bet that both of these people utilize some form of these techniques without even realizing it.

If we stop to think about it, there are situations every day where we can actually practice mental self-discipline. For example, I like to exercise and test my mental techniques of suggestion when I feel hunger. When I get that grumbling in my stomach, or thoughts of giant cheeseburgers and french fries play in my mind, I instinctively pause and recognize the mental and physical reactions that are occurring. Sometimes I will even go so far as to buy a cheeseburger and set it down in front of me, then experience the smell, visualize the taste, and let my mouth begin to salivate. I pick it up and throw it away or give it to someone else to eat. I then sit down to my prepacked lunch, revel in my success, and treat my body right.

Please don't get me wrong by thinking that self-discipline is the act of doing without, or of self-abuse; rather it is the act of control and substitution. Instead of sleeping until 10:00 A.M. and getting up to watch football, you merely substitute that schedule for one of getting up at 5:00 A.M. and running before having a healthy breakfast. I hope that this is all getting through to you, and that you are now beginning to understand what is wrong with your computer and how to go about fixing it.

A series of thoughts or a statement can be called a belief. A belief is another word for our mental guidelines or personal set of rules. Some of us have very strong beliefs that influence our actions and some of us don't. Our beliefs are formed by us and are guidelines for our words, actions, and behavior.

Our beliefs, or personal set of rules and regulations, frame the way we see reality, create reality, and live reality. Negative beliefs reside in the subconscious mind and undermine the good intentions we hold at the conscious level. We must identify and change our negative beliefs that turn into bad habits and destructive behaviors. Below I have listed several negative beliefs that always result in destructive thoughts and behavior.

Belief	Consequence
"I just can't do that, it's too hard."	You will never ever do it!
"I will always be fat."	You will never lose weight!
"I don't like my body and appearance."	Nobody else will like them either!
"I can't help myself, I just can't resist."	You will never help yourself!
"I am just too tired right now."	You will always be too tired!

When we continually tell ourselves these negative phrases, we are actually programming the subconscious mind to turn them into reality. We begin to associate our present reality with these negative beliefs and bring the consequences into our lives. Remember that your life becomes what your thoughts make it. The conversations we have with our inner self form the framework of our attitude, beliefs, and physical reality. If hearing the word "work" elicits feelings and thoughts of failure, tedious labor, stress, and anxiety, we are acting out a preprogrammed muscle memory response. Conversely, if we conjure up images, thoughts, and feelings of joy, success, fun, and money, then associate these over and over again with the word "work" in our mind, we will have reprogrammed our feelings with the technique of suggestion. The good news is that we don't need nearly as much practice or repetition for building this mental suggestion skill as we do for building physical skills. The bad news is that if we fail to practice these mental suggestion skills, we will gradually revert back to the original negative feelings, thoughts, and emotions.

Substitute Thinking

Substitute thinking is an ancient Hindu Yoga technique used to develop tremendous mental focus. This technique employs the tactic of substituting positive thoughts for negative thoughts. The mind's eye is like a movie screen that can hold only one image at any given time. If you are disorganized, every time the thought of how all of your affairs are in disarray appears in your mind, recognize, isolate, and substitute it with a clear picture of you working hard to organize every aspect of your day. You must picture in your mind's eye the pride, efficiency, and amazing results of organizing your personal affairs. This is a direct application of disciplining and controlling your thoughts to produce a desired outcome. Every time you recognize a negative thought, I want you to use this technique to substitute a positive one and experience the power of thought control and discipline. Soon you will think of only positive behavior and actions, which will become programmed into habit.

Take Control Exercise

The ability to overcome the cycle of negative thinking, which causes negative behaviors, can be accomplished by the technique of substitute thinking. The first step to changing a pattern of negative behaviors is to make a conscious effort to identify your negative thoughts. It is a known fact that we speak to ourselves ten times more than we verbally speak to other people. When our internal voice is centered on negative outcomes and circumstances, we experience depression, low self-esteem, and a poor attitude toward life. Substitute thinking can be used to reprogram this negative pattern once we begin to identify the words or phrases and substitute positive ones for them. Here is an example of this technique.

Words	Negative Association	Reprogrammed Thought
Party	Loud music, crowds	Interesting and lively conversation
Exercise	Pain, effort	Health, beautiful body, admiration
Work presentation	Nervousness, embarrassment	Informative, powerful, triumphant

As you can see from the exercise above, the first step in the substitute thinking process is to identify the key words or phrases that we have developed a negative association for. Take your time and think about certain words or situations in your life that make you feel uncomfortable or negative. Next, write down the negative feelings that you associate with these words. Lastly, think about the positive side of these situations or phrases and write them out in the format demonstrated above. Once you have developed the ability to quickly identify and substitute, begin using this technique throughout the day to break your negative thinking patterns.

Cultivate Winning Thoughts

TAKE CONTROL TIP

Don't allow the seed of doubt to be planted in your mind. Aggressively guard against negative thinking patterns. Begin thinking about the house or car you will buy with your first million dollars. Remember that positive thinking is a choice you make.

YOUR SIXTH SENSE

You are in possession of a powerful ability. It is commonly known as a hunch, an insight, a gut feeling, or sudden inspiration. The ability is the power that feeds, enhances, and ignites your focused visions or ideas. It's your intuition. This ability enables the executive to foresee a clear solution during a time of need, change, or in the face of hard economic times. In the Navy SEAL teams we call this our sixth sense, which can create correct solutions and decisions before all of the facts are known. Focused intuition is the generator of success.

You have probably never heard a world leader or top executive say in public, "I had a hunch and went with it" in order to make a crucial decision, hire a particular person, adopt a radical policy change, or take a risky gamble. Yet most of today's high-achieving people combine their sixth sense with logic to greatly enhance their decision-making ability in all aspects of life. Listen closely, and you may hear clues of a gut feeling, intuition, or a last-minute judgment call that led to a certain high-powered decision. Today's successful person does not ignore facts, figures, and logic, but each uses focused intuition input to add weight or solidify a certain course of action.

In the SEALs we regard the sixth sense as a crucial part of every important decision. There are many instances in the world of special operations where a particular door, route, path, area, or situation just didn't feel right and the mission was either changed or cancelled. Surprisingly enough, most of these decisions proved to be absolutely correct. Several times throughout my career as a SEAL, countless lives were saved because of a hunch, strong feeling, or sixth sense.

The sixth sense is simply a way of characterizing the mind's subconscious ability to instantly draw stored information, ideas, and feelings from its memory banks and turn it into a suggestion or emotion. Intuition can come as a flash or as a flow of ideas and suggestions, each one affecting the next until you have a clear pattern of innovative thoughts and actions.

Throughout the course of your life, you have undoubtedly used intuition at some time or another to make a decision. Maybe it was at the car lot when you just felt "wrong" about a particular vehicle, or maybe when you met somebody for the fist time and felt something negative about them, or even decided not to take a certain street for some unknown reason. These are all examples of intuition and your sixth sense providing input during the decision-making process. Most people have heard the stories of people deciding not to get on a particular flight or take a certain bus because something inside their mind was telling them not to, only to find out the plane crashed or the bus went over a cliff. This same powerful ability can be exercised and harnessed to provide clarity and input to our everyday decisions.

Throughout my career in the special operations world, I had the pleasure of studying and interacting with many different cultures. Some cultures use intuition as a major source of information and decision-making. In South and Central America, the indigenous people who live along the Amazon and deep in the jungles believe that a spirit talks to them inside their head. This spirit offers advice, guidance, and often prophecies of things to come. Some Native American tribes believe that the Great Spirit and ancestral spirits guide them with advice and solutions. Others believe that certain animal spirits talk to them during times of duress or uncertainty with hints of advice and guidance.

Throughout time these cultures have used devices and drugs to help promote the sixth sense by using sweat lodges, opium, peyote, and other trance-inducing concoctions. I have spent considerable time with some tribes that use the sixth sense to determine the course of each day, whether it is hunting, fishing, working, celebrating, or spiritual reflection. Some days were judged to be good hunting days simply because it felt "right" or an inner voice told them so.

How can you keep in touch with your sixth sense and tap into the amazing power of intuition? Many Far East holy men, ancient culture spiritual leaders, high-powered corporate executives, and world leaders use a variety of techniques to exercise and harness the power of intuition on a regular basis. Here are six powerful techniques and exercises that come from the jungles of South America, the boardrooms of high-powered executives, and the prayer rooms of Tibet. Try out and practice each one of these techniques to strengthen and harness your sixth sense. You might find some of these a little odd or awkward. Just remember that the sixth sense cannot be quantified, but nearly everyone agrees it is there.

Intuition Games

Playing intuition games is a powerful technique for tapping into your sixth sense. Ask your coworkers or family members to guess who will come into the room next and what they will be wearing. Guess what your friends or family will say next when having a conversation. If you are going to meet somebody new, guess what clothes they will be wearing or their physical features from their personal facts, like age, race, and sex. When you are sitting beside someone in a plane or bus, try to visualize what this person does for a living first, and then ask him or her.

Brainstorming

Use the power of visualization to open up your sixth sense. Close your eyes and imagine a large white wall with the words "advantages" and "disadvantages" written in big black letters. Under the word "advantages," mentally list all of the positive ways to solve this particular problem. As you mentally write each possible solution, take a deep breath and visually see this solution in action from beginning to end. Go through the list of advantages for each solution and clearly focus on all possible outcomes of using this solution.

As you visualize these ideas, does one stand out more than others? Does this idea just "feel" right? Keep these ideas firmly planted in your image and now visualize the word "disadvantages." Mentally write all of the possible factors that could produce an undesired outcome from each of the ideas. By concentrating the brain's power of imagination toward all of the possible pros and cons associated with a certain idea, you begin involving the sixth sense and the subconscious mind. This technique will force the subconscious mind to search for a possible gut feeling and enhance your feeling of intuition.

Dream Wisdom

Dreams can become a powerful link to your inner intuitive mind. For many successful people and religious leaders, the power of dreams can become a gateway for wisdom. Have you ever heard the saying, "Let me sleep on it"? This is a way for you to turn over the problem-solving task to the subconscious mind. Throughout the day and before going to bed, take some time and go over all of the possible avenues, outcomes, and choices to your problem. As you go to sleep, the subconscious mind starts working, searching through all of its available information and can sometimes show you the best solution in the form of a dream. Do not discount the powers of the subconscious mind. Use a notebook to record as much of your dream as you can remember. Sometimes the intuitive answer is hidden in the context of your dreams.

Suggestion

Sometimes we can get so wrapped up in trying to find an answer to our problems that we actually stymie our creative genius. By using the power of self-suggestion to free up your intuitive instincts, you can be looking for answers while going about your everyday business. For example, in the morning I will write down the problem that I need solved on a piece of paper and mentally verbalize this problem to myself five times in a row. I now try to forget about this problem and go about my day as usual. While I am consciously performing my everyday tasks, my subconscious mind is actively searching its data-bases for the necessary information. At some time during the day or night, a little light bulb will appear above my head and a good idea or intuitive feeling will strike me. Try condensing your problem into a single word that is the main theme for your problem. Use this central word to apply the self-suggestion technique and free up your sixth sense.

The Spirit Animal

Some North American and South American Indian cultures believe that every person has a spirit animal that best represents and guides them through life. If you are trying to figure out the puzzling actions or words of a coworker or family member, try using this metaphor technique to gather some insight into this person's behavior. Imagine in your mind if this person was an animal, what sort of animal would he or she be? Be open to any images that suddenly come to mind.

The sixth sense will help you interpret these images into emotional and physical reasons. When you think of this person and a lion comes to mind, words like dangerous, ferocious, cunning, and dominating might come to mind. Also remember that the lion can also be loving, protective, caring, and motherly. This person might appear to be confrontational and menacing, but they may also have low self-esteem and be very vulnerable. Use this age-old technique to free up your intuition about people in your everyday life.

The Sixth Sense Diary

Keep a personal journal or notebook of your gut feelings and flashes of brilliance. This technique will help you become much more aware of your sixth sense and help you identify when your intuition is trying to tell you something. Some of your information will be trivial, while some may be more solid and fact-based. All of your recorded hunches attest to the activity of your sixth sense. If you observe in your journal that 25% of all your gut feelings occurred while looking out your office window, then you might wish to invest more of your time and mental effort into creating this winning environment. Always note in your journal the time, place, activity, and atmosphere when the hunch first came to you, but also make sure to record how, when, and if that particular insight became validated.

DAY-TO-DAY MENTAL DISCIPLINE

If we stop to think about it, there are situations every day where we can actually practice mental discipline. For example, I like to exercise and test my mental techniques of suggestion when I feel tired. When I get that lethargic feeling, or thoughts of laziness and sleep in my mind, I instinctively pause and recognize the mental and physical reactions that are occurring. Sometimes I will think about resting on my couch or crawling under the covers of my bed when I am tired during the day. I will then close my eyes and picture myself performing intense exercises, running long distances, and feeling physically strong to put myself in a high-energy mind frame. I often use vivid memories of my years as a SEAL where I endured days without sleep and with little food or tell myself that I am capable of ten times more that I realize. Remember, mental discipline isn't the act of doing without, or of self-abuse; rather it is the act of control and substitution. Instead of staying up late to watch a particular movie and waking up tired and grumpy, you merely substitute a schedule of going to bed at 9:00 P.M. and getting up early to prepare for the day.

TAKE CONTROL OF YOUR MASTERPIECE

Take advantage of the workings of your subconscious mind. When your subconscious mind accepts an idea, it uses all of its resources to that end and mobilizes the mental and spiritual laws of your deeper mind, for better or for worse. Don't flood your mind with negative thoughts and statements; rather, begin thinking like a superhuman bent on enhancing your present performance in life. Solutions are inevitable when your thoughts are positive and loving. Accept the superhuman idea that you control your destiny, let your subconscious mind begin feeling its reality now, and the law of your mind will do the rest.

A car owner once argued with a mechanic for charging $300 for fixing his engine. The mechanic said, "I charged ten cents for the missing bolt and two hundred ninety-nine dollars and ninety cents for knowing how to fix what was wrong with your car." Think of your mind as the master mechanic, the all-knowing one, who knows ways and means of healing any organ of your body, as well as generating the answers for your success. Decree success, and your mind will establish it, but clarity and relaxation are the keys. Do not be so concerned with the details and daily struggles, but know the ultimate end result. Get the feel of the happy solution to your problems whether it is financial, health, love, or work. Remember how you felt after you accomplished something significant. Keep in mind that this feeling is the cornerstone of all subconscious reactions. Your new lease on life must be felt subjectively in a finished, powerful, beautiful, and tranquil state, not in the future, but as coming about now.

By enacting and understanding, and not only reading, you will have the opportunity to be a true master of your own performance and destiny. You can make your world exactly what you want it to be—the decision is yours. If you want this incredible power and existence, the secret is to remember that your mind is the master mechanic of your performance and success. If you are able to design and regulate your thoughts, you master your mind and actions. Once you do that, you begin to take control of the circumstances in your life and, ultimately, your destiny.

Pain is the ultimate teacher of lessons. Begin taking responsibility for your life and all of the circumstances and events that are in it. If you are unhappy, wish for more money or a better job and decide to make the changes and take positive action to elevate your performance and grasp your destiny. If you desire a sexier, healthier, and more energized body, take the steps necessary to achieve greater results and benefits. If you want a more loving and caring relationship, make the commitment to become the kind of person that attracts and nurtures such a life. None of this will come to you by chance, genetics, or inactivity. If you continue to perform at your present level, nothing will change and your present life will continue to be reality.

A masterpiece is a work of art or symbol of enduring talent, beauty, and revered greatness to be admired by all human beings. Each and every one of us has a blank canvas on which to create our own living and breathing masterpiece. The one consistent value that we all must recognize in the journey to achieving our destiny is pure and simple change. What empowers each of us with the ability to make decisions that change our lives is the ability to take consistent action. The power to control the outcome of our lives is directly related to the amount of control we have over our consistent actions and decisions. The golden rule to controlling change in our lives is: take action, any action. As long as we are constantly acting and moving in the direction of our wants and desires, we exert tremendous power toward the attainment of our desired reality.

MISSION DE-BRIEF
★★★★

It is human nature to seek out pleasure and comfort in life, but we are weakened when we overindulge and lose our ability to control moderation. I will never profess to having mastered the power of mental discipline, but I know and see the results of applying it not only to the elite world of special operations but also to everyday life. Our brains, although extremely complex, operate in a very logical and simple manner. In the SEAL teams we spend about five times as much effort training our mental focus as we do training our bodies. By understanding and applying these techniques of visualization, thought control, and suggestion, we are refocusing and reforming our mental processes and perfecting the art of mental discipline. Achievement of our goals will naturally follow.

PHYSICAL DISCIPLINE
The Fight for the Body

Hidden within each of us is an extraordinary force. Physical and mental discipline are the triggers that can unleash it. Exercise is a form of rebirth, when you finish a good workout, you don't simply feel better, you feel better about yourself.—George Allen

Your physical presence is the picture and impression you give every day to your family, friends, coworkers, and fellow human beings. How you look and feel physically is a direct reflection of your competence. I am not talking about your beauty, but rather the idea of care, maintenance, performance, and self-esteem you physically show and control.

As you think about physical control and begin to develop a plan, remember that the benefits of physical control are numerous. You will

- Enhance your energy and stamina
- Require less sleep
- Maintain a sharp, crisp, and professional appearance
- Develop significant increase in focus, determination, and creativity
- Sustain a longer and more pleasure-filled life
- Enhance your memory, alertness, and mental aptitude
- Create a greater sense of confidence and self-worth
- Show dramatic improvement in family, work, and life performance
- Become an example of self-discipline for all to see
- Revitalize your feeling of purpose and accomplishment

In this chapter, you will be shown time-proven techniques and training systems to master physical control and learn ways to adapt these to meet your goals. When you step up and make the decision to exercise and eat properly, you must remain persistent, consistent, and motivated in your scheduled program to receive real, everlasting results. In just one week, a vibrant energy will radiate into all areas of your life and you will feel better than you have ever felt before. No matter what form of exercise you choose to undertake, you will feel the powerful increase of personal energy in all areas of your life. Good food choices will become powerful fuel and bring essence to your being. The feelings of weakness, fatigue, and complacency will disappear when you come home from a long day of work. Instead you will have the energy and desire to take part in productive activities that are sure to help you take control of your life and increase your self-discipline. Any person who builds the habit of physical exercise has a far greater chance of succeeding in life than those who don't. Every one of us will experience hard times, depression, financial problems, and daily setbacks throughout our lifetime, but it is our ability to bounce back and continue our tireless journey toward our goals that makes the difference. This ability comes from physical and mental strength, the by-product of exercise.

THE ANIMAL WITHIN

Imagine an animal that can run 100 miles without stopping, swim 30 miles in freezing water, climb sheer cliffs thousands of feet high, lift up to three times its own body weight, and dive hundreds of feet on a single breath. This animal actually stares back at you in the mirror each morning, because in reality this animal is you. The human being is one of the most resilient, athletic, and diversely adaptable creatures on the face of the earth. We can survive arctic blizzards, desert heat, days without food or water, and months on the open sea, yet for the majority of today's society, walking up a set of stairs becomes taxing. Today's human being has created a level of personal comfort so great that throughout our lifetime we may use only one-tenth of our actual physical capability. We have created an environment where survival is no longer based on physical ability and as our level of comfort and security rises, our physical bodies become soft and weak.

In the elite world of the Navy SEALs, daily survival is based upon physical endurance and mental fortitude. This environment is strikingly similar to the animal food chain, where strength, speed, and resolve determine survival. Basic Underwater Demolition SEAL School is the most intense physically and mentally demanding training in the world. With a failure and dropout rate of nearly 85%, SEAL training pushes men to the extreme limits of the body and mind. Physical exercise and training are what we utilize to transform men into skillful and thinking predators. Most people never take the opportunity to push their minds and body to the limit, to see exactly what they are made of. Our poor state of physical condition today is a direct result of our perceived limitations and not our actual capabilities. Before I became a SEAL my mind was cluttered with perceived notions and misconceptions about my physical and mental capabilities, which resulted from an environment of comfort and security. The only way to develop the habit of physical exercise and experience a life of health, energy, and vitality is to shatter our perceived limitations and unleash the animal within.

If somebody had told me that I could stay awake for five days and nights, while swimming, running, lifting logs, and being tortured in the surf zone nonstop, I would have laughed in their face. I never could have imagined that anybody, let alone me, was capable of enduring and accomplishing the physical challenges that are part of the job as a Navy SEAL. I am alive today and owe all of my personal success as a speaker and consultant to the intense physical training I received throughout my career. I have survived avalanches, poisonous snake bites, jungle diseases, explosions, parachute accidents, and countless other incidents solely because of God's will and my physical conditioning. Aside from surviving these incidents, physical conditioning has enabled me to overcome professional setbacks, work through financial downtimes, deal with difficult people, protect my loved ones, and accomplish goals I previously thought impossible.

Not only is physical conditioning the key to a lifetime of health, increased energy, and vitality, it is the secret ingredient of a today's top performers in the workplace. In an arena where long hours, stressful commutes, difficult people, and intense competition are the daily norm, the ability to stay focused and perform at a high level is what separates those who move up the ladder quickly from those who simply take up office space. Not surprisingly, many of today's top corporations have taken notice of this fact and have spent millions of dollars building in-house exercise facilities and health-food cafeterias. A person's ability to take control of their physical condition is a direct reflection of their time management skills, decision-making ability, and work ethic. If two people of equal experience and background are interviewing for the same job and one has a weight problem and the other appears healthy, fit, and vibrant, who do you think will get the job? The facts that today's health care costs have skyrocketed and that corporate competition is at an all-time high dictate that physically fit employees are not only an advantage, but a must.

MASTERING PHYSICAL CONTROL

How does one master physical control? Physical control is the result of a self-disciplined lifestyle, which includes successful time management, mental conditioning, and proper goal setting. To master physical control, you must first schedule time for exercise, adopt proper nutrition guidelines, and continually strive to meet your exercise goals. The number one reason that people fail to lose weight, stay with a diet plan, or stick to an exercise program is that they lacked these basic ingredients to begin with. In a time where crazy diet plans, fancy exercise contraptions, and fat-blocking pills are found on just about every television channel, the concept of daily exercise and physical control has become lost in the confusion.

Understand that in order to take control of your physical body, you must make this a top priority in your life. It is the people who are looking for short-cuts, instant results, or the easy way out that fail time and time again. Begin adopting a lifestyle that is centered around physical control. Take note of your present exercise routine, eating habits, and time management system, or lack thereof. Remember that your physical appearance is a huge billboard that advertises your competence, self-worth, and work ethic. This is in direct reflection of your self-discipline. How you present yourself in everyday life, whether it is at home or at the office, is simply the ability to personally control your appearance, words, and actions. Make the following items part of your life:

- Early to bed and early to rise. Nothing improves your performance like preparation. Plan your day before you go to bed, and get up early to prepare yourself.
- Have the look of a self-discipline master. Start with a crisp and well-tailored appearance. Groom your hair and features. Walk with a purpose. Advertise your professionalism.
- A healthy body enhances the healthy mind. Pay attention to the information on nutrition. Investigate and acquire the knowledge of nutrition. Move with agility and strength. Study vitamins, supplements, herbs, and healthy lifestyles. (More about this in chapter 6.)

- Find the time to shower twice a day. Smell good and clean. Work on unsightly bad habits. Eat clean foods such as fruits and vegetables. Take pride in your possessions.
- Assume the responsibility of personal control and appearance, and everyone will notice the benefits. Come to love and care about your body, and you will be well on your way to happiness and longevity.

Once you have programmed your mind to think and focus on positive thoughts, you can work on your outward presentation. You are guaranteed to be noticed and thought of with positive regard. In the following pages you will find simple yet powerfully effective techniques and exercises that will help in dramatically changing the way you live life. Remember that your main objective is to enhance the quality of your life and begin learning the principals of mastering physical discipline. It is imperative that you start out slow and easy at first, then increase the effort and repetitions as you gain more confidence and power.

TAKE CONTROL TIP

Treat Yourself Often
Watch your diet, but don't be fanatical about it. This is the fastest way to lose control. Follow a strict diet Monday through Friday, but treat yourself on the weekend. Once physical discipline becomes a habit and part of your life, controlling your diet is a breeze.

FIVE PRINCIPLES OF EXERCISE AND PHYSICAL CONTROL

In the SEAL teams we exploit five simple and effective principles of physical exercise that we use as the foundation of all physical-related activities. These five principles—overload, individuality, target training, consistency, and FIT—are designed to maximize the effects that physical exercise has upon the human body. It makes no difference what your exercise program is, the use and understanding of these five principles will ensure the safe and immediate elevation of your physical stature. You will then easily meet the goal of any exercise program, which is to enhance performance and health.

Overload

The basis of this principle is that the level of exercise must increase gradually to bring about various physical changes. When your body adapts to a higher level of physical exercise, it will perform more efficiently and with greater ease. Overload is initiated by increasing the intensity, duration, frequency, and style of the exercise. By increasing these aspects of exercise, you in turn increase your cardiovascular capacity and muscular strength. The overload principle states that you must continue to push your body a little more today than you did yesterday. A bodybuilder is able to greatly increase his muscle size and strength by continually taxing the muscle to its maximum limit. Once a certain limit has been reached, the muscle responds by quickly re-building itself to handle the increased strain. This is how our bodies work and why the overload principle must be used to improve performance.

Individuality

The results of certain types of exercises can differ from one individual to the next. By customizing the exercises to meet your personal goals and expectations, you are better able to find out what does and doesn't work for you. Some people find more pleasure in running than they do in weightlifting and vice versa, and still others are better suited to swimming than bicycling. One of the reasons that people today have a hard time staying with an exercise program is that they force themselves to perform exercises that don't necessarily fit their body type and physical characteristics. It is extremely important to learn your likes, dislikes, strengths, and weaknesses before adopting an exercise program. People who dislike working out with a group will have a very hard time maintaining their intensity level at an aerobics class and those who need contact with people will most likely not enjoy swimming or running.

Your ability to individualize certain forms of exercise to best meet your needs and likes is directly proportional to your level of consistency. Expand your knowledge base to include Yoga, Tai Chi, and various other forms of physical exercise to allow yourself more choices. Avoid jumping on the latest exercise craze until you have developed a strong work ethic and commitment level with your favorite form of exercise. Use your friends and family to encourage you, but not to dictate how, when, and where you exercise. Begin developing your own unique and individualized program.

Target Training

This principle reflects specific result-based training. By targeting a specific type of exercise to enhance a desired outcome, you begin focusing on a certain desired result. For example, weightlifting increases muscle mass and muscle group strength but will not necessarily increase your running ability and vice versa. Therefore, it is important to focus on certain muscles involved in a specific type of exercise to receive enhanced performance benefits. If you are trying to develop your upper body or streamline your lower body, then you must start targeting a specific set of muscles with a specific set of exercises.

Most people that I work with always have a desired outcome in mind. They want better definition, larger muscles, a smaller butt, or more-developed legs, but knowing the desired end-result is only half of the battle. If you desire to simply lose weight, you must understand that walking for 15 minutes each day is not going to cut it. You could walk from Los Angeles to New York and not lose a pound. You have to be willing to go beyond the easy, the relaxed, and break your comfort zone. In today's society, people are driven to seek instant success formulas, the magic weight loss pill, and the path of least resistance, but fail to realize that true physical health comes only through hard work and commitment. Target training is about changing one aspect of your body at a time by concentrating on specific exercises designed for specific results.

Consistency

Physical exercise is not a task or chore, but a purposeful habit. You can make all the excuses you want, but you have to exercise with consistency in order to see results. By utilizing the tools of personal mastery and self-discipline, you generate the habit of staying with your personal commitment to exercise. Think back to the various diet or exercise programs you have tried in the past. How long did you stick with them? How many times did you miss a scheduled workout or cheat on your diet? Your ability to exercise at the same place and time each day while fighting off distractions and bad days is the foundation behind a lifetime of being known as a reliable person. There are four keys to building a consistent exercise program:

1. Plan: Set a schedule one week ahead that includes the time and place.
2. Prepare: Have a gym bag prepacked in your vehicle.

3. Execute: Fight through bad days and schedule changes. Exercise is a top priority.
4. Review: Keep a descriptive journal and review your progress from day to day.

FIT = Frequency, Intensity, and Time

The FIT principle must be included to extract the most benefit from your exercise program. The time you spend exercising and the type of exercises you perform are just as important as the amount and intensity of your effort. If you are not improving or enhancing, you are simply stagnating. As you become more comfortable with your routine, exercise more frequently and make the most of your rest days. Walk into any gym in America and you will see more than half of the people standing around talking, wearing designer fitness clothing, and barely breaking a sweat. Increase your intensity and develop a level of focus that demonstrates you mean business.

TAKE CONTROL TIP

Join the 5 O'Clock Club
Develop one of the most important habits of highly efficient people—wake up at 5:00 A.M.! Discipline your time to include an early morning wake-up where you can prepare yourself both mentally and physically for the upcoming day. Use this time to exercise or simply have a little quiet time.

THE RELIGION OF CALISTHENICS

In the special operations community we use calisthenics as the primary building block for a balanced, proportional, and overall powerful body. Calisthenics is a word used to describe a series of exercises that focus on building muscular strength and flexibility for every major muscle group in the body. In today's society of million-dollar gyms, thigh-masters, fancy machines, and spandex, calisthenics bring the individual back to the basics. Most people think that you have to become a member of a high-priced gym or wear hundred-dollar outfits to get in shape. Calisthenics allow you to get in touch with your body and mind by eliminating all of the confusion and easy-way-out philosophies that are found in many of today's physical fitness centers.

You probably have an idea what calisthenics are. Push-ups, sit-ups, chin-ups, right? Yes, but calisthenics are more than that. Simply put, calisthenics bring the individual back to the basics and allow him or her to get in touch with their body and mind. Calisthenics strike a balance between mind and body and provide a complete system for exhausting every body part. Using a series of exercises, calisthenics focus on building muscular strength and flexibility while burning calories at a very high rate. Through these seemingly ordinary exercising methods, individuals train their bodies while sharpening their mental control with relaxation, visualization, and self-discipline.

As elite commandos, we view our individualized calisthenics program to be more of a religion than an exercise. This personal physical religion is a customized program of powerful mental and physical techniques and exercises that enhance all aspects of an individual's life. The church for this personal religion is found in a quiet, serene, and motivating place. You must find an area in your backyard, local park, or house that you can turn into your personal church. A simple calisthenics routine requires nothing more than a towel, motivating music, and a quiet place. Your personal exercise church must become an area of power, reflection, motivation, and goal acquisition. By adding mirrors, motivating pictures and statements, music, and a pleasing environment, your personal church becomes a place of mental and physical empowerment.

The object of a personal physical religion is to provide you with the ability to strengthen your body and mind in an individually created environment of power. I will give you the exercises and techniques that you need to achieve physical mastery, but it is up to you to find or create the perfect environment in which to do them. While you are performing these exercises, focus your mind to generate positive thoughts and pictures about your body. You must visualize your muscles getting bigger, tighter, and stronger as you perform these exercises. Use music and pictures to stimulate your mind and body to take on an air of positive energy. Remember that the magic secret to personal success and mastery is found in the basic personal religion of physical exercise—to use this hour, day, and week to create a new life.

Chin-Ups

Target Areas: Back, biceps, and forearms
Equipment: Chin-up bar

1. Place hands about shoulder-width apart on the bar with your palms facing you, and with your thumb wrapping around the bar (reverse grip). Wrapping the bar with tape is an effective way of improving your grip. Remember to stretch out before mounting the bar.
2. Begin by hanging from the bar with full extension of your arms (dead hang). Pause, and take a deep breath while relaxing your muscles.
3. Slowly pull your entire body upward until your chin is above the bar. It is important to keep your lower body in a straight line with your upper body; otherwise, you will put unwanted stress on your shoulders.
4. Once your chin is over the bar, pause and hold this position for two seconds.
5. Slowly lower to the starting position and allow your arms and back to relax.
6. Repeat until exhaustion. If you have a partner working with you, have him or her grab your feet to help with the last few.

Standard Pull-Ups

Target Areas: Back, biceps, abdomen, and forearms
Equipment: Chin-up bar

1. Place hands about shoulder-width apart on the bar with your palms facing ahead, and with your thumb wrapping around the bar (standard grip). Slightly bend your knees to improve your center of balance.
2. Begin by hanging from the bar with full extension of your arms (dead hang). Take a few seconds to pause and relax your muscles.
3. Slowly pull your entire body upward until your chin is above the bar. Remember to stay still and straight; do not buck or kip your body up.
4. Pause for two seconds once your chin is above the bar. Feel your back muscles contract.
5. Slowly lower to the starting position with your arms fully extended and relax your muscles.
6. Repeat until exhaustion.

Close-Grip Pull-Ups

Target Areas: Back, shoulders, abdomen
Equipment: Chin-up bar

1. Place hands about ear-width apart on the bar with your palms facing ahead, and with your thumb wrapping around the bar (close grip).
2. Begin by hanging from the bar with full extension of your arms (dead hang). Pause and allow your muscles to relax.
3. Slowly pull your entire body upward until your chin is above the bar. Remember to stay still and straight; do not buck or kip your body up. Keep your eyes focused on a place in front of you and slightly higher than the bar. Keep your movement slow and smooth.
4. Pause for two seconds once your chin is above the bar. Feel your muscles contract and release.
5. Slowly lower to the starting position with your arms fully extended and allow your muscles to relax.
6. Repeat until exhaustion.

Wide-Grip Pull-Ups

Target Areas: Back, shoulders
Equipment: Chin-up bar

1. Place hands on the bar about 6 to 12 inches out from your shoulder. Face your palms ahead, and with your thumb wrapped around the bar (wide grip).
2. Begin by hanging from the bar with full extension of your arms (dead hang). Pause and allow your muscles to relax.
3. Slowly pull your entire body upward until your chin is above the bar. Remember to stay still and straight; do not buck or kip your body up. Keep your eyes focused on a place in front of you and slightly higher than the bar. Keep your movement slow and smooth.
4. Pause for two seconds once your chin is above the bar. Feel your muscles contract and release.
5. Slowly lower to the starting position with your arms fully extended and allow your muscles to relax.
6. Repeat until exhaustion.

Diamond Push-Ups

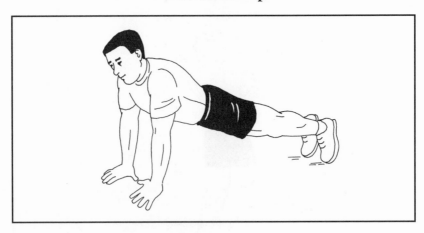

Target Areas: Chest, shoulders, arms

1. Place hands on the ground with your thumbs touching (close grip). Keep your head and back straight.
2. Lower your body so that you touch your chest to your hands.
3. Hold this position briefly, then raise your body.
4. Repeat until exhaustion.

Variations: Change the placement of your hands to a wide grip (hands as far apart as possible) or a standard grip (shoulder-width apart). In both placements, the thumbs are pointed inward toward each other. Alternate among the three grips to ensure a balanced and strong chest, arms, and shoulders.

Dive Bombers

Target Areas: Chest, shoulders, lower back

1. Spread your feet and hands to shoulder-width apart.
2. Raise your buttocks into the air, then slowly sweep your chest downward, then arch upward.
3. With your lower abdomen almost touching the ground and your arms locked out, pause momentarily.
4. Reverse this motion.
5. Repeat until exhaustion. Remember to perform each exercise slowly with control and good form. Do not let your body cheat when you feel the burn. Simply lean to one side and shake out each arm.

Variation: You can use this exercise to strengthen your forearm and grip by raising your body up with your fingers extended.

Abdominal Sit-Ups

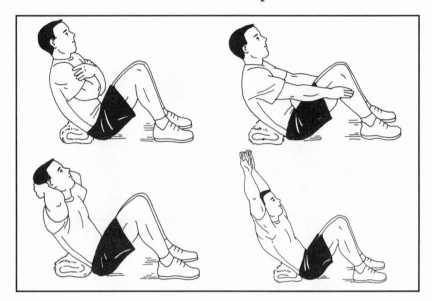

Target Areas: Abdominals, lower back

1. Lie on your back with your feet spread about shoulder-width apart.
2. Place your arms in one of the four positions depicted above.
3. Raise your upper torso to about 75 to 90 degrees from the floor. Keep your feet firmly planted and your head straight.
4. Lower your torso to within inches of the ground.
5. Repeat until exhaustion.

Variations: There are four arm positions that allow you to experiment with various points of balance: (1) arms across the chest, (2) arms at sides; (3) arms behind the head, and (4) arms above the head.

Crunches/Cross-Overs

Target Areas: Abdominals, lower back

1. Lie on your back with your feet spread about shoulder-width apart.
2. Place your hands behind your head.
3. Raise your upper torso from the floor and crunch toward your lower torso. Keep your feet firmly planted and your head straight.
4. Repeat until exhaustion.

Variations: Twist your torso upward and across your body (right shoulder toward left knee). Lower and alternate (left shoulder to right knee). Cross your legs or raise them off the ground. Remember to keep your form strict and tight, working in a slow motion. Make sure your legs do not move forward to meet your upper torso.

Hip Rollers

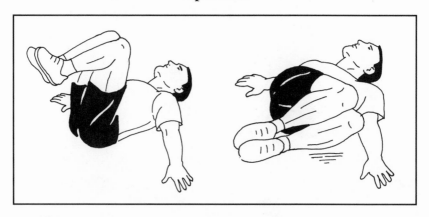

Target Areas: Oblique muscles

1. Lie on your back with your knees together and raised.
2. While keeping your upper torso flat on the ground, slowly lower your knees to one side and then the other.
3. Focus on keeping your legs together and your back on the ground.
4. Repeat until exhaustion.

Flying Flutter Kicks

Target Areas: Lower back, buttocks

1. Lie on your stomach with your feet and hands of the ground.
2. Keep your chest tight and lift your thighs and upper torso off the ground.
3. Repeat until exhaustion.

Scissor Moves

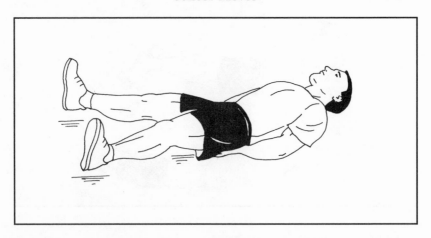

Target Areas: Upper and inner leg muscles

1. Lie on your back. Place your hands under your buttocks to provide a stable "platform."
2. Raise your legs about 3 inches from the ground.
3. Slowly spread your legs apart as far as you can, while keeping them raised from the ground.
4. Bring your legs back together.
5. Repeat until exhaustion.

Leg Levers

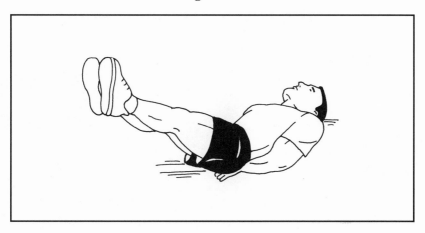

Target Areas: Lower abdominals, quadriceps

1. Lie on your back. Place your hands under your buttocks.
2. Slowly raise and lower your legs from about 3 inches off the ground to about 2 feet.
3. Focus on keeping your legs off the ground for the entire exercise.
4. Repeat until exhaustion.

Flutter Kicks

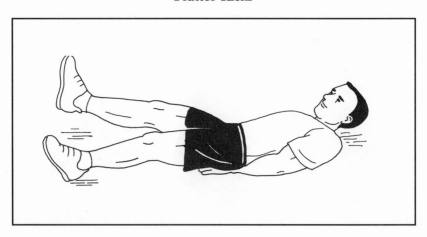

Target Areas: Lower abdominals, upper leg muscles

1. Begin by lying prone with your back flat on the ground. Place your hands under your buttocks and lift your head about 3 inches off of the ground.
2. Leave one leg straight and on the ground while raising the opposite leg to approximately 2 feet off the ground.
3. Keep your legs straight and your toes pointed up (flexed). Try not to bend your knees.
4. Lower your leg to the ground while lifting the other.
5. Alternate lifting one leg 18 to 24 inches and then the other. Maintain strict form and keep your legs straight. Build a consistent and smooth rhythm by first lifting one leg and then the other.
6. Repeat until exhaustion.

Variation: Sitting flutter kicks are performed from a sitting position with your hands behind your head. Alternate lifting your legs 6 to 12 inches from the ground and keep your upper torso locked in an upright position and your abdominals tight. Repeat until exhaustion.

Knee Benders

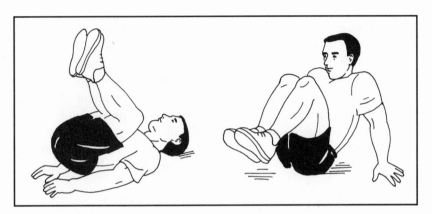

Target Areas: Abdominals

1. Lie on your back. Place your hands under your buttocks.
2. Extend your legs straight.
3. Raise your legs about 3 to 6 inches from the ground, and curl in toward your chest.
4. Repeat until exhaustion.

Variation: Instead of lying prone, hold your torso up in a sitting position. Balance your weight at the top of your buttocks. Extend your legs out, that bring your legs in.

SEAL TEAM RUNNING TECHNIQUE

In the SEAL teams, running is a way of life and not just a form of exercise. Running provides daily obstacles and tests that challenge our self-discipline and fitness level. By reaching deep inside and finding the will to run no matter what the weather or time of day, you will become physically and mentally strong. Running will build your endurance and help you lose weight faster than any other exercise. Many people fail to understand that keeping to a solid running program offers many more benefits than just the physical kind. The ability to prepare and execute a running program helps develop discipline, time management skills, and personal resolve.

Running allows you to open up your mind to clearly focus on your thoughts. It is just as important to have a personal running religion as it is to have one for your calisthenics. By selecting a beautiful, serene, and comfortable running route, you enable the mind to achieve clarity. There is no better way to test your resolve than by running no matter what the conditions or situation. Running is one of the most powerful stress-eliminating tools that a person can learn. In the SEAL teams, we consider running to be an absolute necessity for every aspect of our job. I not only run to enjoy the healthy benefits, but I also run to help generate new ideas, solve difficult problems, and mentally prepare for the upcoming day.

In order to receive all of the wonderful benefits of a running routine, you must first learn and understand how to run correctly. Proper running footwear, surfaces, form, and stretching are key elements to preventing wear and tear on your body. Use the information that is provided here, culled from years of special operations running experience, to provide a solid foundation for your personal running program.

Warm-Up

It doesn't matter what your age, weight, or fitness level is, your body needs to be properly stretched and warmed up before you begin exercising. A warm-up to stretch tight muscles before exercise is crucial for preventing injuries that can result from tight and cold muscles. A stretched and longer muscle is less likely to get injured than a short, tight muscle. Warming up helps protect the legs by stimulating your tendons. Begin by walking for a couple of minutes, followed by slow and focused stretching. Take this time to not only warm up your body, but also your mind. Allow your mind to see positive images and relax to find clarity and motivation. Before I begin my morning run, I follow a simple and relaxing stretching routine. Here are the five steps to this routine:

1. Take five deep breaths with your eyes closed.
2. Spread your legs 3 to 4 feet apart and slowly bend at the waist. Return to the upright position, pause, and continue to bend forward several times. Allow your hamstrings to tighten and release.
3. Place your left foot over top of your right. Bend at the waist while keeping your legs straight. Stretch your arms out and reach for your toes. Pause and hold this position for 10 seconds. Return to the upright position. Continue this procedure, but do not bounce or force your muscles to stretch.
4. Lie flat on the ground with your legs stretched out in front of you. Raise one leg and begin to rotate your ankle in a clockwise motion. Continue for 20 rotations, stop, and rotate 20 times in a counter-clockwise motion. Alternate both legs through this exercise until your ankle joints feel loose and warm.
5. Stand straight up and raise your hands above your head. Slowly inhale as you raise your arms. Pause for five seconds. Slowly lower your hands and exhale completely. Continue this exercise until you feel calm and relaxed.

Running Form

Running is a function of proper strides, footstrikes, body angle, and arm motion. The key to having proper running form is to run in a relaxed manner and move naturally. Don't try to imitate the running form of another person, as each individual runs slightly differently from the next. Remember that running is not meant to be mating ritual, so don't be concerned if your running form looks a little unorthodox.

Stride. The point of foot contact should be in line with the knee, which should be slightly flexed. As your fitness level improves and you get faster, the length of your stride will increase and you will begin lifting your knees higher. Concentrate on not overstriding when you run (i.e., don't let your foot hit the ground in front of the knee flex). Overstriding is very hard on the knees and tendons and can cause injuries. Choppy, short strides usually result from inflexible or tight muscles and are very inefficient. Run with a comfortable and relaxed stride, but do not over-exaggerate your leg movements.

Footstrike. Unless you are a sprinter or competitive runner, the heel-ball foot-strike method is for you: (1) the outside of the heel strikes the surface, (2) the foot rolls inward to the ball of the foot while the knee is slightly bent, and (3) the foot is pushed off of the ground by the big toe. This technique provides maximum efficiency and excellent shock absorption.

Body Angle. The trick to maintaining proper body angle is to keep your back as straight as comfortably possible and your head up and looking ahead. Sometimes, depending upon the terrain, you will have to look down to navigate over and around obstacles. Lean forward only when going uphill, as this position puts stress on your leg muscles. Do not lean back, as this will put unwanted pressure on your back and act as a "brake." The trick is to run relaxed and tall; allow your shoulders to relax and shake your arms out from time to time.

Arm Motion. Allow your elbows, upper arms, wrists, and hands to occasionally relax and hang down at your sides. Fast and tight pumping of the arms is very inefficient and unnecessary for relaxed running. If you feel your arms becoming tight and tired during your run, this is a strong indication that you are forcing your arms to move unnaturally.

Running Frequency

Schedule your runs for at least three or four times per week, or about every other day. It is important to schedule several rest days in your weekly exercise program. A rest day is not necessarily a no-exercise day, but rather a day of an alternate type of exercise. This allows your running muscles to recover and repair. Once your body has become conditioned and you feel no major pain, begin increasing your distance and running frequency.

Intensity and Speed

You should run at a comfortable and relaxed pace that allows you to talk and think. If you run too fast and furiously, you will expend all of your energy in a short amount of time. Running fast tends to tighten muscles and must be followed by a long cool-down stretching period. Speed is not as important as distance and time.

Keep in mind these eight tricks of the trade:

- Do not overstride.
- Relax and think.
- Run tall.
- Run naturally.
- Pick a pleasant area and route.
- Wear the proper shoes and clothing.
- Hydrate, hydrate, and hydrate some more.
- Stretch before and after your run.

Cool Down

Cooling down properly is just as important as warming up. A cooling down period after your run is a basic way of ensuring you don't experience muscle stiffness and pain throughout the day. Always take the time to cool down and regain your focus on how your body feels. This is an excellent time to write down any new thoughts or strategies that your mind has worked on after your stretching routine is completed; keep a notebook in your gym bag. Cooling down both physically and mentally will reduce cramps and your heart rate. Since you took the time to practice self-discipline by exercising, don't stop now by forgetting to stretch and cool down. Remember that this is a very powerful time for your mind to think positively and clearly, so focus on your personal improvement and life-goals.

OTHER AEROBIC EXERCISES

To complement your running workouts and calisthenics, make use of other types of cardiovascular training. Regular exercise stimulates the heart and lungs and improves the body's use of oxygen. Such exercise can also enhance your skin, muscle tone, breathing, and of course your appearance. These exercises should be:

- Regular—repeated three or more times per week.
- Vigorous—raising the heart rate to approximately 60% to 75% of its maximum.
- Sustained—performed for at least 30 minutes without interruption.

It is not uncommon to see men and women in their 80s running and biking and swimming. Cardiovascular exercise dramatically increases your longevity, health, energy, and positive attitude. There is no better way of testing and strengthening your self-discipline than scheduling and sticking to a regular cardiovascular workout.

To produce a cardiovascular training effect, it is important to increase your heart rate to a critical intensity. This intensity is often referred to as the target heart rate. Your target heart rate is simply

$$220 \text{ minus your age, times } 75\% \text{ to } 80\%$$

For example, my target heart rate is 140. That is, $(220–34) \times .75 = 140$. That means I should work out so as to maintain my heart rate at 140 beats a minute. Target heart rate gives you a range and system for exercising at your most beneficial level. There are other methods and techniques available to monitor all areas of your body's functions during exercise, like using a perceived exertion scale (Borg Scale) or electronic heartbeat monitoring device. When you first begin running, keep in mind that your body is initially in a stage of adjustment and that your heartbeat and breathing will feel erratic. Once you have developed a consistent running schedule, begin to increase your heart rate by speeding up slowly.

TAKE CONTROL TIP

Use Music as a Motivator
Nothing has a way of lifting our spirits faster than music. Purchase a small cassette player with headphones and listen to your favorite up-beat music during your exercise routine. Use music to help you feel inspired, motivated, and full of energy throughout the day.

The following exercises use large muscle groups, which will help you achieve an overall balanced cardiovascular system.

Stair/Versa-Climber

Walking and running stairs have been very popular methods of aerobic exercise. Now there are many machines that simulate this great exercise such as the Stairmaster and Versa-Climber. In addition to aerobic development, these machines may also be used to strengthen the upper and lower body. These machines allow the individual to vary the amount of resistance and effort placed upon the body.

Cycling

Cycling can be a fun and effective form of aerobic conditioning, with the added benefit of reduced muscle trauma. Most stationary cycles provide adjustable workouts and resistance levels. Remember, you get out of it what you put into it, so focus on maintaining a challenging speed.

Walking

Walking is becoming one of the most popular fitness activities. The impact on the legs is not as great as in running and the exercise is excellent for older people and people who are overweight. Walking rapidly with hand weights is an excellent way of increasing the cardiovascular output. Keep in mind that as your aerobic capacity increases, you must move on to jogging or running to increase your heart rate and fat-burning capacity.

Swimming

I hope you didn't think I was going to leave this one out. As you can imagine, swimming is one of the Navy SEALs' favorite and relied-upon exercises. The risk of injury to your joints is very low, and it can be very beneficial to injury recovery. Swimming, like running, greatly improves the mind's ability to relax and focus on positive thoughts and ideas. Swimming is what I do when I need to focus and work out a problem in my mind.

YOUR ACTIVE LIFE

Physical exercise is the key that unlocks the door to wealth, power, longevity, sex, beauty, and a lifetime of happiness. If something as simple as exercise can be the answer to all of our dreams and desires, why don't most people include it in their lives? The answer is simple. Physical exercise requires effort, time, and self-discipline. So you say that you are just too busy to exercise. If you truly are busy, then you cannot afford *not* to exercise. Make one of the best decisions of your life and commit yourself to a daily exercise routine. If you are already involved in a fitness routine, step up and take it to the next level or start competing in the sport of your interest.

Physical exercise will propel you to a superior life quicker than any other strategy or technique known to man. It is absolutely free for you to achieve and can be exceptionally fun and powerful if you approach it with the right attitude. Once you begin a consistent exercise program, you will become so used to it that it turns into a daily habit, like eating or waking up. Physical exercise is like the fountain of youth, in that it allows you to slow down the aging and dying process of your body. When you make the commitment to include daily physical exercise into your day, all aspects of your life will improve, including your mental sharpness, physical appearance, social relationships, and overall happiness.

Many people have the misconception that exercise must involve pain, heavy weights, running long distances, and beating up your body, but this notion could not be further from the truth. Some Far East cultures have been practicing and perfecting organized systems of physical exercise that are not only serene and pleasant, but graceful and beautiful to watch. The physical exercise systems of Yoga, Tai Chi, and traditional martial arts all improve your stamina, flexibility, relaxation, and mental focus powers. These systems, when combined with a healthy diet and persistence, will have a dramatic effect on the quality and quantity of your life.

Simple activities such as brisk walking, bicycle riding, swimming, and running are exercises that can be done by young and old alike. By doing some form of physical exercise each day, you will stay younger longer, become much more productive, eliminate stress, and generate a powerful spirit of vitality. Throughout my travels as a professional speaker, many people tell me that they are unable to exercise due to injury and would like to learn alternative forms of exercise. Many of the simple tasks that we perform throughout the day such as walking up stairs, walking your dog, or even cleaning the house can be used as forms of exercise. Remember that the main idea is to gradually build upon an activity until your body becomes strong enough to endure the increased stress of exercise. As long as you make the conscious effort to get up, get out, and begin moving, your body will naturally start to build in strength.

Here are ten techniques to help you stay motivated and committed to daily physical exercise:

- Create a realistic schedule and stick to it.
- Start off slow (20 minutes a day) and think positive thoughts.
- Visualize what your new body will look like.
- Include a partner with similar goals.
- Have a playful attitude and have fun.
- Mix up your exercises and sports.
- Use knowledge control—read books and magazines about exercise.
- Keep a daily log of your progress and accomplishments.
- Stand on the scale and look in the mirror often.
- Use music as a motivator—buy a Walkman, get excited.

TAKE CONTROL TIP

Push Your Limitations
Your body and mind are capable of ten times more than you realize. Push yourself to run an extra 10 minutes or perform 20 more push-ups than normal. Get used to doing more than other people expect of you at work, home, and in life. You will soon find that you are capable of more than you originally thought.

CREATING AN EXERCISE REGIME

The type of exercise that you decide to undertake in the beginning is not as important as actually finding the discipline to adhere to a routine. You must develop a daily exercise schedule and begin taking the steps to achieving what you have written down. In the next couple of days, I want you to list your favorite physical activities in a personal exercise journal and start implementing them into your exercise schedule. You do not need to plan for a whole month's worth of exercise at first, but rather one day or one week at a time. Remember that it is the small victories that provide us with the power to take on the large battles in our quest for life-mastery. Use the principles of the personal management system that you learned previously to help plan, prepare, and execute a solid exercise program. Here is an example of a simple exercise program.

Physical Control Schedule

☐ **MONDAY: 3-Mile Run:** Wake up at 5:00 A.M. Stretch out for 15 minutes. Jog through park on my favorite trail. Cool down by stretching for 10 minutes. Record time, date, place, and run time into my exercise journal.

☐ **TUESDAY: Lift Weights:** Wake up at 5:00 A.M. Drive to gym. Stretch for 15 minutes. Lift light weights for chest and triceps. Complete three exercises of 10 repetitions for each body part. Keep workout to 45 minutes. Record information into my exercise journal. Shower and prepare for work.

☐ **WEDNESDAY: Rest Day:** Read new exercise magazine. Go food shopping and prepare healthy meals for rest of week. Stretch legs and back at 7:00 P.M. Review exercise journal.

☐ **THURSDAY: 3-Mile Run:** Wake up at 5:00 A.M. Stretch out for 15 minutes. Jog through park on new trail that Tom recommended. Cool down by stretching for 10 minutes. Record time, date, place, and run time into my exercise journal.

☐ **FRIDAY: Long Walk:** Wake up at 5:00 A.M. Stretch with my wife for 10 minutes. Walk through park on 4-mile trail on west side. Bring small thermos of tea.

☐ **SATURDAY: Rest Day:** Sleep in and wake up at 8:00 A.M. Enjoy day off.

☐ **SUNDAY: 5-Mile Run:** Wake up at 8:00 A.M. and go to church. Walk to park. Stretch out for 15 minutes. Jog 5 miles on favorite trail. Run first 3 miles at 8-minute pace. Run last 2 miles at 7:45 pace. Cool down by stretching for 10 minutes. Record time, date, place, and total run time into my exercise journal.

MISSION DE-BRIEF
★★★★

The techniques and information that I have shared with you can be customized to an individual's needs, age, physique, and lifestyle. The exercises that you have learned are designed to strengthen and limber every muscle group in the human body. It is important to point out that if you have a weak area, or past injury to a certain body part, you must slowly and carefully begin to focus on strengthening and limbering this area. It is not the purpose of this book to be a thorough guide on exercise, but to provide you with a foundation upon which to begin mastering physical control.

Too often today, people are looking for instant gratification and immediate results. The process of taking control of your physical body challenges these modern misgivings by requiring you to focus on time management, persistence, and discipline. The majority of people in today's society have the basic desire to improve their physical condition, but become confused and turned off by the barrage of money-making commercialism that serves only one master—profit. It is very important that you stay clear of million-dollar gyms and quick-fix exercise programs at the beginning. Start developing a personal exercise program based upon the K.I.S.S. (keep-it-simple-stupid) principle.

Make a dramatic change in your life. Become motivated, energized, and excited about each and every day. Wake up with power, focus, and clarity about your journey to achieving all that you desire. Can you honestly justify not setting aside one out of the 24 hours in a day to increase your life span, mental clarity, and overall happiness? Make today the day you begin taking control of your life by giving up the excuses and developing a personal exercise program.

6

NUTRITIONAL WARFARE

Tell me what you eat, and I will tell you what you are.—Anthelme Brillat-Savarin

Today, many scientific studies now conclude that the body and mind are powerfully connected and if one is not operating at peak levels, the other suffers drastically. Taking control is about treating and maintaining both of these precious miracles with careful nutrition to create the powerful life you deserve. Make no mistake about it, eating properly is a constant battle in which your life hangs in the balance. Nutritional warfare is a concept of techniques and information that will provide you with the ability to successfully do battle with the forces of evil that lurk in our stores, restaurants, and refrigerators every day.

By changing your diet, you can dramatically enhance your body, mind, emotions, moods, energy levels, and longevity. All of the information and techniques found in this book are of no value if you do not have the self-discipline to begin utilizing and applying them to your life. This chapter is about the fuel we put into our machines and how it effects our lives. By caring for your body with proper and disciplined nutrition, you will have the power and vitality needed to achieve your life goals. In Far East societies, what a person eats is thought to be directly related to his or her mental intelligence and physical toughness. Fruits and vegetables, along with a meatless diet, are responsible for providing a powerful flow of energy and personal enlightenment.

THE ZEN OF NUTRITION

The ancient people of the Himalayas are a perfect study in mental clarity, physical strength, and longevity. Many live well beyond 100 and maintain sharp minds and strong bodies throughout their lives, performing incredible feats well past our society's retirement age. These self-disciplined masters go for weeks on end without food or sleep and can endure very high levels of pain in adverse conditions. What is the secret of their powerful lives? It is simply that they eat in moderation and follow a strict natural diet with self-discipline.

The 5,000-year-old diet that the Himalayan people follow is a pure diet based on living foods—those created by nature, sun, air, water, and Mother Earth. The disciplined diet focuses on fruits, fruit juices, vegetables, and grains. By making changes to your diet that ensure these life-giving foods make up at least 85% of your intake, you will win the first important battle of nutritional warfare. In order to gain physical mastery and life-control, you must dig deep inside yourself and find the will to eat natural and fresh foods only. Meat products are simply dead foods. Our stomach and intestines are dramatically different than those of carnivores and are more anatomically similar to fruit- and vegetation-eating primates.

In the United States today, the average American consumes over 261 pounds of meat annually. We wonder why we have such high rates of colon, stomach, and bone cancer. Animal flesh and meat have been found to have high proportions of chemicals and toxins. We are not only ingesting meat, but a plethora of health-defeating additives such as growth hormones, steroids, mad-cow disease, preservatives, and meat by-products. Dead meat also lacks most of the important vitamins and minerals that we need to function at peak levels, and is also very hard to digest because of the large amount of energy required to break it down. Have you ever noticed how slow, sluggish, and lethargic you feel after eating a big steak? Compare this to how you feel after eating a large and healthy salad that is easily digested.

ASSESSING YOUR DIET

Nutritional warfare has become a battle for each and every one of us, due to the fact that everywhere we shop, look, and eat we are bombarded with deadly foods, toxins, chemicals, and false information. This is the battle that you must begin fighting today.

It is true that many people in the United States tend to gain weight with age, but it is not necessary that we do. Getting fatter as we get older is not without increased health risks. Diseases associated with aging such as heart disease, stroke, and diabetes are more prevalent in overweight people. Metabolism slows about 5% every decade after 30, therefore we have to decrease our food intake by that much just to stay at our present weight. We tend to lose muscle and bone with age as well. We can slow down the effects of declining muscle mass and metabolism if we eat right and remain physically active. Muscle tissue is more metabolically active than fat, therefore metabolism increases with an increase in muscle mass.

Since less than 20% of the United States population currently exercises regularly three times per week, it is easy to see why most people believe it is normal to gain weight with age. There are four crucial components needed to lose weight effectively and forever:

- Regular aerobic and strength-enhancing exercise
- A living-foods, low-fat, high-fiber, and supplemented diet
- Moderate calorie restriction
- Disciplined lifestyle change that incorporates the first three factors

Many people choose to do only one of these components. They initially may lose weight, but at some point the weight loss stops and they get bigger than they were before. The word "diet" implies that you are going on or coming off of something. A diet also implies that you are restricted from doing something, which usually leaves you feeling deprived. For this reason, most people who are on diets always fail at keeping the weight off. A healthy living-foods diet and regular exercise is a lifestyle change that will lead to a powerful, beautiful, efficient, and long-living body filled with vitality.

Here are ten questions you must find answers to:

1. How many calories do I really eat?
2. How much bad fat do I really eat?
3. Do I skip meals?
4. How many servings of fruits and vegetables do I eat?
5. Do I eat when I am stressed out or upset?
6. When is my first meal of the day?
7. What portion sizes am I eating?
8. How much time and effort do I spend planning my food intake?

9. How often do I prepare my own meals?

10. How much time do I spend learning about food and nutrition?

By looking closely at our eating and nutritional habits, we begin using the Take Control concept of personal management. Think critically and honestly about your daily intake of food and discipline yourself to change your eating habits.

A DISCIPLINED DIET

What element exists that enables a person to choose the proper food over desired food? That element is self-discipline! The powers of the mind and body are joined to focus our thoughts and actions in to a predetermined response. The response we are looking for is one of proper selection and decision-making when you open your mouth to ingest selected body fuel.

In order to gain control over the mental and physical action of eating, we must first understand how the process works. We are preprogrammed to respond in a certain way to the sounds, smells, and tastes of certain foods. The program that exists in our brain is the result of our memories, ancestors, chemical reactions, and trends of society. In nature, there are predators and gatherers of food. The lion is a meat-eating predator and the monkey is a gatherer of fruits and vegetables. The grizzly bear is a predator and the gorilla is a gatherer of vegetation and fruits. This is not to say that predators always eat meat and gatherers always eat fruit and vegetables, but that one is designed for a different lifestyle than the other. As a human being, do you have extended carnivorous teeth, deadly claws, or the ability to run down and kill for meat? No, but you do have flexible hands and an opposing thumb, the ability to grow food, and the physical characteristics of a food gatherer. I am not saying that you must give up meat altogether, rather that like most gatherers our diet must consist of 90% fruits, grains, and vegetables. Instead of eating red meat for protein, start experimenting with soy, meatless vegetable patties, tofu, or fish instead of red meat in any form.

If meat is so hard on our bodies, why do we eat it? Many people argue that vegetarian diets do not provide proper protein, but ironically those who eat a lot of red meat ingest the lowest-quality protein available. Meat contains a high concentration of uric acid, which cannot be broken down by the liver and can lead to deadly health problems. Fruits, vegetables, and certain dairy products provide a superior quality of protein to that found in meat. Take a look at the most powerful animals on this planet; the gorilla and the elephant have about 35 times the strength of a human and subsist completely on fruits, grains, and vegetables. I am not a vegetarian and strongly advise people to eat small portions of chicken, fish, and turkey since most people have an extremely hard time of eliminating meats all together from their diet.

It seems that every time we turn around there is a new instant-success diet book or program and most of these border on the extreme. It is amazing to me that in a time where technology and science is discovering the secrets of the universe, we still haven't learned the basic principles of good nutrition that ancient societies discovered more than 5,000 years ago. There are many reasons why people endanger their health by gaining weight and it doesn't matter if stress, low self-esteem, laziness, depression, or genetics are to blame because these can all be overcome with self-discipline. Remember that nobody forces you to eat fast food or lie on the couch instead of exercising, and all of the excuses in the world cannot change the fact that you have the power of choice. Changing your present eating habits is not as simple as it seems. Everywhere you look there is a new fast food restaurant opening up, the store shelves are packed with unhealthy foods, and we are constantly being bombarded with conflicting information. No, developing a disciplined diet is not easy, but it is a matter of life and death.

Challenge Your Willpower
TAKE CONTROL TIP
Test you willpower by purchasing food you crave the most and keeping it with you throughout the day. Place it on your desk, in your car, or on the kitchen table. See just how strong your willpower is by denying this craving as long as you can.

NUTRITIONAL WARFARE BASICS

Nutrition is the science of nourishment, and the study of nutrients and the processes by which organisms utilize them. Nutritional warfare is based on the powerful concepts and principles that have been established for over 5,000 years. Poor nutritional decision-making can mean the difference between life and death. All living organisms need proper nutrition to function and live normally. Here are the six nutrients found in foods:

- Proteins
- Fats
- Carbohydrates
- Minerals
- Vitamins
- Water

Proteins, carbohydrates, and fat provide the body with calories. Vitamins, water, and minerals provide no calories for your body. Carbohydrates and proteins supply the body with four calories per gram, and fats supply the body with nine calories per gram. Carbohydrates are sugars and starches in food that are usually called simple and complex carbohydrates. They provide the main fuel and energy source in the body. Examples of complex carbohydrates include the starches in bread, pasta, rice, cereals, and whole-grain foods. Simple carbohydrates include the sugars in fruits and vegetables. Refined simple sugars include table sugar, which is found in processed foods like cookies, candy, cakes, sodas, fruit punch, and ice cream.

Proteins

Protein is made up of amino acids that are broken down during the digestion process. Amino acids are often referred to as the "building blocks" of protein. Protein is vital to the human body; it functions to repair and build tissue, as well as in the formation of hormones, antibodies, and enzymes. Amino acids are classified as either nonessential or essential. Amino acids that can be produced in the body are called nonessential and the eight amino acids that the body cannot produce are called essential. They must be provided by the food in our diet. Complete proteins are foods that contain large amounts of essential amino acids. Some forms of complete protein are foods such as chicken, fish, eggs, and milk. Proteins that cannot supply the body with all of the essential amino acids are known as incomplete proteins. These come from non-animal sources such as legumes, grains, and vegetables. By combining two incomplete proteins, a complete protein diet can be obtained, if all essential amino acids are provided by the food combination. This is the heart of the commando diet system. When we eliminate unhealthy red meats and dairy products from our diets, we must choose alternate forms of protein to supplement this loss.

Most scientific studies have shown that Americans eat much more protein than their bodies require. An overload of protein in the diet generates toxic nitrogen by-products that overburden the kidneys. Studies also have concluded that societies that eat high animal-protein diets have a much higher rate of cancer. With the commando diet, you will notice a lighter feeling and an overall improvement in your digestion. If you are going to eat animal protein, stick to chicken and fish prepared by grilling, broiling, or steaming. Other options for your protein intake are soy, tofu, whey protein, and supplemental protein drinks. As you select your protein meals, try these different sources to reduce the stress on your digestive system.

Fats

Many people are under the impression that if you want to lose weight and prevent heart disease, you cannot eat fat at all. The truth is that there are some good fats that are essential to healthy living. The problem lies in the fact that the typical American diet gets 40% of its calories from fat. In stark contrast to the American diet, the traditional Japanese diet contains less than half this amount. The rate of obesity in Japan is three times lower than in the United States. But for Japanese people living in the United States, the rate of obesity is seven times higher than in Japan and the rate of cancer and heart disease is dramatically increased. To enhance your health, increase vitality, and flush the fat out of your body, you need a daily supply of good fats. Good fats are known as omega-6 and omega-3 oils, or GLAs and EPAs. Many people come to me for help after years of starving their bodies on low-fat, low-calorie diets. They complain of dry skin and hair, constipation, and weak and brittle nails. By adding the essential GLA and EPA oils to their diet, these problems are reversed. It is the EPAs, or omega-3 oils, in the diet of the Eskimos that prevent them from having heart disease, despite a heavy diet of animal fat and protein. Many societies that eat large quantities of fish have a very low incidence of heart disease, confirming the powerful effects of EPA.

Omega-6 oils are even more important than the EPAs for protecting the cardiovascular system, heart, immune system, and skin. These powerful oils flush the fat out of the body, and when both omega-3 and omega-6 are combined together, the health benefits are unmatched. Some unrefined vegetable oils such as safflower, borage, evening-primrose, corn, soy, and sesame all provide high levels of GLAs for your body.

Recent research has shown that olive oil can dramatically reduce the levels of LDL, the dangerous blood cholesterol, while keeping HDL, the beneficial form, intact. This fact could be the reason why the Mediterranean peoples such as Italians and Greeks, who use large amounts of olive oil, have half the death rate from heart disease as do Americans. Olive oil carries monounsaturated fats, as do nuts and avocados. Canola oil has recently been found to contain large amounts of monounsaturated fats as well and can be used in light cooking. It is important to understand that reducing your intake of all types of fat is healthy, but if you are going to consume any fats, make them the good ones.

Carbohydrates

Carbohydrates come from plant sources and are made up of the chemical elements hydrogen, carbon, and oxygen. Carbohydrates are the best energy source for all bodily functions and, like proteins, contain four calories per gram. This power source is not only a complete fuel but also helps with digestion and food assimilation. It is very important to understand that carbohydrates are needed to metabolize fat, regulate protein, and break down fat in the liver. If you are eating too few carbohydrates, then you are in a sense building fat stores because your body has no fuel to burn the fat. In today's age of science, study after study from top research labs confirm that the best way to lose weight and keep it off is to exercise regularly and to eat a low-calorie, low-fat diet packed with complex carbohydrates like fruits, vegetables, and whole grains. It's not just the American Heart Association that says so. It's the National Cancer Institute, the National Academy of Sciences, and dozens of other health-promoting agencies. Fruits and vegetables supply a whole range of nutrients that high-protein dieters miss out on, including phytochemicals like beta-carotene, isoflavones, and bioflavonoids.

All carbohydrates are made up of sugars. The body is going to break carbohydrates down into simple sugars (fructose, glucose, or galactose) whether the carbohydrate is refined grains such as white bread and white rice, or complex carbohydrates like dextrins or starches. The end product will always be the same—glucose.

Another thing that complex carbohydrates offer in substantial quantities is fiber, which health experts say we should be eating to the tune of 25 to 35 grams each day, instead of the 13 grams we currently average. Fiber slows the absorption of the sugars that are contained in complex carbohydrates and won't cause a rapid spike in blood sugar. Eating lots of fiber helps produce a slow steady rise that gives you a constant source of energy and doesn't provoke a surge of insulin. Likewise, you don't get the cholesterol and fat that are high in protein foods.

Consuming carbohydrates can improve your mood and your relationships. A 1992 study of 233 families in Portland, Oregon, directed by Gerdi Weidner, Ph.D., found that those who switched to a high complex carbohydrate and low-fat diet experienced a reduction in aggressive hostility and depression—as well as lowering their cholesterol.

In America today, we consume far too many calories. Why? Because we lack control of our urges, cravings, and taste buds. We ingest 10% more calories today than we did 20 years ago. Carbohydrates, gram for gram, contain half of the calories of fat and offer the added benefit of fiber. The key is not to treat all carbohydrates the same. Eat complex carbohydrates like fruit, vegetables, and whole grains, not prepackaged cakes, cookies, and bagels, which are loaded with excess fat calories.

Water

Water is the most basic element of life. Without water, death occurs within days. Your body is about 70% water. Water is essential for the process of absorption and digestion of nutrients, and excretion of bodily wastes. Water plays a significant role in the regulation of body temperature and mental awareness. There is nothing special with regard to weight loss and water drinking. Drinking water will not flush fat out of your body, but it will keep you well hydrated. By increasing your water intake at mealtime, you will reduce the urge to overeat. Water is supplied from both food and liquids. For some reason, we seem to believe that dairy products are a good substitution for water and fruit juices when this is simply not true.

Dairy foods must be reduced or eliminated completely. Many people have a hard time digesting milk, while cheese congests the system and dehydrates the body through constipation. Cheese should be considered as an infrequent high-fat treat, not a dietary staple to your diet. Yogurt is easier to assimilate than any other dairy product, but still requires considerable energy to digest. There are many different sources of calcium besides dairy products, including leafy greens, sesame seeds, raw nuts, corn tortillas, broccoli, and sea vegetables. I strongly recommend calcium supplements for most people, no matter what foods they eat.

A diet high in organic fruits and vegetables goes a long way in keeping your body hydrated. There is no provision for water storage in the human body; therefore, we must replace the amount lost every 24 hours to maintain optimal health. Normally, about 2.5 liters of water (ten 8-ounce cups) are required each day for a sedentary adult in a normal environment.

Experience Chinese Green Tea

TAKE CONTROL TIP

Discover a healthy secret over 5,000 years old—drink Chinese green tea. Try green tea in the morning instead of coffee. Green tea has less caffeine and is packed with antioxidants. If you just cannot do without coffee, try drinking it without sugar or cream powders.

THE COMMANDO DIET

At the very heart of the commando diet are fresh fruit and vegetables. Our body is at least 70% water; since fruits and vegetables also are very high in water, they are most perfectly suited to our body composition. The water contained in fruits and vegetables is important for energy and cleansing. Water carries the cargo of nutrients into our intestines, where they are quickly absorbed. The water then carries away the waste. One of the most important concepts of using fruits and vegetables is to select organic produce only. By selecting organic produce, you eliminate the influx of pesticides, toxins, and chemicals that are introduced into your body from commercially grown produce.

To get the most out of your produce, I highly recommend that you eat most of it raw, as cooking depletes the nutritional value. If you are going to cook it, it is important that you cook produce for only a couple of minutes. Vegetables need not be eaten plain to be healthy. A highly nutritious and tasteful way of preparing vegetables is to make a meatless stew. The broth of the cooked vegetables is very high in nutrients and minerals. A vegetable broth not only energizes your body, but also greatly assists in cleansing your body of its stored toxins.

Another source of powerful nutrients and minerals is water vegetables. Edible seaweeds have long been a regular part of the diet of coastal peoples such as the Pacific Islanders, the Japanese, and the Irish. Sea vegetables are extremely rich in iodine and other minerals and are a very important food for healthy skin, hair, nails, bones, and teeth. The iodine in sea vegetables stim-

ulates the thyroid gland and ensures proper metabolism and a healthy repro-
ductive system.

Supplements

I use the term supplements to describe various vitamins, minerals, and herbs
that do just that—supplement our diet to make up for certain deficiencies. In
today's society, supplements are looked at as the quick fix to all personal
health problems. The problem with our diet is that we eat large amounts of
very unhealthy foods and wonder why we are overweight, tired, mentally
drained, and ill. Most Americans think that if they take some supplements after eating two Big Macs and fries, that this will make everything better.

There are so many different types of supplements out on the market today that it would take a whole book to just cover 10% of them. If you make a
disciplined decision to find out all that you can about various supplements
and how they can help or hamper your personal commando diet, you will
have taken another step in winning the nutritional war. I am a strong believer
in supplementation and daily-use supplements to enhance my performance,
health, and longevity. For simplicity's sake, I have grouped vitamins, minerals, and ergogenic agents together in hopes of reducing confusion.

Recent studies have shown that by taking adequate levels of vitamin E, vitamin C, magnesium, and selenium the rate of heart disease could be reduced by up to 50%. This alone could result in over $50 billion in healthcare
savings per year. This represents savings from just one health problem. Any
way you look at it, taking vitamin-herb-mineral supplementation is going to
reduce your healthcare costs and enhance your longevity. Most of us know
that we are not getting the required nutrients from our present diet and that
we have poor nutritional habits that must be improved. Most of us exist in an
environment where stress, regular exposure to toxins, and quick snacks are
the norm. Aside from daily exercise and diet modification, taking supplements is crucial to our health and a tremendous amount of scientific research
supports this fact.

Vitamins and minerals play important and diverse roles in our health. Vitamins work with enzymes as catalysts, accelerating the breaking or making of
the chemical bonds that join molecules together. The connection between vitamin intake and fatigue is evident in the importance these substances have in
the energy production process. Minerals, like vitamins, are required to maintain normal functioning of our cells. They play a crucial role in the composition

of bones and blood, but also function with vitamins as part of the body enzyme system. A high-quality vitamin-mineral supplement acts as a solid "insurance formula" against nutritional deficiencies. All totaled, the human body requires 22 different minerals and 13 different vitamins for optimum nutrition.

Herbs

Natural herbs have been used to treat any ailments, prevent injuries, increase memory and intelligence, and greatly extend a person's life since before recorded history. Herbs are plants, plant products, and plant derivatives. Herbs have been used since the beginning of recorded time to help human beings achieve optimum health. Ancient societies, whom many consider primitive, understood that consuming certain herbs helped extend their life and improve their existence. For some reason, with our advanced and intellectual society of today, we instead consume chemicals, toxins, pesticides, artificial foods, deadly fats, and life-reducing foods on a regular basis. It hasn't been until recently that our doctors, scientists, and great experts have recognized the importance of these wonder plants. There are hundreds of herbs and various combinations that extremely enhance the quality and productivity of your life. The study of herbs and their benefits has increased dramatically over the last ten years and has proven the amazing benefits of their use in a proper diet program.

I have listed some of the supplements that can have dramatic effects upon your health and performance:

Daily-Use Supplements		
Type	**Power**	**Natural Source**
Vitamin A	Strong bones, skin, eyes	Bananas, milk, fish, liver
Vitamin B$_3$	Fat and protein metabolism	Seafood, poultry, liver
Vitamin C	Reduces risk of heart disease	Oranges, tomatoes, broccoli
Vitamin E	Skin, hair, immune function	Nuts, seeds, green veggies, liver
Calcium	Strong bones, nerve conduction	Beans, legumes, milk, veggies
Selenium	Strong cardio system, antioxidant	Seafood, poultry, cereals

Ginseng	Regulating heart rate and blood sugar Increases metabolism Stimulates blood flow	Ginseng root
Goldenseal	Detoxifier, flushes system	Goldenseal extract
Zinc	Neurologic function, immune system	Legumes, seafood
Magnesium	Metabolism, muscles, nerves	Nuts, grains, leafy veggies
Saw Palmetto Berry	Prostate function and health	Plant form
Glucosamine Sulfate	Joint health, arthritis	Supplement pill
Ginkgo Biloba	Improved memory, clarity	Biloba tree
St. John's Wort	Elevated mood, fights depression	Plant form
Coenzyme Q10	Strong heart, arteries, cardiovascular	Supplement pill
Carnitine	Strong heart, arteries, cardiovascular	Supplement pill
Chromium	Regulates glucose, fat metabolism	Whole grains, cheese
Potassium	Regulates acid balance, water, nerves	Bananas, oranges, dates
Echinacea	Fights infection, immune system	Plant form
Bilberry Extract	Antioxidant, blood flow to eyes	Plant form
Guarana	Increased energy, circulation	Plant form

Take the time to educate yourself on the world of supplements, vitamins, herbs, and minerals. You must begin your personal diet by reprogramming the way you eat, and what you eat. Understand that all of your nutritional needs can be met through a diet of proper foods, but this is extremely difficult today and only proper supplementation can make up for this deficiency. As always, consult with your doctor to help develop a proper supplementation program. Don't just take every new miracle pill that your local vitamin store endorses. Take control of your life and begin educating yourself about supplements. You must take a war-like approach to nutrition and diet.

Amino Acids. These supernutrients are essential in building neurotransmitters in your brain, and a deficiency in any amino acid will result in lethargy and a lack of mental focus. Most people think of sports and weightlifting when they hear the term amino acids, but these nutrients have an even greater role in mental function. Some of the amino acids that help mental function are: phenylalanine, arginine, glutamine, taurine, and tryptophan. You should always avoid taking tryptophan with phenylalanine, as this can lower blood serotonin levels and possibly lead to depression. Talk to your physician or nutritionist about how to best supplement amino acids into your diet.

Choline. This essential supernutrient is broken down into acetylcholine, which is the chemical that transmits electric impulses in your brain. Choline has been shown to dramatically improve short-term memory in humans and should be taken in conjunction with vitamin B_5. Diarrhea is a common side effect when Choline is taken in very large doses, so pay attention to the daily-recommended doses.

Antioxidants. The benefits of supplementing your diet with antioxidants include antiaging effects and protection of brain cells. Vitamins that are classified as antioxidants are vitamins A, C, and E. It is wise to do some research on antioxidants first, as their recommended dosages vary significantly. Most people are unaware that vitamin A is toxic, so taking beta-carotene instead is highly recommended, unless otherwise prescribed by your doctor.

Ginseng. This ancient power herb has been used to increase mental and physical performance for over 5,000 years. Ginseng root is used to treat high blood pressure, cancer, fatigue, and a host of other ailments throughout the world. This power herb is effective in regulating heart rate and blood sugar levels, increasing metabolism, and stimulating blood flow. Siberian and Korean ginseng are the two most potent and pure versions available today. Ginseng comes in the form of pills, powders, teas, and whole roots, but teas and liquids provide a more efficient transfer system to the bloodstream.

Gotu-Kola. In ancient China, people used this power herb to heal skin problems, fight infection, and maintain strong mental and physical health. Gotu-Kola has also been shown to improve brain function and reduce stress in many studies.

Ginkgo Biloba. This power herb comes from the leaf extract of the oldest tree on earth. Ginkgo has been shown to increase cranial blood flow, improve memory and problem solving, increase alertness, and encourage the production of your brain's natural fuel—ATP. Ginkgo is widely accepted as a natural brain booster by the Asian and European medical communities. This power herb usually can be found in powder and liquid form and is readily available in most vitamin outlets.

COMMANDO DIET ESSENTIALS

Keep in mind that the list below is only a recommended sample of the foods that you can purchase to begin implementing the commando diet. Take the time to educate yourself about food labels and how to determine harmful ingredients. Purchase as much as possible of these products in their fresh form as opposed to processed forms and gradually reduce your refined sugar intake to nothing.

Basics of a Commando's Diet			
Proteins	**Fats**	**Carbohydrates**	**Liquids**
Chicken	Nuts	Bananas/Oranges/Apples	Water
Turkey	Olive Oil	Vegetables/Whole Grains	Orange Juice
Fish	Sesame Oil	Oatmeal/Brown Rice	Grape Juice

Remember that manufacturers are counting on the fact that you will not investigate their products thoroughly, because they need to add chemicals, preservatives, and additives in order to extend the shelf-life and enhance the taste. Become familiar with the techniques and wording they use to conceal ingredients. The commando diet is not about completely restricting yourself from a few desserts and treats here and there, but is an overall program of clean, unprocessed, and balanced foods.

Use the Internet

TAKE CONTROL TIP

Take the time to write down the ingredients, additives, and chemicals that you do not know much about in your favorite foods. Search the Internet to find information about these items. You will be shocked at the various toxic chemicals that are in our foods.

Power Foods

Some foods provide such a powerful combination of nutrition, taste, and health benefits that they deserve to be classified as power foods. These foods are so life-enhancing that some ancient religions thought they were given to them by the gods. The healthiest and longest-living societies make these foods the foundation of their diets. The addition of power foods into your diet can make a dramatic difference in your overall energy level, mental well-being, and health.

Sprouts. Sprouted seeds, whole grains, and legumes are among the most powerful and healthiest foods on this planet. They are a perfect example of living foods that carry nutrients directly to your body's most basic cells. Sprouts are extremely high in the purest forms of protein, enzymes, and lecithin. The rich enzymes in sprouts trigger your digestive system to power-up and cleanse itself. Sprouts contain minerals and vitamins and are extremely low in calories. Sprouts encompass a group of seeds, legumes, and whole grains that include rye, yellow soy, wheat, sunflower, radish, lentils, and radishes. Get into the habit of keeping a plastic container of various seeds in your refrigerator and sprinkle them on your foods and salads for added nutritional benefit.

Lecithin. This power food comes from soybeans and can be purchased as a supplement in granular form at most health food stores. Lecithin flushes fat from the liver and prevents it from collecting in the bloodstream. When digested, lecithin produces acetylcholine, which removes lactic acid from the body, muscles, and joints to provide a healthier and more flexible body. Lecithin also helps flush away toxins and waste from the nerve cells and helps enhance the reflexes. Instead of using milk on your morning cereal or oatmeal, trying substituting soy milk fortified with vitamin A, D, and calcium. Or use mashed tofu in place of ricotta cheese in your veggie lasagna.

Garlic. Garlic is very high in selenium, a powerful antiaging nutrient that has been proven to control heart disease, intestinal problems, high blood pressure, liver diseases, and sinus conditions. Garlic is also extremely efficient at reducing triglyceride and cholesterol levels in the blood. A study of people over 100 years old found that the only practice they shared in common was that they consumed large quantities of garlic. This powerful food is one of the cornerstones to life extension and vitality. To receive the maximum benefits from garlic, I recommend that you use minced garlic instead of processed powder. Just chop up a few cloves to sprinkle over your meals.

Whole Grains. Unprocessed grains contain important nutrients like vitamin E, vitamin B, and bran fiber that help in cleaning the walls of your intestines. Several types of grains such as buckwheat and barley are considered to be complete protein food in addition to supplying the body with powerful nutrients and minerals. Grains such as barley, millet, and buckwheat are the foundation of life-enhancing diets that have been in existence for thousands of years. Stay away from bleached flours and processed breads like bagels, pizza dough, and white sandwich bread.

Onions. This plant belongs to the same family as garlic and, like garlic, helps bring cholesterol levels down and prevents the clumping of platelets. This vegetable, especially if eaten raw, helps to prevent the gathering of unwanted fats in the arteries that can lead to heart attacks and strokes. Onions also help in killing harmful bacteria without hurting your body's naturally friendly bacteria. Get into the habit of including onion slices in your salad, on your sandwiches, or cooking white meats with them.

The commando diet is designed to offer a realistic, intelligent, and life-extending system of foods that you can use to enhance the quality of your life. By incorporating fruits, vegetables, grains, power foods, supplements, proteins, and self-discipline, the commando diet turns food into a weapon instead of a detriment.

MENTAL NUTRITION

Thousands of years ago, ancient cultures understood the relationship between body and mind. These ancient people discovered that certain foods and herbs not only helped physical performance, but also helped increase mental function. In today's age of technology, we have polluted our bodies and minds instead of improving them. A person's ability to remember and focus properly can be affected by deficiencies in vitamins, minerals, protein, or iron, or by processed chemical and food additives. Our sugar-obsessed society has concluded that too much sugar is very harmful to human health, yet we continue to produce and consume more sugar products each year. In fact, major studies continue to show that the average American diet greatly impairs and damages mental and bodily functions.

Today's scientists aren't sure exactly how nutrition interacts with mental function, but they do know that several nutrients are vital for enhancing the brain's ability to register, retain, and recall information. These important mental nutrients include lecithin, carbohydrates, vitamin B, and certain proteins. Without sufficient levels of vitamin B, thiamin, folic acid, and choline, the human brain will lose its ability to focus and function properly.

Recent scientific studies have shown that acetylcholine, the brain's vital memory chemical, can be dramatically increased by following a diet rich in soybeans, fish, and lecithin—all of which are high in choline. In one study, participants who were given small doses of choline, were able to memorize and recall a large list of words more quickly and accurately that those who were not given choline. Today, scientists have concluded that people who have deficiencies in vitamin B_6, vitamin B_{12}, copper, zinc, vitamin C, folate, and riboflavin have diminished capacities for memory and problem-solving.

Although food is polluted with toxins and chemicals, there have been some amazing scientific discoveries in the field of smart drugs. By feeding off of society's desire for wanting everything to be instant, easy, and without effort, researchers have created several smart drugs that produce fantastic brain-boosting results. Since the seventies, top research scientists have been conducting studies on the effects of these drugs. Most of these pharmaceuticals were originally produced to treat diseases such as Alzheimer's, Parkinson's, and dementia, but through extensive testing researchers found their amazing potential for improving mental function.

There are many studies available today that show increased mental function has occurred in average healthy adults from these drugs, with little or no side effects. As always, it is advisable to discuss these drugs with your doctor before taking any of them yourself.

> **Eat Like a Zen Master**
> Many ancient cultures believed that by eating very slowly they were able to extract all of the life-energy from their food. This practice of eating small portions and chewing slowly is not only beneficial to your health but also a good way to slow down and relax.

TAKE CONTROL TIP

Described below are some amazing smart drugs, supernutrients, and power herbs.

Piracetam

This smart drug is used to treat several illnesses like stroke, alcoholism, and dementia, but has also been shown to improve learning and memory in healthy adults. Piracetam is the most commonly used smart drug on the market today and has a wide variety of medical uses. Piracetam has been shown to increase the flow of information between the left and right sides of the brain, which is believed to enhance the creative problem-solving ability in humans. Studies have found no side effects, although headaches, nausea, and insomnia are possible.

Vasopressin

This brain hormone is naturally present in your body and helps in learning new information. It has been used to treat several conditions that lead to dysfunctional memory, as well as a certain form of diabetes. People who take Vasopressin report benefits of increased attention and clear-headedness, although side effects of headaches and stomach cramps have also been reported. People with diagnosed cardiovascular problems are discouraged from taking this smart drug. Vasopressin is widely available in Europe and Asia, but is available only by prescription in the United States.

DMAE (Dimethylaminoethanol)

This smart drug is commonly found in most nutrition and vitamin supplementation stores in the United States. DMAE is believed to increase memory, learning, intelligence, and extend your life span. Adverse side effects are almost nonexistent, but hypertension and muscle cramps have been reported. Some reports have shown that an overdose of DMAE can cause reverse effects like clouded thinking, impaired memory, and drowsiness. Studies have shown this smart drug to be a much safer and more effective stimulant than caffeine.

Caffeine

Found in several forms, this stimulant is most commonly associated with the world's two favorite drinks: coffee and tea. There are many conflicting reports about the long-term effects of caffeine, but nobody disputes the mental and physical performance boost that it delivers to the body. A few cups of coffee or tea can quickly improve your energy level and focus and lift your spirits. It is important to point out that too much caffeine can cause irritability, memory loss, and physical problems, so be selective in your caffeine intake and consult your doctor before taking it.

Modern science and technology have greatly improved our understanding of the most powerful and effective substances known to man, namely nutrients and herbs. These wonderful gifts of nature provide the most basic physical and mental nutrients that our bodies need to function. Through advanced research and study, we have discovered several supernutrients and power herbs that directly enhance our mental functions. Although most of these have been used for thousands of years by ancient cultures, we are now beginning to better understand their importance and capabilities.

PROPER EATING ESSENTIALS

Energy is the first essential element of physical control, for without an abundance of it you are like a car without gas. For optimal energy, it is important that you eat according to the natural functioning cycles that occur in your body. The following is a natural cycle for an average adult who eats three meals a day: breakfast at 7:00 A.M./lunch at noon/dinner at 6:00 P.M.

- The Feeding Cycle: 5 A.M.–8 A.M. and 12 noon–8 P.M. (Foods are ingested and digested.)
- The Absorption Cycle: 8 P.M.–4 A.M. (The foods are expended.)
- The Removal Cycle: 4 A.M.–12 noon (The foods are excreted.)

These natural body cycles are typical of how our human digestive and assimilation systems function throughout the day. One of the reasons that people experience increased weight gain, digestive problems, and constipation is because their eating habits are out of sync with their natural body cycles. By understanding these natural cycles and eating foods that allow these cycles to operate effectively, you will tap into your powerful energy reserves and see a tremendous increase in overall health. The process of flushing out our bodies is accomplished by eating greater amounts of high water-content foods and understanding the body's three functioning cycles.

High Water-Content Food

Your body composition is approximately 70% water, so to properly cleanse your body and ensure that it is operating at peak levels, your diet must consist of at least 70% high water-content foods. By eating plenty of fruits and vegetables and drinking plenty of water, we are able to maintain this peak performance range. High water-content foods such as most fruits and vegetables are easier to digest, assimilate through the body faster, and can be eaten raw or served as a quick snack.

Eating Cycles

Now that we have begun to eat high water-content power foods, we must ensure that your eating cycles are scheduled into your body's three functioning cycles. Eat a large breakfast of fruits and vegetables (between 5 A.M. and 8 A.M.) as the body is now trying to get rid of unwanted wastes and toxins. This allows the elimination and excretion process to operate at peak efficiency. During mid-day, have your proteins, grains, fruits, supplements, and vegetables in five or six small meals (noon to 8 P.M.) for maximum benefit. You should not ingest any foods after 8 P.M., as this will greatly effect your absorption cycle by overworking your digestive system (8 P.M.–4 A.M.). By practicing the commando diet, we allow our bodies to repair and flush themselves of harmful toxins in a natural way

(4 A.M.–12 noon). By flushing the toxins out of the body, we ensure that it remains pure inside.

These essential elements of the commando diet are not as difficult to follow as it first may seem. In the morning when your body is eliminating toxins and waste, start off the day with several bananas, oranges, or apples, or a glass of fruit juice. By utilizing self-discipline techniques, you will automatically reach for the fruits and juices instead of eggs, bacon, toast, and coffee. For lunch and dinner, make sure your meals are full of fresh grains and vegetables to ensure peak energy and health levels are maintained throughout the rest of the day. The results you will experience from the commando diet will be noticed on the very first day. This system is not some "magical" diet or insane new-age lifestyle, simply the natural flow of energy, life, and vitality. Your health, mental state, and energy levels will increase to levels that you have never experienced before. Remember to treat yourself on the weekends and don't become frustrated if you slip every now and then, for as long as you follow the commando diet five days a week, you will see dramatic improvements.

Controlled Digestion

In order to conserve essential energy for your day, it is important that you understand the concept of controlled digestion. If you are like most people, gobbling down your lunch while watching television or taking care of work-related business is a daily occurrence. Proper and controlled chewing of all food might sound like a simple task but it is extremely essential for health and vitality. The saliva that is concentrated in your mouth is designed to initially break down the food that you eat. Large chunks of undigested food are tremendously stressful on your stomach's digestive system, requiring large amounts of energy to break down. How often do you feel tired and lethargic after eating a quick lunch or dinner? How many times a week do you feel like taking a noontime nap? If you are like most Americans, the answer to these questions is most likely every day!

Properly chewed food is digested much more easily, which also means your body needs less of it. The body will require less food intake when you slowly and thoughtfully chew your food. In today's society, people eat much more food than they actually need, which in turn becomes converted to fat. By simply taking an extra 10 to 15 seconds to chew your food, the benefits of greater energy and a leaner body will be added to your life. Think of your digestive system as the engine to your machine. Just like your vehicle's engine, proper fuel and maintenance is directly related to its life span and performance.

Fasting

Fasting is one of the oldest and time-honored means of detoxifying and cleansing the body. It is used as a means of physical and mental healing and has been used in religious practices since recorded history. With the advent of increased technology and medical data, today's medical doctors receive almost no training or clinical practice in nutrition. The valuable information that has taken many societies and cultures thousands of years to develop is rarely even discussed, let alone introduced into today's medical training.

The positive effects of a properly controlled fast has been well-documented in modern medical literature and shows that fasting can be extremely effective against a wide variety of ailments. The medical data about fasting suggest a wide array of applications. Allergies, obesity, ulcers, depression, chemical poisoning, asthma, eczema, irritable bowel syndrome, and neurosis are among the many health problems for which fasting has proven effective. I strongly recommend a two- to four-day juice fast once every six months as an effective way of improving your overall health and vitality. A juice fast includes four 12-ounce glasses of freshly squeezed juice each day during the fast. During a fast, our fat cells release stored fat into our systems. This can create unpleasant reactions from the toxins and chemicals being released into the system. Individuals who have high levels of toxins in their body are advised to seek medical assistance under a carefully controlled fasting program.

Before you begin your fast, I recommend that you eat only fruits and vegetables the day before and have a fresh supply of organic produce on hand to last throughout your fasting period. It is very important to drink lots of water and get plenty of rest during your fast, as you will experience a decrease in energy. I also recommend drinking two to three cups of noncaffeinated herbal teas to enhance the cleansing process. Understand that a fasting period is also a time of rest, so plan your fast on a weekend or during a stay-at-home vacation time. Your body is a warehouse of various chemicals, toxins, and environmental poisons that have been stored up over the years. A properly controlled fast can be one of the most beneficial and health-inducing practices that you can do. In addition, the process of fasting is a powerful way to build discipline and self-control.

Take Control Exercise

Now that you understand the basics of the commando diet, we must begin to implement its powerful concepts into your life. In the SEAL teams, we must be able to effectively operate in all environmental extremes. In one week we could find ourselves in the searing heat of the African desert and the next week in the subfreezing cold of the Arctic. In order to effectively prepare our bodies for such extremes, we use a technique called acclimatization. By preparing our minds and bodies with the needed information, equipment, clothing, and food, we are better able to understand and combat the dramatic effects of rapid change. It is through the process of understanding how and why our bodies react to various food changes, temperatures, and conditions that we are able to predict and counteract the stresses of change.

For this mission we are going to begin the process of acclimatizing to a new country or environment. The only foods to be found in this new country are fruits, vegetables, supplements, grains, chicken, and fish. This foreign country has no McDonald's, 7-11's, Pizza Huts, or restaurants of any kind. In order to prepare yourself for this upcoming mission, you must slowly start adapting to this food change by altering your present diet. To successfully accomplish this mission, you must begin studying, understanding, and consuming these new foods. Each day we will begin eating less of our regular foods and more of these new foods, until we have successfully adapted to this country's indigenous diet. List the foods you have eaten for each meal and use the following questionnaire to learn more about your present eating habits and identify which foods and habits need to be adjusted.

Once you have a clear picture of the foods and liquids you ingest during an average day, you must begin replacing these harmful foods with power foods. One of the keys to winning the battle of nutrition is preparation. If you develop the habit of spending time each evening preparing your breakfast and lunch for the following day, you will not only save time but also dramatically improve your overall health.

It is important to understand that just eating these foods is not enough, you must also begin researching and studying all that you can about the relationship between your body and these foods. By keeping a daily journal of

---

24-Hour Eating Period

Breakfast
Time: _____
Food: _____
Drink: _____

Lunch
Time: _____
Food: _____
Drink: _____

Dinner
Time: _____
Food: _____
Drink: _____

Snacks
Time: _____
Food: _____
Drink: _____

Assessment
Fast Food Items: _____
Processed Foods: _____
Sweets / Sugars: _____
Sodas / Alcohol: _____
Red Meats: _____
Dairy Products: _____

---

what, where, why, and how you eat these foods, we are better able to understand the effects of these new foods on our bodies.

The powerful effects of the commando diet upon your body will truly amaze you. By the end of the week you will feel a tremendous vibrancy and energy like you have never felt before. The benefits of eating living foods and eliminating dead, processed foods from your diet will make you a true believer. The path to power living must begin with self-discipline. All of the information that you have just read is worthless unless you begin disciplining yourself to take action today. You are a big person now, so start taking responsibility for your body and its care. You are what you eat.

MISSION DE-BRIEF
★★★★

The powerful effects that you'll feel from the commando diet are a direct result of self-disciplined eating. The concept of nutritional warfare is one of knowledge and action. By ensuring that we eat only living and unprocessed foods, we tremendously enhance our health, clarity, energy, and vitality. The introduction of self-discipline into our eating habits is a sometimes difficult and demanding task. By utilizing the techniques of visualization and thought control, we can program our minds to erase urges and impulses. The most powerful weapon in the war of nutrition is information. It is up to you to develop the foundation of knowledge needed to properly select and purchase living foods. You can read all of the personal empowerment books that you want, but it is ultimately self-discipline that makes your actions speak louder than words.

It is very important to keep a daily journal of all the information pertaining to our eating habits. Everybody has a bad day and makes a few poor decisions, but through self-discipline and personal management we are able to dramatically reduce the occurrence of these glitches. I am a firm believer in treating yourself to whatever you want every now and then, but that does not apply to every day! By giving in a little every day, you are only treating yourself to illness, obesity, low self-esteem, and death. It is not so hard. Stand up and take responsibility for your actions and life. Start getting everything you want out of life by making a commitment. By adding a little self-discipline to your life, you begin reaping the tremendous benefits of power living. Health, vitality, success, beauty, and longevity are yours for the taking; all that you need is commitment and self-discipline.

7

PROFESSIONAL DISCIPLINE

Hold yourself responsible for a higher standard than anybody else expects of you. Never excuse yourself. Never pity yourself. Be a hard master to yourself—and be lenient to everybody else.—Henry Ward Beecher

Ah, the wonderful world of work. The alarm goes off with a nerve-rattling buzz and you reach over to hit the snooze button. The clock says 5:45 A.M., and you drag yourself into the bathroom to begin the neverending morning routine. Shower, dress, heat up a day-old cup of coffee, grab your briefcase, and you're out the door to start the hour-long battle with traffic. Working for money is one of the few things that just about all humans living on this small planet share in common. Most people will spend more than 70% of their time alive on earth simply working. It has replaced hunting and gathering as the most fundamental aspect of survival and the basis by which we judge our existence. Work is responsible for determining where we live, how we dress, who we know, and even our state of mental and physical well-being. If our jobs encompass so much of our lives and are so vitally important to our existence, wouldn't it make sense to sharpen our skills, improve our position, strive for accomplishment and fulfillment?

Many people who work today view it as a necessary evil that controls a great portion of their life. Work has become a source of dread, depression, and high stress for most people. How about that small percentage of people who absolutely enjoy going to work, who live a life of comfort and security, who supervise hundreds and even thousands of people, and who experience a lifetime of achievement and success because of work? Most of us know of somebody who, with seemingly average talents and intelligence, rose through the ranks in record time to become the CEO of a company or started their own business and dominated the market.

On the other hand, other people we know either progress in their career at a standard pace or remain stagnant right up to retirement age. Then there is a group of people who can never seem to hold onto a job, who are constantly concocting instant-success schemes and can fill their resume with a long list of failed attempts at a career.

So, the question remains, what makes the difference is all these situations? It is professional discipline.

Professional discipline is made up of several different ingredients, all of which can be learned, applied, and improved upon. Professional discipline is a toolbox of skills that, when applied, will not only dramatically change your work performance but also completely enhance the quality of your life. The power of professional discipline is made up of five separate skill-areas:

- The predator's mindset
- Presentation control
- Rapid reasoning
- Knowledge control
- Creating balance

THE PREDATOR'S MINDSET

Several years ago, I was in an African nation working on a SEAL security team for a high-ranking American diplomat. On a particular day during his visit, the host country had scheduled an escorted tour of its vast game preserve for the diplomat and his entourage and since we were acting as his security team, we were required to go along. As we drove down the dirt road in a long procession of jeeps, armored Suburbans, and various vehicles, the diplomat asked if we could stop at a particular location in the road. Once we stopped the procession, he quickly jumped out of the vehicle and pointed to a spot about 100 yards to the side of the dirt road. There, lying in the grass, was a large lioness with a freshly killed gazelle in her grasp and about eight or more hyenas gathered behind her waiting for the spoils. She had an incredibly majestic air about her and, by her demeanor, we could tell that she was not the least bit concerned about our presence. As we watched this amazing scene of nature unfold, I casually stated that most people never get to see this scene up close in their lifetime. The old diplomat looked at me and replied, "That's where you are wrong. What you are looking at happens every day, in every city, in every company and place of work throughout the world."

I have since come to understand that the old diplomat was referring to what I call the great human food chain. You see, even with all of our technology, education, and advanced way of life, we continue to act out our primitive animal instincts on each other. Just as the lioness is the queen of her domain and dictates the actions of all the other animals on the Serengeti, the highly disciplined person sits on top of the human food chain and controls his or her work environment with a superior work ethic, dominating performance, and superior skills. This category of high-performing person accounts for about 1% of a workforce.

Next is what I call the fair-weather worker, or hyena, who is not willing to put forth the effort and continually waits in the background, hoping to jump on the success of the predator.

Lastly comes the prey or the working sheep herd, who views work as a place to hang out for eight hours and the source of all bad things. The prey make up about 70% of the workforce and the hyenas around 29%.

The predator's mindset is about attitude. It is an attitude of domination, effort, and high performance. Most of us can name a person or two that we work with whom everybody looks up to, who is the decision-maker and the go-to person in a time of crisis or high-pressure situations. These people possess an aura of leadership and are usually found in the highest reaches of an organization. When something needs doing or a question needs to be answered, everybody comes to this person. Predators are the backbone behind every great team, organization, and company because they not only demonstrate a high-performance work ethic, but they cause others to work on a higher level. This is a person in control of their environment and destiny. This is the predator's mindset.

The predator's mindset is about not accepting failure. All too often today, individuals and organizations factor in a certain amount of failure into every action, decision, and project. Many companies and organizations readily accept a certain percentage of defects, errors, and incompetence. This failure mindset dictates that mistakes and incompetence can be regarded as a normal part of daily business. A certain percentage of employees will not show up each day. A certain percentage of mistakes will be made in each department and a certain amount of customers will be lost in a given day. For most businesses, this failure percentage is in the range of 1% to 5%. What most people fail to realize is that even the acceptance of a 1% failure rate can be disastrous. This is not to imply that failure cannot be tolerated or considered a possibility, but rather that it should be viewed as an unacceptable performance trait. The following is what would result from a 0.1% failure rate being accepted in some professions and come from current industry production figures.

- 2,000 incorrectly performed surgical procedures would occur each month.
- 14 passenger airplanes would crash each week.
- 384,000 letters would be lost each day within the U.S. Postal System.
- 78,840 telephone calls would be misrouted every hour.
- 385 patients would be prescribed the wrong drug every week.

When we begin to count on failure as a part of doing business or as an acceptable trait in our lives, a funny thing happens—we begin to fail. Instead of raising our personal expectations and improving our career, health, and relationships, we actually lower our performance and the performance of others around us by accepting failure. The predator's mindset is about controlling our attitude. It is so easy and enticing to stand around the water cooler with your coworkers and complain about how unfair and mundane your job is. It is easy to do only what is required of you and hope that somebody above you retires in order to be promoted. Becoming a high performer is hard. It takes twice as much effort and discipline to stand out from the crowd or keep your cool in the face of adversity.

The first step to taking control of your career begins with your attitude. You have the choice to become the king of your domain or stay put with the work force prey. The work ethic and attitude you adopt is completely up to you. Here are some tips for developing the predator's mindset:

- Show up to work 15 minutes before anybody else.
- Let it be known that you want more responsibility and perform accordingly.
- Maintain an organized, clean, and professional work space.
- Always dress less casually and more professionally than everybody else.
- Become a listener and never ever complain out loud.

- Strive to someday become the CEO and not just a manager—raise your sights.
- Control your emotions and limit your socializing.

The predator's mindset is a skill that can be easily learned and adopted. It is not based upon your education level, gender, race, or position, but entirely on your attitude and work ethic. In today's highly competitive work arena, success is determined by the little things and usually the difference between winning and losing comes down to attitude. Remember that when you wake up in the morning, you control whether your job has a positive or negative influence in your life, because nobody controls your attitude except you.

Assess Your Attitude

TAKE CONTROL TIP
Take the time to think about how others perceive your attitude. Are you a complainer? An optimist? What sort of picture is your attitude painting about you? Change your image by adopting the predator's mindset.

PRESENTATION CONTROL

The human being is a visual animal. We live in a society where sound bites, video clips, and multimedia presentations are the mediums by which we learn and communicate. People start to make immediate judgments based upon our body language, dress, colors, and overall appearance the moment they see us.

Most experts agree that we are perceived three ways: 55% visually, 40% vocally, and 5% verbally. The United States intelligence community and special operations forces have used body language, dress, and power words to influence and control people for over 40 years. Psychologists and behavioral experts have concluded that we are walking, talking visual aids that influence how people think, feel, and react to us, long before we even say a word. Today, corporations and organizations have started to realize the impact that body language, dress, and vocabulary have on their bottom line.

The impression we give to people through mannerisms, attire, and words is vitally important to our professional performance. Oftentimes, how we are perceived can be the difference in getting promoted, closing a sale, or effectively managing people. There are several key aspects of our presentation that we can control to customize the impression we wish to convey and subconsciously influence people to our way of thinking. The three key areas of presentation control are appearance, body language, and vocal discipline.

Appearance

Our appearance conveys a powerful visual message to the people we come in contact with. By understanding how certain colors and features of dress subconsciously trigger various feelings in people, we can customize our appearance to convey a particular message. The following is a list of colors and the nonverbal signals they convey.

Color	Feeling
Red	Powerful, aggressive, responsible
Black–Dark Blue	In control, conservative, serious
Yellow–Orange	Carefree, social, warm
Green–Light Blue	Friendly, social, emotional
White	Organized, clean, orderly

Most of us associate certain colors with feelings, personalities, and traits. The common stereotypes that we associate with hair color provides insight into our subconscious associations. For example, many people joke that blonde or yellow hair relates to fun-loving, ditsy, and social personalities. The hair color of red is often times associated with aggression, anger, or hotheadedness, and the hair color of black relates to serious-minded and unemotional people. This is a common method of categorizing and verbalizing our initial impressions based upon colors. By understanding and utilizing this behavioral characteristic, we can modify our appearance to convey a desired feeling, attitude, or trait.

Our ability to convey a certain feeling is not limited to just colors. Behavioral psychologists have come to learn that straight lines, adornments, and shiny objects also play a role in our overall presentation. The familiar image of the American soldier in a sharp, crisp, well-tailored uniform with straight creases and shiny medals is the stereotypical image we associate with discipline and courage. In the special operations community, we refer to shined shoes and a shiny belt buckle as the "raccoon syndrome," because these items catch the eye and stand out from the surroundings, just as a raccoon is known to be attracted to shiny objects in the water. Having well-shined shoes conveys the signal of power and discipline for both men and women, but excessively large and bright jewelry does not.

For both men and women, short hair, dark-colored suits, and shined shoes present the image of competence. The following list is a description of certain dress characteristics and the messages they convey.

Presentation	Impression
Sharp, distinct creases	Disciplined, competent, organized
Shined shoes	Powerful, a leader, in control
Short groomed hair	Confident, disciplined, organized
Fit and trim body	Energetic, powerful, disciplined

It is important to remember that your clothing, personal grooming, and physical condition all play a very important part in the message that you advertise every day. Many people are tremendously gifted in their profession but fail to recognize the importance of presentation control and nonverbal impressions upon their overall performance. Too often, people treat their workplace as a social club or singles bar and continually wonder why they never get promoted. Begin spending extra time and money preparing yourself to present an image of control, discipline, and professionalism.

Body Language

Nonverbal communication encompasses not only how we dress, but includes the visual signals we send with our posture, facial expressions, and hand movements. Understand that wearing the appropriate clothing and displaying disciplined grooming habits is only a small part of our overall presentation. We send out thousands of visual signals each day to our clients, coworkers, bosses, friends, and family via our body language. These signals can make you appear confident, in control, incompetent, nervous, or even insincere. When your body language is sending a different message than the words out of your mouth, people become confused and are more inclined to remember your nonverbal message over the verbal message.

As a professional speaker, I am paid to deliver a certain message to large groups of people in a relatively short time. If my body language and physical presentation is not in line with my verbal message, the audience will most likely become confused and irritated. Most people fail to understand that we are always giving a presentation, from the time we leave our drive-way to the time we return home at night. No words can convey our competence, confidence, and interest as quickly as body language does, and it takes a tremendous amount of words and charisma to change this physical impression. Our body language is the result of our inward feelings and emotions. If we feel nervous, unsure, or angry, then our body will display this message unconsciously. It is important to understand that in one way or another, we are all salespeople trying to sell our most important product—ourselves.

Being a good communicator is one of the greatest assets in today's business world. A person who understands body language has a tremendous conversational advantage and can quickly assess another person's true message through their body language signals. Our bodies send messages by three different body movements: facial expressions, hand gestures, and posture. Usually, all three of these body movements coordinate to send a particular message. Let's take a look at some of the most common nonverbal messages that we send and the body language we use to display them.

Message	Body Movement
Anger	Crossed arms, clenched fists, dilated pupils, frowning
Boredom	Slouching, little eye contact, chin in hand, blank stare
Condescension	Hands on hips, tilted head, rolling eyes, stroking chin
Confidence	Direct eye contact, leaning forward, erect stance, open hands
Defensiveness	Arms or legs crossed, leaning back, clenched fist, little eye contact
Doubt	Arms or legs crossed, raised eyebrows, hand to face, squinting
Enthusiasm	Erect body stance, eyes wide, smiling, palms open, rapid talking
Frustration	Clenched fist, touching hair, modulating voice, frowning, sweating
Guilt	Little eye contact, low voice, tilted head, arms crossed, frowning
Interest	Leaning forward, open hands, nodding head, direct eye contact

Nervousness	Twitching lips, hand to mouth, darting eye movement, sweating
Readiness	Hands on hips, leaning forward, direct eye contact, open hands
Suspicion	Little eye contact, hand to nose, looking away, squinting

Understanding and assessing body language is one of the most important tools you can use to help influence and communicate with people. A person who coordinates their body language with their verbal message is many times more effective in all aspects of communications and personal influence. Understanding how to control your body language can result in more sales, better relationships, enhanced leadership, and greater influence over other people.

An effective way to develop better body language skills is to use a mirror to practice your conversations or videotape your presentations. The basic skills of appearance control and refined body language can quickly elevate your performance both at home and at work. Take control of your life by developing the ability to discipline your communication skills.

Vocal Discipline

Nothing can be more persuasive or get us into more trouble than our mouth. Most people have experienced the embarrassment and discomfort that is associated with saying the wrong words at the wrong time. The ordinary, everyday act of speaking can be your greatest asset or your worst nightmare. Oftentimes a person's success or failure comes down to what they say and how they say it. Your appearance and body language are far more easy to control than your words. Nothing can ruin a career or reputation faster than a lack of vocal discipline.

Most of us know intelligent and competent people who stagnate in their careers because of swearing, poor verbal command, or vocal emotional outbursts. The key to persuasive language is found in its emotional content. Understanding the fact that people are controlled and influenced through their emotions is the foundation behind verbal control. All of today's politicians, media personnel, and marketing professionals prepare their words carefully to influence our behaviors and emotions.

Many people make the mistake of speaking from emotion rather than thought. How often do you say something to cut somebody down, express your displeasure, or hurt somebody's feelings without even thinking about it? How often do you say words just to be accepted or be in the majority, even if you don't feel this way? As parents we often ignore the effect of our language on children. What a surprise it is to hear our children swear or use a derogatory statement, only to remember that they are simply repeating our words. How many times have you said things you really didn't mean, only to wish you could take them back? The development of vocal discipline is crucial to our personal life as well as our professional career. Begin thinking about the words you use and how you use them throughout the day. Try controlling your tendency to swear or speak badly of people. The simple act of consciously thinking about your words, instead of blurting them out, will dramatically improve the impression you give people.

You can greatly enhance your overall presentation by understanding and working on these four keys to vocal discipline: pause, tone, content, and delivery.

- **Pause:** Always pause before you speak. This helps draw attention to your words and creates interest. Use a pause to think about and choose your words carefully.
- **Tone:** Use the tone of your voice to illicit emotions. Never speak in a monotone voice. Raise your tone to highlight power words or to keep people's attention.
- **Content:** Proper preparation is the key. Take the time to think about what you want to say and practice your delivery. Never, ever, use swear words or language that can be deemed inappropriate. Stay away from acronyms or complicated words, as this will not impress and only serves to confuse people.
- **Delivery:** Use the skills of appearance control and body language to accentuate your words. Highlight key words with facial expressions and hand movements.

The first step to gaining control of our professional presentation is to make a detailed assessment of our present vocabulary, dress, and body language. Oftentimes the key to improving our professional performance can be found in the mirror. By assessing the presentation that we advertise every day at work, we can distinguish what needs to be changed, enhanced, and developed. Take the time to think about your physical appearance, vocabulary, and body language and the message they portray about you. Use the information you have learned here to assess and correct the areas of your professional presentation that diminish your reputation and ability to influence.

RAPID REASONING

Every human being is faced with daily problems that exist in everyday life, and they can take up a lot of our time and energy—even drain us physically and emotionally. Sometimes we can get so caught up worrying and thinking about our daily problems that there is little time or energy left for anything else. Rapid reasoning can be used to deal instantly with important problems and get them rapidly and efficiently out of the way. This little-known skill can work miracles in your life. People with rapid reasoning skills quickly gain reputations as leaders and quick decision-makers. They're able to scan a problem or situation at a glance and quickly come up with the correct solution and decision.

Most of us hear and read about our nation's successful decision-makers, both in business and government. Everybody knows that the real decision-makers are at the top of finance, business, entertainment, and government. For most of these superhumans, their ability to quickly and correctly make decisions has propelled them to the top in all fields. Rapid reasoning is one of the most important elements of professional control, and one of the most dynamic elements of human success. Financial and business corporations spend millions of dollars a year training their executives to make correct and timely decisions. This powerful skill can make an immediate impact upon your life by:

- Handling difficult coworkers, family members, and customers.
- Helping you make smarter decisions concerning your personal life.
- Enabling you to deal with problems as they come up in everyday life.
- Transforming you into an effective leader and decision-maker.

When you are faced with a problem or situation, you probably discuss it with other people or try various solutions until you get one right. Or perhaps you turn it over and over in your mind or ignore it until a later date, hoping it will solve itself.

These are normal human problem-solving techniques that we have been taught or programmed to perform. Sometimes they work out all right, and sometimes they don't. Here are some techniques you can use to hone your problem-solving skills and make you a rapid reasoner.

Power Focus

Use a notebook with the word "Problems" at the top of one sheet of paper to list the problems you are focusing on. Or speak into a tape recorder, outlining your problems. These techniques allow you to focus on your problem solving to open up more of our powerful reasoning skills. Scientists and psychologists have discovered that the human mind is much more efficient and organized when it has something tangible to work with. Your mind can go in a thousand different directions as you mull over a problem, but if you put it down on paper, you enact the power of focus and clarity on that single problem.

When you begin writing your problem down in your notebook, you are not only documenting it—you're also sending a powerful message to your subconscious mind. Basically, you are telling it to work on this problem even after your conscious mind has focused on other matters. In our subconscious mind, we're not aware of all that is happening inside this hidden computer in our heads. Nor are we aware of its awesome power to help figure out our problems and situations. Most of you have heard about some of the amazing things the subconscious mind is capable of, but few people are familiar with its important role in problem solving. They don't know that successful people make full use of their subconscious problem-solving powers.

Here are a few important facts you should know about your subconscious mind:

- Your brain stores enough information to fill 100 million books. This amazing warehouse of information houses the solution to your problems somewhere inside of it. Sadly, only a small portion of this information is easily available to your conscious mind.
- When you are perplexed by a certain problem, you can order your subconscious mind to begin looking through all of the data in its warehouse for ideas and solutions to this problem. As you go about conducting your regular business at hand, your subconscious mind is busy searching and matching information and experiences that relate to this particular problem. At some point in time, your subconscious mind will relay

this information to your conscious mind. This information would never have been recalled by the conscious mind.

- The subconscious mind will accept almost any thought you present to it. The power of suggestion is how we program or task our subconscious mind. The conscious mind is controlled by logic, and suggestion and thoughts control the subconscious. If you were to tell your subconscious mind over and over again that you could fly, it would believe this as fact even though the conscious mind knows it to be untrue.

How many times have you tried to remember a name or word, and no matter how hard you racked your brain, you just couldn't remember it? Then, several hours or days later, you suddenly remember it. This is your subconscious mind in action. The information was buried in your head somewhere, but you just could not recall it. By closing your eyes and focusing your problem into an image or picture, you begin involving the subconscious mind. Close your eyes and imagine the end result of your problem, or try to picture the happy and successful conclusion to your situation. Now go back step by step and retrace in reverse motion exactly how you arrived at your successful decision or solution.

This technique will allow your subconscious mind to not only see your desired outcome, but begin rapidly accessing ideas and bits of stored information that relate to your problem. You will be amazed at the speed and intense focus that your subconscious mind displays in presenting your conscious mind with an answer. Use this method along with the following techniques to turbo-charge your decision and speed reasoning abilities.

Idea Tree

An idea tree is a very efficient method of problem solving. It begins with a primary concept or word. Around this central word you draw seven to ten main ideas that relate to this word. You then expand further on these words by again drawing seven to ten main ideas that relate to each of those words. With this simple, yet powerful technique, you exponentially create related ideas that can quickly produce one or many solutions and decisions. The idea tree is not limited to problem solving or decision-making, but also can be used as a very fast and efficient system for taking notes. This technique has several advantages over standard note-taking methods because you can focus on the important concepts, facts, or ideas quickly. In addition, it reduces sentences and paragraphs into single concepts and ideas and forces your mind to concentrate on the big picture. The resultant idea tree can be seen by the eye and memorized faster.

An idea tree lets you quickly produce many ideas and simultaneously organize them by placing one idea next to a related idea. The idea tree is a very powerful tool for note taking, report writing, and creative problem solving, where it is extremely important to get all related information and solutions. Use this concept for lightning-fast decision-making by drawing seven to ten possible decisions around your central problem or situation.

The idea tree is ideal for giving a speech or brief. Instead of having your speech or brief written out in paragraphs on several sheets of paper, you can create an idea tree centered on the main theme of your speech. When somebody asks you a question during your speech, you can quickly move to the place on your idea tree that relates to the question and then return to where you were without losing yourself in a pile of written papers.

The key to mastering the idea tree is to keep it simple and use single words. Sometimes you may need to write out explanations for some of your words, but keep these to a minimum. This technique will help increase your ability to rapidly learn information by forcing you to remember the content information of each word without looking at it or having it written down. By practicing this method, you can program your mind to group information with by using an idea tree format.

The Decision Grid

One of the greatest problems facing corporate America today is the reluctance and inefficiency involved with making daily decisions. As a consultant, I have worked with corporations and organizations that spend most of the day in meetings haggling over by whom, how, and when a decision should be made. Some companies spend incredible amounts of money, time, and manpower to simply decide what bagels to serve at the next day's meeting. It seems that nobody wants to be responsible for making a decision that could in someway reflect badly upon them, and this behavior results in more and more meetings with little or no results.

The decision grid is an effective way to make rapid decisions based upon a scoring system. We use the decision grid in the SEAL teams to make life-and-death decisions in under three minutes. It is designed to include known data with intuition to arrive at the best possible solution to a dilemma. The decision grid is also effective at eliminating ego and the "I am in charge" attitude that often creates conflict during the decision-making process.

The decision grid uses the simple system of scoring the available solutions in known categories to single out the most advantageous one. Similar to a course-of-action grid, the decision grid helps you find a clear solution to your problem. Here is a an example of a simple decision grid for deciding upon a new job:

Options	Money	Benefits	Location	6th Sense	Score
Job #1	4	2	1	2	9
Job #2	3	3	4	3	13
Job #3	4	3	2	2	11
Self-Employed	4	1	3	2	10

As you can see from the above example, the decision grid is scored from a high value of 4 to a low value of 1, 4 being the best and 1 being the worst.

The importance of the sixth sense in the decision-making process cannot be overstated. The list of categories can include such subjects as family opinion, outside advice, or anything that is of importance to the overall decision. Once each option has been evaluated and scored, a quick decision is made and the planning process can now be initiated. The decision grid is a powerful way to improve your overall efficiency and reduce stress. By quickly making a solid decision and moving on to the next task at hand, you can effectively eliminate procrastination and reduce the stress involved with mulling a decision over and over in your mind.

I include a section entitled "Decision-Making" into my journal so that I can review past decisions and learn from my mistakes through the entire process. Oftentimes we are faced with decisions that we have confronted in the past and can use this journal to review the options and outcome of this past decision. Develop the skill of rapid reasoning by eliminating wasted effort, time, and worry with the decision grid.

The Decision Compass

This is a powerful problem-solving method that I developed by combining SEAL team mission planning techniques with Far East military tactics and is used for individual or group-based rapid decision-making. The decision compass was originally used by Chinese warlords for quick battlefield problem solving. This technique provides a diverse framework of thinking strategies to attack the problem or concept from many different angles. The decision compass is broken up into four equal thinking directions. This method promotes greater input from more people, or several different perspectives for the individual. By using the decision compass to attack problems and situations, you are able to separate ego and ulterior motives from performance.

When using this technique in a group-based environment, it is important to remember that a compass direction is a type of thinking rather than a label for thinking. The thinking directions must never be used to categorize individuals, and everybody thinks in one direction at the same time. The decision compass is a powerful problem-solving tool that can be used to quickly attack a problem from many different perspectives and arrive at a well-balanced decision.

The decision compass is one of the most flexible and rapid methods in existence for enhancing your reasoning and problem-solving skills. This technique provides a super-fast platform for which a group or individual can quickly arrive at a concrete decision. The benefits of using the decision compass are:

- Eliminates egos and biased opinions
- Encourages creative and off-the-wall thinking
- Provides a super-fast problem-solving platform
- Dramatically enhances your creative thinking abilities
- Reduces paperwork, time, and confusion in all business environments

There are four different thinking styles or directions that the thinker can go to or from at any given time. By jumping from one direction to another, you are able to create scenarios and generate ideas from a different perspective each time. To begin the decision compass, you must first write the problem or situation in the center of a piece of paper or on the blackboard. Next, you draw arrows pointing North, South, East, and West from the center. Each direction represents a different thinking style or approach, and you can start from any direction you desire. I cannot overemphasize the importance of ensuring each person involved is thinking in the same direction as everyone else. The four cardinal directions and thinking styles are:

- **North Thinking:** This direction covers facts, figures, and needed information. When moving to the North direction, forget all proposals and arguments and begin looking at the cold, hard facts.
- **South Thinking:** The South direction encompasses intuition, your sixth sense, emotions, and feelings. This thinking direction allows you to give your gut feeling or intuition without needing to justify it. It is important to record or annotate each person's intuition without requiring an explanation.
- **East Thinking:** This is the logic and caution direction—why something will work and why it will offer benefits. East thinking is used to point out why a suggestion does or does not fit the facts, system in use, or governing policy. It can be used to look forward to the possible results of a certain proposal or action, but can also be used to pinpoint the value in the present situation.
- **West Thinking:** This is the direction of alternatives, creativity, new proposals, and off-the-wall thinking. The West direction is the area for innovation and radical idea thinking. Again, it is very important to record all of the ideas or concepts created while in this direction of

The Decision Compass

NORTH THINKING
Facts & Figures

WEST THINKING
Off-The-Wall Ideas
Creativity
Alternatives

PROBLEM

EAST THINKING
Logic & Caution

SOUTH THINKING
Sixth Sense & Intuition

thinking. Use the West direction of thinking to move sideways when working on a problem, and try different concepts, ideas, or points of entry.

Nothing shapes our lives more than the decisions we make. In today's fast-paced business world, we must make hundreds of important decisions each day and often our professional progress is determined by how effective we are at making correct and timely decisions. More times than not, it is our natural tendency to put off decisions that create a tremendous amount of stress in our lives. Rapid reasoning is a learned skill that can be passed onto our children to help them limit future mistakes and develop self-discipline. Understand that all of us make mistakes and will continue to do so until the day we die, but by developing the skill of rapid reasoning we can begin to learn from them instead of continually repeating them.

KNOWLEDGE CONTROL

Our brains have become dumping grounds for massive amounts of information. On any given day, our senses are bombarded with commercials, news, music, e-mails, web sites, and hundreds of other information mediums that flood our minds with useless clutter. Never before has it been so hard to stay focused on a simple task without being flooded with information.

Today's professional must learn how to control the incredible influx of information into their lives by filtering out distractions and continually staying on top of their ever-changing field of expertise. Knowledge control is more than just filtering information, it is about becoming the top expert in your chosen profession. One of the quickest and surest ways to achieving success in your profession is to become a recognized expert. All too often we get caught up in the tasks associated with our profession and forget to improve our knowledge and spend time separating ourselves from our competition.

Becoming an expert in a profession involves constant study, networking, writing, speaking, and organization. Most people fail to understand that our success at work is dependent upon not only our daily performance but also our knowledge of the subject-matter and our ability to display it. In America today, the average person watches 4.5 hours of television each day. This is time that could be spent reading, writing articles, networking with other experts, or simply increasing our knowledge base. It doesn't matter if you are a car salesman, secretary, doctor, or CEO. Controlling the information you allow into your brain can mean the difference between success and failure.

Do people come to you for answers? Are you consulted for advice? What is the future of your business? Who are the current experts in your field? Are you familiar with new developments? How much time do you spend improving your knowledge? All of these questions will lead you to think about how you spend your time and what information you allow into your brain.

Information Improvement

As a performance consultant, I find that people feel so overwhelmed with the barrage of information today that they go home and shut down by sitting in front of the television or avoiding anything to do with their profession. But the first step to controlling the information that we allow into our mental databanks is to simply replace entertainment information with improvement information. Instead of listening to music and the weather report on your way to work, put in cassettes or CDs that focus on your particular area of expertise. Turn off the television for one hour each night and read books and articles relating to your profession. Use your time spent surfing the web for gaining insight about new developments and future changes to your industry. Begin filtering out the unnecessary information that you flood your senses with and replace this with videos, cassettes, and books that are focused toward your goals. Start attending seminars and lectures that help improve your performance and quality of life. Ask to attend meetings and workshops at your company to gain further insight into the inner workings of your business. Spend time researching and writing articles for your industry newsletter or magazine. Make it a point to network and form relationships with other experts in your profession. This is how you become a qualified expert in your particular field or profession.

Get Organized

Another way to gain control of the amount of information in our lives is to become organized at work. Many people are under the misconception that technology will solve all of their organizational shortcomings, so they fail to create a system for controlling the influx of information into their lives. One of the best ways to gain control of this data overflow is to get organized. From your desk to your car, if you can't find that file or phone number the instant you need it, you're wasting valuable time and increasing your stress level. Ironically, the number one reason people give for being disorganized is lack of time.

A disorganized person will lose approximately one hour a day looking for things in his or her office and, since time is money, being disorganized can hurt your bottom dollar. Here is an example of the cost of disorganization for today's professional based upon losing one hour each day during a 40-hour week:

Yearly Income	Lost Productivity
$ 40,000	$ 5,000
$ 75,000	$ 9,375
$100,000	$12,500
$150,000	$18,750

The above figures are conservatively based upon a moderately disorganized person who loses about one hour each day, but can easily be doubled for a team or group of individuals working together on a daily basis. Disorganization can be likened to a virus, as it slowly begins to infect other people who come in close proximity to it. While working with many large corporations, I often hear people claim that they have a "special" way of organizing their space and it may look like a complete mess, but it makes sense to them. This is the number one excuse that disorganized people make to justify their lack of discipline.

A Control System

A good control system is your best defense in fighting disorganization and clutter. To get started, we must eliminate the clutter in our lives. As human beings, we have the natural tendency to collect everything and this is the major reason for clutter. Begin eliminating clutter by getting a trash bag and being brutally honest about what you really use, need, and want. Go through your home first and work one room at a time. Go through every closet, box, and cabinet. Next, move to your office. Start with the most obvious piles of paper on the desk and in the file cabinets.

A control system that I find works very well for most people is based upon the proper filing of information. Since each of us stores information according to different criteria, it is important to establish a logical order to a filing system. Here are eight tips to a proper control system:

- Develop a list of the main topics for your information, papers, and files.
- Use a numbered or colored-tab system to identify each topic.
- Alphabetize or number subcategories within each main topic. These subcategories must be related to the main topic.
- Alphabetize your contacts, customers, and clients into an easily accessible folder.
- Create a laminated card with the contents of each main topic folder and tape it to the front of the cabinet or drawer.
- Get into the habit of putting things back after using them and storing new information as soon as you receive it.
- Schedule a half hour at the end of the week for filing and disposing of accumulated clutter and information.
- Use your computer to store and categorize information with the same system. Remember to delete clutter. Properly store information on your computer at the end of the week.

Gaining control of our lives and getting organized can seem like an overwhelming task, but the more attention you pay to organization, the more productive and efficient you become. It is important to understand that any reason you give for being disorganized is simply an excuse and does affect your career. Take the first step to gaining control of the information overload by developing the personal habit of organization.

CREATING BALANCE

Many of the performance problems that people experience at work can be traced to unbalanced living. More often than not, poor performance in the workplace is a result of personal problems and problems at home. With today's rapid pace of life, creating a proper balance between our professional, spiritual, and personal lives can seem like an overwhelming task. Since 1973, our work week has increased from a national average of 40 hours to 51 hours, and our leisure time has gone from 26.2 hours to a low of 19.5 hours per week. This fact alone can account for a tremendous increase of stress in our lives if it is not counteracted. The bottom line is that we work more hours, have less time to ourselves, play less, and allow this unbalance to create stress.

Stress is not only a problem, it is a killer. Stress is known to be a major contributor, either directly or indirectly, to coronary heart disease, cancer, lung ailments, accidental injuries, cirrhosis of the liver, and suicide—six of the leading causes of death in the United States. Most of us feel worn out and run down at some point during the week and still others experience the more serious effects of chronic stress—that state of physical, emotional, and spiritual exhaustion. Chronic stress and burnout build up slowly in our lives and many of us are not aware of it until we experience some sort of breakdown.

Because of the widespread nature of excessive stress and burnout, it is important that we identify the possible symptoms in our own lives. Some of the most common physical symptoms are fatigue, insomnia, and nagging physical ailments such as frequent heartburn and headaches. Some of the most common emotional and spiritual symptoms include irritability, anxiety, depression, excessive anger, disillusionment, cynicism, and bitterness. Based on national samples, it is estimated that stress-related illnesses cost industry and business between $50 billion and $75 billion a year.

You can walk into any bookstore in America today and find several medical books dedicated to the study of stress, but very few discuss how to create balance within our lives to diminish its effects. In my personal life, I have learned the hard way that my spiritual relationship with God is crucial not only to my performance and character but also to ensuring a sense of balance. My belief in God helps me see the big picture when I get too wrapped up in the small details, and through spiritual guidance, I have learned how to release my mind from worry.

Many people who try very hard at maintaining a good balance in their life fail to include activities that promote spiritual well-being. Whatever religion you practice or follow, understand that your spiritual side demands constant attention or you will experience problems in both your professional and personal life.

The old adage "All work and no play makes Jack a dull boy" seems to be the national anthem for today's working adult. Instead of using exercise or family time to balance out our work stress, it seems more people are turning to watching television or surfing the Net to find balance. With the incredible advances in technology today, we have effectively closed ourselves off from the outside world and disabled the action spark in people. The problem lies in the fact that television, video games, movies, and the Internet do not, for the most part, relieve stress, they simply postpone it.

Balance can only be created by an equal distribution of time and effort. This is not to say that if you work 8 hours each day, you will need 8 hours of stress-relieving activity, but only that we must find ways to improve the quality of our lives with the free time we have. Using the skills of time discipline, personal management, and organization that you have learned in the previous chapters will greatly increase the amount of free time you have.

Creating balance does not mean that you should avoid all types of stress. Don't be afraid to enjoy the stress of a full life or to relish the challenge and competition that each new day brings. Rather, look at your life as a great balancing act where an equal distribution of time and effort is the goal.

Sounds pretty simple, doesn't it? In fact, it *is* pretty simple. If work consumes your life, find ways to work less and play more. If you feel lethargic and depressed, exercise your body more and strengthen your spiritual beliefs. If you feel stress from bills and debt, develop financial discipline and live within a budget. If your performance at work is poor, improve your appearance, work ethic, time management, and organizational skills. If you smoke, eat poorly, and feel unhealthy, dedicate your free time to exercising, beating your habits, and eating right. Find an unbalanced area of your life and learn how to counteract it. Remember that proper relaxation is as important to creating balance as work is to making money.

Ancient Relaxation Secrets

For more than 4,000 years, the mystic monks of Tibet have been practicing mental and physical techniques to enhance longevity, overcome pain, conquer disease, and perform amazing physical feats. Tibetan medical practitioners were considered to be the most knowledgeable and effective healers of their time. Thousands of years ago, the great Chinese warlords would refuse to go into battle without having a Tibetan healer on their medical staff and enjoyed staging healing competitions between the traditional Chinese doctors and the Tibetan healers. Even today, the Tibetan monks are famous throughout the world for their devotion, discipline, and mystic enlightenment.

The Buddhist monks of Tibet still practice healing and meditation techniques that have been in use since before recorded history. Through many hours of meditation and by using relaxation techniques, these mystical monks are able to endure the harshest of environments, go days without food or water, and stay warm with very little clothing for extended periods of time. Today's working professional cannot afford to ignore the ancient wisdom and techniques of relaxation, which are the result of thousands of years of practical use and study.

In today's fast-paced world, stress and mental fatigue can effectively degrade our mental and physical performance level on a daily basis. In order to stay focused and healthy, we must find some way to relax. Although tension is sometimes thought to be mostly mental, it clearly has detrimental effects on the body. The slightest stress and tension can cause our muscles to become tense and our breathing to become short and awkward. When you become stressed and experience tension, your body produces chemicals that make your heart beat faster and your skin begins to flush and sweat.

Only by understanding and focusing on this often overlooked enemy can you begin to increase your mental and physical efficiency. Most people allow stress and tension to build up to dangerous levels, until they finally explode on their loved ones or fellow coworkers. So what can you do to ensure that stress and tension are alleviated from your life? The answer is very simple: learn to relax. By learning to relax, you will begin to reap powerful benefits like tranquillity, serenity, clarity of mind, balanced emotions, and enhanced happiness in your life.

It is very important to find a quiet place or use earplugs when practicing these techniques. Close the door to your office and lie down on the floor, or stretch out in your chair in a comfortable position. Use this powerful Tibetan relaxation technique to regain your vitality and mental clarity when stress has you in its clutches:

1. Lie down or stretch out in your chair. Close your eyes and calm your mind.
2. Visualize a time in your past when you were very relaxed and tranquil.
3. Take a few big deep breaths and exhale them slowly and completely.
4. Get into a slow but deep breathing pattern.
5. Picture your bare feet and tell them to wiggle and then relax completely.
6. Think of a very relaxing and serene image. It can be a big bed on a cold winter night, or whatever you imagine as relaxing.
7. Verbally tell yourself to relax. Say the word very quietly and slowly. Keep repeating the word to yourself.
8. Next, tell your calves and knees to relax. Imagine a soft yellow glow of energy is irradiating up your legs from your feet. Visualize your calves and knees slowly relaxing.

9. Continue this process until you have gone from feet to head. Picture the soft yellow glow engulfing your body. Feel how relaxed and warm your body is. Keep softly verbalizing to yourself the word *relax*.

10. Stop at a specific area of high tension, like your neck, back, or head. Spend extra time visualizing this area. See the warm yellow glow spread over tense muscles. Keep your breathing rhythm slow and deep.

This very simple technique forces your body and mind to work together in alleviating tension. It is very important to understand the concept of stress and tension release. The majority of people that suffer from emotional distress, irritability, upset stomach, headaches, and depression often experience these symptoms on a daily basis due to stress. There are many devices and drugs on the market today that are sold as stress relievers, but the simple truth is that your mind is the master of both creating and relieving stress and tension. Set aside a few minutes each day at home and at the office to practice this powerful, yet simple technique.

Now that you have learned how to relax the stress-induced tensions in your body, the next step is to learn an ancient technique for relaxing your mind. Every waking second of the day, your mind is churning over thoughts and images of your life as you know it. For most people, these thoughts and images are centered on work, problems, worries, unpleasant experiences, what-ifs, and any number of stress-inducing topics. The key to taking control of the images, thoughts, and inner voice of your mind is to understand and practice the concept of Black Tea. This technique is used to turn off or black out all unwanted images, sounds, and thoughts to relax and rest your mind. It is very effective in canceling out stress and leaves your mind in a relaxed, calm, and serene state.

The Black Tea technique is based upon simply thinking of pouring black tea over the movie screen in your mind. Black tea is a very dark and rich brew, with the color consistency of dark black paint. Use the Black Tea technique to cure insomnia, relieve mental stress, gain clarity and focus, or simply take a well-deserved mental break. Practice this ancient method several times throughout the day and use it to turn off and recharge your brain for better mental performance:

1. Close your eyes and get into a comfortable position.
2. Regulate your breathing to a slow and deep rhythm.

3. In your mind, picture a warm, thick, and dark cup of black tea or paint.
4. Look into the dark color of this liquid and think of the color black.
5. Imagine this dark liquid being poured over your mental movie screen.
6. Picture this liquid blacking out all sound, color, and thoughts in your mind.
7. If you see small images appearing, continue pouring the tea over them.
8. Keep thinking of blackness and continue your deep breathing rhythm.
9. Focus on drowning out your inner voice and thoughts.
10. Let the sound of your breathing enter your mind and relax your brain.

MISSION DE-BRIEF
★★★★

Chances are you will probably never get fired for average performance or for just doing enough to get by, but average pay and average living is the best you will ever do. Still others aren't so lucky and continue to get downsized and blame their lack of success on just plain bad luck or the ever-changing job market. Professional discipline is about paying attention to the small things that most people take for granted and fail to recognize. Seeing yourself through the eyes of your coworkers or clients is one of the hardest things to do but is the cornerstone of personal improvement.

Working for money is a fact of life and cannot be changed unless you win the lottery or move to the deepest jungle, but it can also be the vehicle that takes you beyond your wildest dreams. How much control do you really have over your career? The surprising answer is total control! You can choose to be the hardest-working, most professional, and most sought-after employee, or you can choose to hide in the crowd. You can choose to treat work as a daily challenge, a competition, and a chance to reach your goals, or you can choose to stand with the complainers at the water cooler. Achievement is a choice and not a birthright. Take control of your future by developing the skills of professional discipline and watch how many people you pass on the ladder of success.

100 SECRETS OF POWER LIVING

Self-respect is the fruit of discipline; the sense of dignity grows with the ability to say NO to oneself.—Abraham J. Heshel

There are thousands of little secrets and techniques that can be used to change the way we live. These secrets of power living are facts and concepts that are used and practiced by some of the most elite commando units on this planet. I have taken these powerful techniques and concepts and altered them for everyday use. Keep an open mind, take notes, think deeply, and try implementing a few each day.

The world's most successful people use these concepts and techniques every single day to advance to the top of the human food chain. Start creating an aura of positive energy that radiates and touches everyone around you. Use these secrets of power living as a tool for controlling the changes in your life.

1. DEVELOP YOURSELF ONE HOUR A DAY

Set aside one hour each morning for personal development work. Visualize your day, listen to motivational music and tapes, or read inspirational books or statements to gain positive focus and clarity of purpose.

2. KEEP A JOURNAL OR NOTEBOOK

We all have thoughts, ideas, tasks, and inspirations that pop into our heads throughout the day. Keep a small journal with you at all times to record these bursts of mental energy.

3. EXERCISE DAILY

Do something each and every day to enhance your physical health. What you do is not as important as how much you do. Make a steady commitment to include some form of physical activity into your daily schedule. Include a friend, spouse, or partner into your exercise routine to provide support and motivation. Do 50 sit-ups and 50 push-ups every morning before you hit the shower; this will not only wake you up, but also generate a flow of positive energy throughout your body and mind.

4. SLEEP LESS

Most people do not need more than seven hours of sleep to maintain peak health. Try getting up one hour earlier for seven days and it will develop into a powerful routine. Imagine having an extra seven hours a week to spend on the things you want. This is one of the most powerful and life-changing commitments you can make to become more productive and organized.

5. LEARN TO SIT STILL AND LISTEN

Most people don't even spend two minutes a week in total silence and peace. Enjoy the power of silence and tranquillity for at least 10 minutes a day. Reflect on where your life is going and what you are doing to master control of it. Practice the skill of sitting quietly in a peaceful and powerful place.

6. LAUGH FOR HEALTH

Learn to laugh for at least five minutes a day. Laughter activates potent chemicals in our bodies that elevate us to a happy, balanced, and carefree state. Some therapies actually use laughter to heal a person's illness and it is a wonderful drug for life's dose of reality. Purchase a funny tape or book to keep you laughing throughout the day. Laughter as medicine will create an environment of health and vitality.

7. MASTER TIME MANAGEMENT

There are at least 672 hours in every month. I am sure you can allot ten of these toward the achievement of the goals you desire. Become ruthless with your time. Treasure and guard each minute as if it were your last. Plan around your top priorities and focus on doing immediate, short-term, and long-term goals that you wish to accomplish. Buy an electronic or paper organizer; tack up planning boards, calendars, and to-do lists in your house and at work. Never forget what matters most to you and give that the majority of your time.

8. SURROUND YOURSELF WITH THE POSITIVE

Associate with only positive, friendly, and focused people who do not drain your time and energy. Become acquainted with people of great success and knowledge. Have books in your library about self-improvement, positive attitudes, wealth, health, religion, and success.

9. PICTURE YOUR REWARD

Have pictures of all the things you want to have or become. Cut out pictures of houses, properties, vehicles, vacations, or the body you want to have and carry them with you every day. Become accustomed to seeing the desired efforts of your labor and you will eventually make them a reality.

10. LEARN A NEW WORD EACH DAY

Have a dictionary on your desk or beside your bed and circle one new word a day. Say this word and its definition five times to yourself and use it in a sentence during the day. This simple technique will not only improve your communication skills but also become an example to everyone around you of your personal commitment and work ethic.

11. STUDY PHILOSOPHY

The secrets to wealth, health, beauty, longevity, and vitality have been in existence for thousands of years. Pop music, fast food, fashion, television, and computers are not secrets to better living. Open your mind to ancient herbs, diets, exercises, breathing techniques, and philosophies, and your life will make a dramatic change for the better.

12. TURN OFF THE TV

What medium do you think is responsible for the food we eat, clothes we wear, way we talk, items we purchase, music we listen to, and hours we spend sitting around? Yep, you guessed it! Television is the most powerful form of mind control known to man. Just as visualization is a powerful technique for our minds, television uses images, sounds, and fantasy to control what we do and think. Do yourself and your children a favor by drastically reducing the amount of brainwashing you are exposed to. The average American family watches four hours of television per day. You say that there are not enough minutes in the day to get everything done? Well, here is a way to free-up 240 minutes a day for personal development and quality time with the ones you love. Unplug the brainwashing machine!

13. LEARN A LANGUAGE

In the SEALs, we must be proficient in foreign languages. Nothing stimulates the mind like learning everything possible about a different culture, including the language. Take a course, buy books or tapes, practice with a friend, or visit a country and culture of your interest. It is a wonderful and magnificent world we live in, so take advantage of it and expand your talents and knowledge.

14. SUPPLEMENT YOUR LIFE

Increase your knowledge of herbs, vitamins, and nutritional supplements. Dramatically reduce your healthcare costs and sick days, while improving your health, vitality, and longevity. If you like radiation, chemicals, toxins, surgery, and hospitals, just go ahead and ignore this one! Try a cup of Chinese green tea with your meals and experience the benefits of this 5,000-year-old wonder drink. There are many excellent books and tapes available that can help explain the tremendous powers of herbs, vitamins, and supplements.

15. POLISH YOUR APPEARANCE

Start by practicing the principles of physical discipline and spend 30 minutes more each day making sure you present the image of competence, intelligence, and professionalism. Learn how to iron your shirts and pants, get a clean, short haircut, polish your shoes, and prepare ahead for the next workday. Remember that first impressions are the lasting ones.

16. SPEAK WITH DISCIPLINE

It doesn't matter how professional or competent you look. If you swear like a sailor or always have a smart remark, you are advertising your ignorance to everyone. Stop and think about what you want to say before you say it. If you condition yourself to pause before saying anything, people will naturally respond with interest. Take the time to practice and think about what sort of words and body language you wish to use.

17. BREATHE IN LIFE

Good breathing practices will unleash the energy that lies deep inside you. Deep breathing maintains a peak state of both body and mind, fitness and health. Ancient breathing practices fully oxygenate the body and recharge you with energy to tackle your demanding tasks. Ancient societies have always used deep breathing techniques to create optimal health, happiness, and mental clarity. Take some time each day to study and practice deep breathing techniques.

18. MAINTAIN A POSITIVE MENTAL ATTITUDE

Having a positive mental attitude about everything in life will allow you to succeed where others have failed. Becoming an expert in any human activity takes practice and a positive mental attitude. It doesn't matter how bad things are, the person with a never-say-die attitude and positive outlook will always find a way to the top. Practice mental techniques for finding the good in every situation and circumstance. Stop complaining and start looking at what is good and right, instead of bad and wrong. Have an attitude of defiance and perseverance toward failure in all aspects of your life. Focus on erasing or reprogramming negative thoughts and actions.

19. REBUILD CHARACTER FLAWS

Every human being has flaws in his or her character and personality. Use mental discipline to recognize and reprogram those glitches and flaws. Listen to what your spouse, friends, and family say about your behavior and personality. Take a written inventory of your character every 30 days to focus on areas that need improvement. Become aware of your habits, traits, and overall personality.

20. GET A PET

Have a pet as a best friend. Animals have been shown to greatly reduce stress and improve happiness in humans. Having a pet is one of the best ways to practice responsibility and commitment. Teaching your children to be responsible for taking care of the family pet is an invaluable teaching tool. Learn to appreciate the other inhabitants of our planet and enhance the quality of your life.

21. MEET YOUR GOALS

Discover what it is you really want out of this life, and go into battle for it. Take time each day to schedule and refocus your efforts in this direction. Start off with small and easy goals, then gear up for the larger battles. Prioritize your energy and efforts toward accomplishing your life's dreams, but always take time to enjoy the little things in life.

22. STRENGTHEN YOUR RELATIONSHIP

Set aside at least one night each week to be alone with your spouse. Get a babysitter, turn off the television, and focus all of your attention on your life partner. Start really communicating and enjoying the company of this special gift in your life. Behind almost every successful person lies a strong and supportive spouse.

23. BECOME THE AGGRESSOR

We have all heard the saying "The meek shall inherit the earth," but have you also heard the saying "It's a dog-eat-dog world?" Make no mistake about it, we live in a supercompetitive world today and only the aggressive and committed come out on top. Look people straight in the eyes when you talk to them, but talk with authority and intelligence. Attack each new day and project with the same ferociousness that a lion uses on its prey. Become a predator of success by going the extra mile, or doing more than is asked of you. Being humble is a virtue, but dominating your enemies and devouring your problems is a way of life.

24. STOP OVEREATING

Eat only what you need and push the rest away. Our society is the most blessed and rich nation on this planet, and it shows! Add money to your bank account and more years to your life by stopping before you are full. The human stomach was not designed to hold and digest more than a handful of food, so think light and small when eating. "I eat, I eat some more, I get fat, and therefore I am" should be our national motto. Controlling what and how much we eat is an excellent test for our self-discipline. Welcome the challenge and start power living, instead of power eating.

25. BECOME THE CHAMELEON

Start imitating the successes of great people and leaders. Study your top-ten most interesting and successful people, and learn what and how they did it. Have a personal role model who inspires you to greatness. Imitate the best virtues and strengths of our world's most respected and successful humans by researching every step they made.

26. CONTROL YOUR EMOTIONS

Learn to be emotionally neutral during troublesome times. Control your anger and depression by pausing, then slowly counting to ten. Control and understand the effects of food upon your emotions and personality. Discipline your mind to block out urges and suppress emotions during each conversation. Be emotional when you are with the people you love and trust, but never show weakness to others. See #23 above.

27. RELAX AND RECHARGE

Nothing drains your energy more than stress and worrying. Create a sanctuary in your house or office that is peaceful, serene, silent, and full of positive energy. Go outside and sit under a tree, or go for a walk in the woods to gather your thoughts, slow your heart rate, and gain clarity of mind. Create a garden that is pleasant in sight, sound, and smell. Schedule 30 minutes each day for relaxation and meditation development. This is one of the most powerful concepts of power living.

28. PINCH PENNIES

The best way to have money is to save money! You don't have to be frugal to save money, just organized. Take time to really study and investigate your personal finances. Stay at home more often to benefit your relationship and family life. Clip coupons, shop around, take care of what you have and it will take care of you. Start a savings plan that automatically deducts money from your pay. When you begin mastering financial self-discipline, wonderful things happen.

29. PRACTICE MIND CONTROL

Use the techniques of mental reprogramming and thought control to bring a positive energy to your thoughts and actions. Wear a rubber band around your wrist and snap it every time a negative or bad thought comes into your mind; this will program a physical and mental reaction to negativity. Surround yourself with positive images and statements and monitor the information that is allowed to bombard your brain.

30. CHALLENGE YOURSELF DAILY

Set lofty goals and strive to attain them every day. Expect more of yourself than anybody else does. Challenge stimulates the mind and body into positive action. Stop staying "I can't" and start saying "I will." Try to better your last physical or work-related performance and enjoy the benefits of power living.

31. MASTER PERSONAL MANAGEMENT

Become organized and efficient in all aspects of your life. Schedule time to organize all of your possessions and valuables. Buy a computer or pocket organizer to record and efficiently manage all of your personal and professional matters. Spend 20 minutes each night preparing your clothing, food, and to-do list for the following day.

32. RELEARN YOUR MANNERS

Practice the codes of personal conduct that your parents or grandparents instilled in you. Say "yes ma'am" or "yes sir" when addressing an older person. Treat people with respect and dignity in every situation. Become someone that your children and family can look up to and respect.

33. ADVERTISE INTEGRITY

Behave and talk in the same manner when you are away from your spouse as you do when you are with your spouse. Self-discipline is about making and keeping personal commitments. Treat your relationship or marriage as the ultimate commitment and example of mutual respect. A man or woman of integrity puts principle and moral ethics in front of pleasure and personal gain. Practice the concept of keeping your promises and doing what is right, instead of what is popular.

34. BE A GIVER AND NOT A TAKER

Tithe at church, or give to charities and worthwhile organizations. Do good things for others and others will do good things for you. Become the person that friends can come to in a time of need and watch your personal satisfaction rise.

35. BECOME A SEEKER OF KNOWLEDGE

Use the principles of knowledge control to fill your mind and life with useful and interesting information. Take a course at a local college or trade school. Learn a new skill each month. Surround yourself with good books and self-improvement literature. You are what you eat, but you act upon what you know.

36. TAKE TIME TO REFLECT

Schedule 10 minutes each day to pause and reflect upon your performance in all aspects of the day's events. Learn to critique yourself and learn from mistakes. Think about how other people may have perceived you on this day. Close your eyes and replay the events of the day in your mind's eye. Become your own mental coach.

37. USE MUSIC AS A TOOL

Purchase a Walkman or CD player for your office. Listen to classical and emotional music to stimulate your mind power. Use music as a motivational tool for your physical activities and watch your performance improve dramatically. When you drive home from work, or become stuck in traffic, play your favorite relaxing music to eliminate stress.

38. BECOME AN EARLY RISER

No time of day is more silent and serene than early morning. Get up early and enjoy the sunrise with your life-partner. Go for a walk through the woods before work to prepare your mind and stimulate clarity of purpose.

39. THINK AND ACT YOUNG

To stay in top physical condition and promote slow aging you must not let an old person move into your body and mind. Create a youthful and fun lifestyle that stimulates the mind and body. You are as old as you think and act. Enjoy tremendous vitality by living with zest, passion, and a youthful attitude.

40. TREAT YOURSELF

Allow yourself a rare treat every now and then to reward yourself. Buy something nice or have a delicious dessert once a week to celebrate your successes and accomplishments. Take a day off and do nothing except fun and interesting things that both you and your family enjoy.

41. DEVELOP SOCIAL SKILLS AND DIPLOMACY

Stop and really listen to what people are saying and doing. Show your leadership through attentiveness and compassion. Take a stance on matters of importance, but learn to remain flexible. Practice interacting with people of dissimilar likes and personalities to enhance your people skills.

42. MASTER PATIENCE

Every great person fails more times than he succeeds. Remember that persistence and patience breed success. Learn to pause and relax when you are feeling impatient and irritable. A great way to practice patience is to prepare a meal that takes a long time to cook when you are really hungry. When you are impatient or frustrated, walk away for a couple of minutes, then come back and tackle your task with renewed energy.

43. ENCOURAGE COMPETITION

Nothing motivates like competition. Develop the personal desire to be better than the next guy. Privately compete with your coworkers and exercise partner. The spirit of competition is what makes our society so amazingly productive and effective. Learn to compete against your previous performances and work success. Challenge success often and compete against poverty and illness.

44. ENJOY NATURE

Go on camping trips with your friends and family. Learn to rock or ice climb and challenge your fears. Surround yourself with plants at home and at work; if you can't go to nature, bring nature to you. Watch the Discovery Channel or wildlife films with your children or spouse and enjoy the marvels of Mother Nature. Take up bird-watching or take a survival course and become proficient in backwoods navigation. Your children and grandchildren will forever be respectful of nature if you take a stance and become concerned about the environment.

45. TAKE THE PATH LEAST TRAVELED

Get into the habit of being original. Who says that you have to keep up with the Joneses? Find your own way and beliefs. Learn the concept of doing things the right way instead of the easy way. Stand for something and believe in it with integrity and honor.

46. BECOME PHYSICALLY COMPETENT

Accept the role of protector and defender of your spouse and family. Start taking lessons in boxing, martial arts, and self-defense. Don't go looking for fights, but be able to protect yourself and the ones you love. Feel the tremendous power and energy of physical competence in your life. Know when to act and when to walk away. There is nothing worth fighting for except your loved ones, but be prepared to do so.

47. DEFEAT YOUR BAD HABITS

We all have varying degrees of bad habits. Understand that you always pay the consequences for bad habits sooner or later. Start reprogramming your mind to reduce and eliminate these from your life. Make a commitment and tell everyone about it; this will help in providing your motivation and support. Begin mastering self-discipline and open the doors to power living.

48. BECOME A TRAVELER

A well-traveled person is a wise and worldly person. Pick a different country or destination each year and begin expanding your horizons. Take advantage of today's wonderful technology and travel abroad. Stay out of the tourist mode and start looking closer at life on this great planet.

49. BECOME AN EXPERT

Take a strong interest in any subject you like and learn all there is to know about it. Become studious and intimately knowledgeable about your business or profession. Write books and papers on your favorite subject and spend some time each day becoming an expert.

50. MASTER SELF-DISCIPLINE

Understand that self-discipline is the solid foundation of all good actions and thoughts. Practice the techniques found in this book to enhance and stimulate the power of self-discipline. Become the person that people wish to emulate. Take the knowledge of power living and live powerfully.

51. HAVE A DO-NOTHING DAY

Set aside one day a week for doing absolutely nothing. Have no set schedule, no to-do list, no important phone calls, and only do what you like to do. It is very important to break the pattern of everyday life and allow yourself complete freedom to do what you want. Go see a movie or sleep in late.

52. LEARN YOUR OPPOSITES

If you are a man, learn how to cook, sew, and garden. If you are a woman, learn about vehicle maintenance, woodworking, and lawn care. Stop limiting your knowledge because society has programmed you to accept certain skills and not others. Stop and think about what your opposite subjects and skills are, then begin expanding your knowledge base by learning.

53. REPLACE "I CAN'T" WITH "I CAN"

Reprogram your mind and attitude to accept no limits. The only reason you can't is because you are always telling yourself so. Begin changing your attitude by changing your thoughts and beliefs about what can and can't be accomplished. Start thinking like a superhuman achiever.

54. PAY ATTENTION TO YOUR SIXTH SENSE

Start listening to that little voice of advice and intuition in the back of your mind. We all have the sixth sense, but you have to open your mind by exercising this powerful gut-feeling response. Use your sixth sense to solve problems and generate ideas. Pay attention to your gut-feelings, intuitions, unexplainable emotions, and that little voice.

55. WALK A MILE

Don't be so quick to judge a person. Learn how to look past a person's attire, words, and personality. See him or her for what they truly are; one of God's creations. Before you pass judgment on somebody, you must first walk a mile in his or her shoes. Get in the habit of treating people with respect and courtesy, no matter what their status in society.

56. BE STRONG

It may be true that the meek will inherit the earth, but the law of nature says that the weak shall inherit nothing. Superhumans are not frail, scared, or passive in their quest for success. Stick your chest out, look people square in the eyes, and begin gaining forward momentum in your life. The path of power living is above-average performance. Make a conscious effort to exhibit self-confidence and aggressive leadership abilities.

57. BREATHE POWER

Take a hint from ancient cultures and practice the art of deep breathing. Get into the habit of working your body to its maximum. Go farther and faster than you did the day before. Push yourself during physical exercise and condition your mind as well as your body.

58. ASSERT AN ATTITUDE OF RESOLVE

Learn to break your comfort zone and welcome the challenges of life. Understand that hardship can either build your resolve or make you a constant complainer. The attitude of resolve is body armor for your mind. Start generating the powerful feeling of personal fortitude.

59. TAKE RESPONSIBILITY

Be as quick to take the blame as you are to take credit. Understand that responsibility is the foundation of character and integrity. Stand up, be a strong man or woman, but most of all be responsible. Accept the responsibilities of leadership and be known for your compassion, integrity, and strength of character.

60. PRACTICE PATIENCE

When you feel yourself becoming impatient and anxious, take a deep breath and remember the virtue of patience. Learn to use patience as a powerful exercise for self-discipline. Force yourself to remain calm, cool, and collected when you are around children or in slow-moving situations. Focus your attention on strengthening your patience, and you will defeat the symptoms of stress.

61. NEVER SHOW WEAKNESS

Let your guard down only with your loved ones and the people you truly trust. Don't allow your problems to affect your outward emotions at work or around unfamiliar people. In society, as in nature, showing weakness is a sure way of attracting predators. Learn to strengthen your resolve by controlling how you express your emotions.

62. DON'T EAT SO MUCH

Ever wonder why everybody seems to be fat and lethargic? It is because we eat more food than our stomachs were designed to hold. The typical American dinner would serve a family of five in most third world countries. Learn to eat in moderation and stay away from all-you-can-eat buffets. Make the effort to eat six or seven small meals throughout the day, instead of three huge meals at set times.

63. ACCEPT FAILURE

Understand that failure is a fact of life. Don't expect to fail, but welcome failure as a teacher and it will enhance your wisdom. Start calling your problems "challenges," and use them as character builders and strategy planners. Be known as a person that never, ever gives up.

64. DEVELOP CHARACTER GOALS

Start setting daily and monthly character goals. Identify what character flaws you have and make a plan to improve them. Make each day a proving ground for character strength and every problem a personality challenge. Begin each day with a to-do list for your personal character development.

65. PRACTICE CONCENTRATION

Schedule time to clear your mind and practice mental focus skills. Sit quietly and observe the things around you. Focused concentration brings clarity of mind and serenity to our often crazy lives. Learn how to remove and ignore small distractions and experience the wonderful benefits of focused attention.

66. GET AN ENDORPHIN FIX

Start a cardiovascular exercise program that includes running or bicycling. Begin feeling a powerful surge of endorphins in your body when you vigorously exercise. The endorphin fix for the athlete is similar to the narcotic high that drug users feel, except that it is pure vitality, self-esteem, and health. Make the effort to get your heart and blood pumping on a daily basis, and reap the benefits of enhanced physical and mental performance.

67. BREAK FREE FROM CREDIT

Credit cards and bad credit are two reasons why people struggle most of their adult lives. Become debt-free and gain independence by cutting up your credit cards and paying cash for everything. Take the time to see what is on your credit report and begin building up solid credit. Don't allow big banks or financial institutions to stand in the way of your goals; begin treating your personal finances as a top priority.

68. TAKE VITAMINS

Take advantage of today's medical knowledge and yesterday's ancient longevity secrets by supplementing your diet with vitamins and herbs. Become knowledgeable on the important subject of your body's vitamin and mineral needs. Make vitamin supplementation a part of your daily routine and experience a lifetime of vitality, energy, and enhanced health.

69. USE THE POWER OF SUGGESTION

The subconscious mind is the most powerful aspect of the brain. Begin learning about the wonders and capabilities of your subconscious mind and the power of suggestion. Make it a daily habit to say your goals over and over in your mind. Give your subconscious mind positive suggestions and begin generating mental momentum.

70. USE PRAYER

We all pray when things are at their worst or when we really want something, but get in the habit of praying to simply balance your spiritual life. Start praying for guidance, strength, and for the welfare of others. Use the power of prayer to open your mind and heart to discover your creator.

71. EAT POWER SNACKS

Get in the habit of bringing fruit, energy bars, and vegetables to work. Experience the benefits of healthy snacking and increased energy. Put down the candy bar and diet soda and reach for an apple, carrot, or energy bar instead. Feel the difference that clean and healthy fuel makes in your physical motor.

72. EXERCISE EMOTIONAL CONTROL

Take the time to reflect upon your behavior. Ask your loved ones to critique how you control your emotional peaks and valleys. Make the conscious effort to recognize when your emotions are at an extreme, and practice the art of self-control.

73. STAND FOR SOMETHING

Nobody likes a wishy-washy person. Believe in something and stand up for your opinions, but be careful to allow others the same courtesy. Take an interest in the environment, world affairs, and politics, and join an organization that supports what you believe in. Stop complaining about the way things are and start doing something about it.

74. EXPERIENCE THE INTERNET

Keep on top of your profession by learning how to use the limitless resources of the Internet. Use this amazing tool of technology to expand your horizons and knowledge base. Technology is the foundation of our society's future, so make sure you are not left behind.

75. BECOME A LISTENER

Make a conscious effort to keep quiet and truly listen to your loved ones and coworkers. Stop offering advice and suggestions—simply close your mouth and become a good listener. Improve your relationship and marriage by truly being interested in what your significant other has to say.

76. ADVANCE TOWARD YOUR DREAMS

Do something each day to help bring you closer to achieving your goals. Turn off the television and spend one hour each day accomplishing a goal-related task. Make it a priority to talk often with your spouse about your strategy and goal progress.

77. PREPARE YOURSELF

We all know that poor planning will result in poor performance. Make sure that you are well-prepared for the day ahead before retiring for the evening. Devote 30 minutes each evening for preparation to ensure that your early mornings are as stress-free and relaxed as possible. Take the time to set out your clothing, organize your briefcase, prepare a lunch, and develop a to-do list before going to bed.

78. MUSTER CHARISMA

Work on developing a charismatic personality. Practice the art of socializing and public speaking. Make it a point to be interested in what other people are saying. Learn to smile more and memorize a few light jokes to encourage conversation. Work on your charisma and you will develop the ability to interact with difficult people in difficult situations.

79. STAY INFORMED

Make it a point to stay on top of current events and new developments. Get into the habit of reading several different newspapers each day. Subscribe to magazines that cover world affairs, technology, health, and finance. Remember that knowledge is power.

80. HAVE A MENTOR

Learn how to take solid advice from successful and happy people. Have a mentor that offers advice in a time of need. Make it a priority to learn from the mistakes of others. Keep control of your ego and practice the skill of being humble. Remember that having money is not always a reflection of intelligence or wisdom.

81. BOND WITH NATURE

Take the time to get out of your office and into nature. Set aside leisure time to walk in the park, or go camping in the mountains. Nature has a way of putting things in perspective for you. Get back in touch with your humanity by letting nature show you how small your problems really are.

82. ORGANIZE YOUR LIFE

Take the time to clean, maintain, and organize your house and possessions. Schedule one day every two weeks for organizational tasks. Find the discipline to organize those areas of your life that always seem to be in disarray. Increase your productivity and efficiency by organizing your goals, possessions, and time.

83. CREATE TO-DO LISTS

Most people have tried a to-do list, but few people ever follow through with it. Start incorporating a to-do list into your life. Make it a priority to accomplish everything on your list. Begin by starting small and simple, then add more detailed items over time. All organized and efficient achievers use to-do lists as a powerful work tool.

84. DRINK WATER

Your body is approximately 70% water. Most people never drink the required eight glasses a day, and their mental and physical performance suffers. Make it a point to drink water instead of coffee and start benefiting from a well-hydrated system. Always have a source of water readily available to you at home and at work.

85. BE EARLY

Make it a habit of always being 10 to 15 minutes early for every appointment. Set your watch 10 minutes ahead and you will always be early. Show your discipline and motivation by being well-prepared for your appointments.

86. IDENTIFY YOUR HABITS

We all possess particular habits and traits that are annoying to others or harmful to ourselves. Take the time to critique your personal habits, both good and bad. Make a list of what you want and need to change about yourself. Begin using self-discipline to defeat these habits. Remember that nobody is perfect, but some people come close.

87. EDUCATE YOURSELF IN NUTRITION

Take the time to learn about the poisons and toxins stacked on every shelf in every supermarket. Make it a point to only eat pure and clean foods. Become an expert on the fuel that your body requires. Remember that you truly are what you eat, and nutrition is the key to health and vitality.

88. RECOGNIZE HARD TIMES

It doesn't matter how many problems you have, somebody will always have more. Stop and take a hard look at how blessed you really are, and ask yourself if these are truly hard times. In this day and age, we have forgotten what real struggle and survival is all about. Take the time to talk to an older person who lived during the Great Depression and see if you really know what hard times mean. Be thankful for all that you have every day of the year.

89. ADMIT YOUR MISTAKES

These three simple words—"I was wrong"—are often the most difficult in the English language to say. Become a better husband, wife, and human being by admitting when you are wrong—even sometimes when you're not. Make sure your ego does not outweigh your common sense and ability to be humble.

90. SET ASIDE A POWER ROOM

Have a special place in your home or office where you can go for peace and quiet reflection. Make a power room that offers you privacy for meditation and peaceful reflection. Have quiet music and pictures of your goals on the wall. Use this place as a base for motivation and serenity.

91. CHALLENGE YOUR MIND

Stop vegetating in front of the television or home computer. Start challenging your mind with crossword puzzles, word games, sports, chess, and by learning new skills. Remember that you cannot afford to allow your brain to remain inactive, so get up and get thinking. Make it a point to learn something new each day. Challenge your mind and open the door to your creative genius.

92. FIND INSPIRATION

Read motivational and inspirational books. Make self-improvement a top priority in your life by reading inspirational stories of human accomplishment and success. Begin to learn how others have joined the ranks of the high-achievers and find motivation in these stories. Start stocking your personal library with books on success and self-improvement, and generate new ideas from the world's most successful people.

93. STOP WORRYING

Stop allowing every little problem and situation to eat up so much of your thinking. Begin laughing out loud when you feel yourself worrying about something. Get in the habit of defeating thoughts that worry you and regain your never-say-die attitude.

94. CONTROL DESIRE

Nothing can bring down a man or woman faster than desire. Learn to harness the power of self-control and stay away from instant gratification. Your success as a human being is directly related to your ability to control desire and develop strong personal discipline.

95. BE CHIVALROUS AND HAVE INTEGRITY

The monks of Tibet practice the philosophy of building personal integrity and practicing human chivalry every day of their lives. Character is the defining critique of your personality, strengths, weaknesses, and personal integrity. Learn to place top priority on human chivalry and personal integrity.

96. FIND GREEN POWER

Surround your home and work space with beautiful life-giving plants. Use nature's oxygen factory to improve your health and emotional well-being. Plants calm the mind and create an atmosphere of relaxation. Begin learning about plant life and ancient herbal medicine by adding several herbal plants to your home or office. The added responsibility of caring for several plants is an excellent way to exercise and build self-discipline.

97. SURROUND YOURSELF WITH SILENCE

An ancient Far East technique for building discipline and mental focus is to observe one half-hour of total silence each day. Sit in your office or home and concentrate on the beauty of silence. Do no physical or mental activity except to think about your goals and self-improvement. Use the power of silence to reflect and meditate upon your performance as a human being and how you can improve each area of your life. Let other people know that you wish not to be disturbed during this time and begin experiencing the wonders of reflection and silence.

98. LOOK DISCIPLINED

Your appearance should not be dictated by the current fad, fashion, or style. Keep your hair short and neat, your clothes pressed and starched, and your fingernails well groomed. Maintain the look of a disciplined human being by spending extra time and effort on a no-nonsense appearance. Learn how to shine your shoes and wear dark blue or black business attire at all times. Remember that you are a leader who sets the standard of excellence for all to see, and not a sheep who follows the fads and fashions of the sheep herd.

99. UNDERSTAND KARMA

Do good things and give more of yourself than you take, and you will begin experiencing the power of personal karma. Understand that all bad and unjust actions will come back on you ten times stronger. Make charity a monthly habit, and give a little of your good fortune back to the world. Remember the age-old saying, "You reap what you sow," and understand that integrity, honor, and strong moral character generate your good karma.

100. BECOME GOAL ORIENTED

Begin setting daily, monthly, yearly, and lifelong goals for yourself. Attack your goals and desires like a commando, but use common sense and moderation when setting them. Get accustomed to writing down your goals and keep a journal of your progress and efforts. Understand that goals provide motivation, persistence, satisfaction, and emotional well-being. You must begin writing down your goals this very minute, or drift aimlessly through life without direction.

Appendix A

WORDS OF WISDOM

There are things known, and there are things unknown. And in between are the doors of perception.—Jim Morrison

About 2,500 years ago, a Greek physician by the name of Hippocrates stated, "Men ought to know that from the brain—and from the brain only—arise our pleasures, laughters, and successes—as well as our sorrows, pains, griefs, and failures." I often wonder how mentally advanced and how different our world would be if the human race had followed the advice and teachings of ancient wisdom. Imagine how advanced our technology and mental powers would be if we had followed the advice of ancient scholars and used our brains to reprogram ourselves for health, wealth, control, and happiness. I wonder if we would be able to control our bodily functions like the Shaolin and Tibetan monks of the Himalayas, or would have developed the powers of clairvoyance and ESP. I can only imagine how many wars and conflicts would have been avoided if we had continued to learn about the amazing powers of our minds.

Successful people became successful only because they have acquired the habit of thinking like a predator rather than a lamb. The majority of their thoughts are centered around the belief that they can and will attain what they desire. When a negative thought enters the mind, it is quickly re-placed with a positive thought through self-talk. The power of subcon-scious thought is 100 times more powerful than conscious thought. The great philosophers throughout time, from Plato and Socrates to Emerson and Gandhi, are all known to have used self-talk in programming themselves for achievement.

The quickest way to develop the momentum of success is to learn from those who are successful. The rest of this chapter is designed to give you the information and wisdom needed to build your own momentum and encourage the development of the predator mindset. Highlight your favorite quotes and ideas, write them into your personal notebook, and use them in each stage of your plan for achievement.

ACHIEVEMENT

Do not be desirous of having things done quickly. Do not look at small advantages. Desire to have things done quickly prevents their being done thoroughly. Looking at small advantages prevents great affairs from being accomplished.—Confucius

The greater the difficulty, the more glory in surmounting it. Skillful pilots gain their reputation from storms and tempests.—Epictetus

We live in deeds, not years; In thoughts not breaths; In feelings, not in figures on a dial. We should count time by heart throbs. He most lives Who thinks most, feels the noblest, acts the best.—David Bailey

Success is not measured by what you accomplish, but by the opposition you have encountered, and the courage with which you have maintained the struggle against overwhelming odds.—Orison Swett Marden

Empty pockets never held anyone back. Only empty heads and empty hearts can do that.—Norman Vincent Peale

It's your aptitude, not just your attitude, that determines your ultimate altitude.—Zig Ziglar

Every man who is high up loves to think that he has done it all himself; and the wife smiles, and lets it go at that.—Sir James M. Barrie

Having once decided to achieve a certain task, achieve it at all costs of tedium and distaste. The gain in self-confidence of having accomplished a tiresome labor is immense.—Thomas A. Bennett

There are countless ways of achieving greatness, but any road to achieving one's maximum potential must be built on a bedrock of respect for the individual, a commitment to excellence, and a rejection of mediocrity.—Buck Rogers

Death comes to all. But great achievements build a monument which shall endure until the sun grows cold.—George Fabricius

Mere longevity is a good thing for those who watch Life from the side lines. For those who play the game, an hour may be a year, a single day's work an achievement for eternity.—Gabriel Heatter

Finish each day and be done with it. You have done what you could. Some blunders and absurdities no doubt crept in; forget them as soon as you can. Tomorrow is a new day; begin it well and serenely and with too high a spirit to be encumbered with your old nonsense.—Ralph Waldo Emerson

The only way around is through.—Robert Frost

Great things are not done by impulse, but by a series of small things brought together.—Vincent Van Gogh

I feel that the greatest reward for doing is the opportunity to do more. —Jonas Salk

If life were measured by accomplishments, most of us would die in infancy.—A. P. Gouthey

My mother drew a distinction between achievement and success. She said that achievement is the knowledge that you have studied and worked hard and done the best that is in you. Success is being praised by others. That is nice but not as important or satisfying. Always aim for achievement and forget about success.—Helen Hayes

The best job goes to the person who can get it done without passing the buck or coming back with excuses.—Napoleon Hill

A man may fulfill the object of his existence by asking a question he cannot answer, and attempting a task he cannot achieve.—Oliver Wendell Holmes

High achievement always takes place in the framework of high expectation.—Jack Kinder

Man is always more than he can know of himself; consequently, his accomplishments, time and again, will come as a surprise to him.—Golo Mann

Trust yourself. Create the kind of self that you will be happy to live with all your life. Make the most of yourself by fanning the tiny, inner sparks of possibility into flames of achievement.—Foster C. McClellan

I am always doing things I can't do, that's how I get to do them.—Pablo Picasso

The measure of a man is the way he bears up under misfortune. —Plutarch

The truth of the matter is that there's nothing you can't accomplish if: (1) You clearly decide what it is that you're absolutely committed to achieving, (2) You're willing to take massive action, (3) You notice what's working or not, and (4) You continue to change your approach until you achieve what you want, using whatever life gives you along the way.—Anthony Robbins

Nothing is as difficult as to achieve results in this world if one is filled full of great tolerance and the milk of human kindness. The person who achieves must generally be a one-idea individual, concentrated entirely on that one idea, and ruthless in his aspect toward other men and other ideas.—Corinne Roosevelt Robinson

The will to win, the desire to succeed, the urge to reach your full potential . . . these are the keys that will unlock the door to personal excellence. —Eddie Robinson

The average estimate themselves by what they do, the above average by what they are.—Johann Friedrich von Schiller

Disciplining yourself to do what you know is right and important, although difficult, is the high road to pride, self-esteem, and personal satisfaction. —Brian Tracy

Never mistake activity for achievement.—John Wooden

ATTITUDE

Two men look out the same prison bars; one sees mud and the other stars. —Frederick Langbridge

Any fact facing us is not as important as our attitude toward it, for that determines our success or failure. The way you think about a fact may defeat you before you ever do anything about it. You are overcome by the fact because you think you are.—Norman Vincent Peale

To different minds, the same world is a hell, and a heaven.—Ralph Waldo Emerson

Always look at what you have left. Never look at what you have lost.
—Robert H. Schuller

If you believe you can, you probably can. If you believe you won't, you most assuredly won't. Belief is the ignition switch that gets you off the launching pad.—Denis Waitley

Ability is what you're capable of doing. Motivation determines what you do. Attitude determines how well you do it.—Lou Holtz

Holding on to anger is like grasping a hot coal with the intent of throwing it at someone else; you are the one who gets burned.—Buddha

The optimist sees opportunity in every danger; the pessimist sees danger in every opportunity.—Winston Churchill

Our attitudes control our lives. Attitudes are a secret power working twenty-four hours a day, for good or bad. It is of paramount importance that we know how to harness and control this great force.—Tom Blandi

Minds are like parachutes—they only function when open.—Thomas Dewar

A great attitude does much more than turn on the lights in our worlds; it seems to magically connect us to all sorts of serendipitous opportunities that were somehow absent before the change.—Earl Nightingale

And now here is my secret, a very simple secret; it is only with the heart that one can see rightly, what is essential is invisible to the eye.—Antoine de Exupery

The greatest discovery of my generation is that human beings can alter their lives by altering their attitudes of mind.—William James

I am convinced that attitude is the key to success or failure in almost any of life's endeavors. Your attitude—your perspective, your outlook, how you feel about yourself, how you feel about other people—determines your priorities, your actions, your values. Your attitude determines how you interact with other people and how you interact with yourself.—Carolyn Warner

Eagles come in all shapes and sizes, but you will recognize them chiefly by their attitudes.—Charles Prestwich Scott

Attitude is more important than the past, than education, than money, than circumstances, than what people do or say. It is more important than appearance, giftedness, or skill.—Charles Swindoll

CHARACTER

Always do right—this will gratify some and astonish the rest.—Mark Twain

Of all the properties which belong to honorable men, not one is so highly prized as that of character.—Henry Clay

Die when I may, I want it said by those who knew me best that I always plucked a thistle and planted a flower where I thought a flower would grow.—Abraham Lincoln

Judge of your natural character by what you do in your dreams.—Ralph Waldo Emerson

There is nothing in which people more betray their character than in what they laugh at.—Johann Wolfgang von Goethe

It's really a wonder that I haven't dropped all my ideals, because they seem so absurd and impossible to carry out. Yet I keep them, because in spite of everything I still believe that people are really good at heart.—Anne Frank

Character cannot be developed in ease and quiet. Only through experiences of trial and suffering can the soul be strengthened, vision cleared, ambition inspired, and success achieved.—Helen Keller

Who you are speaks so loudly I can't hear what you're saying.—Ralph Waldo Emerson

That which does not kill me, makes me stronger.—SEAL team saying

Kindness in words creates confidence
Kindness in thinking creates profoundness
Kindness in giving creates love.—Lao-tzu

Be kind, for everyone you meet is fighting a harder battle.—Plato

CONTROL

Warriors take chances. Like everyone else, they fear failing, but they refuse to let fear control them.—Ancient samurai saying

Flow with whatever is happening and let your mind be free. Stay centered by accepting whatever you are doing. This is the ultimate.—Chuang Tzu

No man is fit to command another that cannot command himself.—William Penn

No one can make you jealous, angry, vengeful, or greedy—unless you let him.—Napoleon Hill

Your brain shall be your servant instead of your master. You will rule it instead of allowing it to rule you.—Charles E. Popplestone

Never allow anyone to rain on your parade and thus cast a pall of gloom and defeat on the entire day. Remember that no talent, no self-denial, no brains, no character are required to set up in the fault-finding business. Nothing external can have any power over you unless you permit it. Your time is too precious to be sacrificed in wasted days combating the menial forces of hate, jealousy, and envy. Guard your fragile life carefully. Only God can shape a flower, but any foolish child can pull it to pieces.—Og Mandino

Nature has placed mankind under the government of two sovereign masters, pain and pleasure . . . they govern us in all we do, in all we say, in all we think: every effort we can make to throw off our subjection will serve but to demonstrate and confirm it.—John Bentham

Nothing gives a person so much advantage over another as to remain always cool and unruffled under all circumstances.—Thomas Jefferson

You cannot prevent the birds of sorrow from flying over your head, but you can prevent them from building nests in your hair.—Chinese proverb

DETERMINATION

The man who can drive himself further once the effort gets painful is the man who will win.—Roger Bannister

The spirit, the will to win, and the will to excel are the things that endure. These qualities are so much more important than the events that occur.—Vince Lombardi

The difference between the impossible and the possible lies in a person's determination.—Tommy Lasorda

Nothing great will ever be achieved without great men, and men are great only if they are determined to be so.—Charles de Gaulle

If your determination is fixed, I do not counsel you to despair. Few things are impossible to diligence and skill. Great works are performed not by strength, but perseverance.—Samuel Johnson

What this power is I cannot say; all I know is that it exists and it becomes available only when a man is in that state of mind in which he knows exactly what he wants and is fully determined not to quit until he finds it.—Alexander Graham Bell

I am doing a great work and I cannot come down. Why should the work stop while I leave it and come down to you?—Bible (Nehemiah 6:3)

Nothing can resist the human will that will stake even its existence on its stated purpose.—Benjamin Disraeli

The longer I live, the more I am certain that the great difference between the great and the insignificant is energy—invincible determination—a purpose once fixed, and then death or victory.—Sir Thomas Fowell Buxton

You can do what you have to do, and sometimes you can do it even better than you think you can.—Jimmy Carter

We will either find a way, or make one!—Hannibal

A determined soul will do more with a rusty monkey wrench than a loafer will accomplish with all the tools in a machine shop.—Robert Hughes

Every worthwhile accomplishment, big or little, has its stages of drudgery and triumph; a beginning, a struggle, and a victory.—Mahatma Gandhi

Bear in mind, if you are going to amount to anything, that your success does not depend upon the brilliancy and the impetuosity with which you take hold, but upon the everlasting and sanctified bulldoggedness with which you hang on after you have taken hold.—Dr. A. B. Meldrum

A failure establishes only this, that our determination to succeed was not strong enough.—John Christian Bovee

The price of success is hard work, dedication to the job at hand, and the determination that whether we win or lose, we have applied the best of ourselves to the task at hand.—Vince Lombardi

It takes a little courage, and a little self-control.
And some grim determination, if you want to reach the goal.
It takes a great deal of striving, and a firm and stern-set chin.

No matter what the battle, if you really want to win,
There's no easy path to glory, there is no road to fame.
Life, however we may view it, is no simple parlor game;
But its prizes call for fighting, for endurance and for grit;
For a rugged disposition that will not quit.—Navy SEAL Master Chief

DISCIPLINE

In reading the lives of great men, I found that the first victory they won was over themselves . . . self-discipline with all of them came first.—Harry S Truman

If you will discipline yourself to make your mind self-sufficient, you will thereby be least vulnerable to injury from the outside.—Critias of Athens

He conquers twice who conquers himself in victory.—Jyrus

It is better to conquer yourself than to win a thousand battles. Then the victory is yours. It cannot be taken from you, not by angels or by demons, heaven or hell.—Buddha

What it lies in our power to do, it lies in our power not to do.—Aristotle

The first and the best victory is to conquer self.—Plato

First we form habits, then they form us. Conquer your bad habits or they will conquer you.—Rob Gilbert

The great end of education is to discipline rather than to furnish the mind; to train it to the use of its own powers, rather than fill it with the accumulation of others.—Tyron Edwards

No man or woman has achieved an effective personality who is not self-disciplined. Such discipline must not be an end in itself, but must be directed to the development of resolute Christian character.—John S. Bonnell

If you do not conquer self, you will be conquered by self.—Napoleon Hill

No horse gets anywhere until he is harnessed. No stream or gas drives anything until it is confined. No Niagara is ever turned into light and power until it is tunneled. No life ever grows great until it is focused, dedicated, disciplined.—Harry Emerson Fosdick

The only discipline that lasts is self-discipline.—Bum Phillips

A colt is worth little if it does not break its halter.—Proverb

Nothing of importance is ever achieved without discipline. I feel myself sometimes not wholly in sympathy with some modern educational theorists, because I think that they underestimate the part that discipline plays. But the discipline you have in your life should be one determined by your own desires and your own needs, not put upon you by society or authority. —Bertrand Russell

He who lives without discipline dies without honor.—Icelandic proverb

FOCUS

The human mind is not rich enough to drive many horses abreast and wants one general scheme, under which it strives to bring everything.—George Santayana

The shortest way to do many things is to do only one thing at a time.—Wolfgang Amadeus Mozart

Nothing focuses the mind better than the constant sight of a competitor who wants to wipe you off the map.—Wayne Calloway

Most people have no idea of the giant capacity we can immediately command when we focus all of our resources on mastering a single area of our lives.—Anthony Robbins

The successful warrior is the average man, with laser-like focus.—Bruce Lee

If you focus on results, you will never change. If you focus on change, you will get results.—Jack Dixon

Concentration is the ability to think about absolutely nothing when it is absolutely necessary.—Ray Knight

Get out of the blocks, run your race, stay relaxed. If you run your race, you'll win. Channel your energy. Focus.—Carol Lewis

Determine what specific goal you want to achieve. Then dedicate yourself to its attainment with unswerving singleness of purpose, the trenchant zeal of a crusader.—Paul J. Meyer

Often he who does too much does too little.—Italian proverb

To succeed at the level I want to . . . you have to be focused and serious.
—Kent Steffes

He who dares . . . wins!—British commando motto

GOALS

Without goals, and plans to reach them, you are like a ship that has set sail
with no destination.—Fitzhugh Dodson

Aim for the top. There is plenty of room there. There are so few at the top,
it is almost lonely there.—Samuel Insull

The goal you set must be challenging. At the same time, it should be realistic and attainable, not impossible to reach. It should be challenging enough
to make you stretch, but not so far that you break.—Rick Hansen

You must have long-term goals to keep you from being frustrated by short-
term failures.—Charles C. Noble

What you get by achieving your goals is not as important as what you become
by achieving your goals.—Zig Ziglar

First say to yourself what you would be; and then do what you have to do.
—Epictetus

The person with a fixed goal, a clear picture of his desire, or an ideal always
before him causes it, through repetition, to be buried deeply in his subconscious mind and is thus enabled, thanks to its generative and sustaining
power, to realize his goal in a minimum of time and with a minimum of physical effort. Just pursue the thought unceasingly. Step by step you will achieve
realization, for all your faculties and powers become directed to that end.
—Claude M. Bristol

Go for the moon. If you don't get it, you'll still be heading for a star.—Willis
Reed

It is those who concentrate on but one thing at a time who advance in this
world.—Og Mandino

Our goals can only be reached through a vehicle of a plan, in which we must fervently believe, and upon which we must vigorously act. There is no other route to success.—Stephen A. Brennan

If I've got correct goals, and if I keep pursuing them the best way I know how, everything else falls into line. If I do the right thing right, I'm going to succeed.—Dan Dierdorf

If you raise your children to feel that they can accomplish any goal or task they decide upon, you will have succeeded as a parent and you will have given your children the greatest of all blessings.—Brian Tracy

We aim above the mark to hit the mark.—Ralph Waldo Emerson

It is for us to pray not for tasks equal to our powers, but for powers equal to our tasks, to go forward with a great desire forever beating at the door of our hearts as we travel toward our distant goal.—Helen Keller

Difficulties increase the nearer we approach the goal.—Johann Wolfgang von Goethe

Decide what you want, decide what you are willing to exchange for it. Establish your priorities and go to work.—H. L. Hunt

From a certain point onward, there is no longer any turning back. That is the point that must be reached.—Franz Kafka

Nothing can add more power to your life than concentrating all your energies on a limited set of targets.—Nido Qubein

Setting goals for your game is an art. The trick is in setting them at the right level neither too low nor too high.—Greg Norman

Nothing can stop the man with the right mental attitude from achieving his goal; nothing on earth can help the man with the wrong mental attitude. —Thomas Jefferson

My philosophy of life is that if we make up our mind what we are going to make of our lives, then work hard toward that goal, we never lose—somehow we win out.—Ronald Reagan

Having an exciting destination is like setting a needle in your compass. From then on, the compass knows only one point—its ideal. And it will faithfully guide you there through the darkest nights and fiercest storms.—Daniel Boone

GREATNESS

There are no great men, only great challenges that ordinary men are forced by circumstances to meet.—William F. Halsey

Greatness does not approach him who is forever looking down.—Hitopadesa

No great man ever complains of want of opportunity.—Ralph Waldo Emerson

Great men are true men, the men in whom nature has succeeded. They are not extraordinary—they are in the true order. It is the other species of men who are not what they ought to be.—Henri Frederic Amiel

Be not afraid of greatness; some are born great, some achieve greatness, and others have greatness thrust upon them.—William Shakespeare

No great man lives in vain. The history of the world is but the biography of great men.—Thomas Carlyle

Man is only truly great when he acts from his passions.—Benjamin Disraeli

In our society those who are in reality superior in intelligence can be accepted by their fellows only if they pretend they are not.—Marya Mannes

Great men are like eagles, and build their nest on some lofty solitude. —Arthur Schopenhauer

Well, I wouldn't say that I was in the great class, but I had a great time while I was trying to be great.—Harry S Truman

HABIT

We are what we repeatedly do. Excellence then is not an act, but a habit. —Aristotle

A nail is driven out by another nail. Habit is overcome by habit.—Desiderius Erasmus

First we form habits, then they form us. Conquer your bad habits or they will conquer you.—Rob Gilbert

Power is the faculty or capacity to act, the strength and potency to accomplish something. It is the vital energy to make choices and decisions. It also includes the capacity to overcome deeply embedded habits and to cultivate higher, more effective ones.—Stephen R. Covey

Winning is a habit. Unfortunately, so is losing.—Vince Lombardi

Your net worth to the world is usually determined by what remains after your bad habits are subtracted from your good ones.—Benjamin Franklin

Habits . . . the only reason they persist is that they are offering some satisfaction. . . . You allow them to persist by not seeking any other, better form of satisfying the same needs. Every habit, good or bad, is acquired and learned in the same way—by finding that it is a means of satisfaction.—Juliene Berk

I never could have done what I have done without the habits of punctuality, order, and diligence, without the determination to concentrate myself on one subject at a time.—Charles Dickens

It is hard to let old beliefs go. They are familiar. We are comfortable with them and have spent years building systems and developing habits that depend on them. Like a man who has worn eyeglasses so long that he forgets he has them on, we forget that the world looks to us the way it does because we have become used to seeing it that way through a particular set of lenses. Today, however, we need new lenses. And we need to throw the old ones away.—Kenich Ohmae

Good habits result from resisting temptation.—Indian proverb

As a twig is bent, the tree inclines.—Virgil

Thoughts lead on to purposes; purposes go forth in action; actions form habits; habits decide character; and character fixes our destiny.—Tyron Edwards

HEALTH

Ill health, of body or of mind, is defeat. Health alone is victory. Let all men, if they can manage it, contrive to be healthy!—Thomas Carlyle

He who enjoys good health is rich, though he knows it not.—Italian proverb

To get rich, never risk your health. For it is the truth that health is the wealth of wealth.—Richard Baker

The ingredients of health and long life are great temperance, open air, easy labor, and little care.—Sir Philip Sidney

To insure good health: Eat lightly, breathe deeply, live moderately, cultivate cheerfulness, and maintain an interest in life.—William Londen

A man's health can be judged by which he takes two at a time—pills or stairs.—Joan Welsh

The sovereign invigorator of the body is exercise, and of all the exercises walking is the best.—Thomas Jefferson

The human body has been designed to resist an infinite number of changes and attacks brought about by its environment. The secret of good health lies in successful adjustment to changing stresses on the body.—Harry J. Johnson

KNOWLEDGE

I am enough of an artist to draw freely upon my imagination. Imagination is more important than knowledge. Knowledge is limited. Imagination encircles the world.—Albert Einstein

Every mind was made for growth, for knowledge, and its nature is sinned against when it is doomed to ignorance.—William Ellery Channing

You can swim all day in the Sea of Knowledge and still come out completely dry. Most people do.—Norman Juster

Knowledge is power and enthusiasm pulls the switch.—Steve Droke

Not to know is bad, not to wish to know is worse.—Nigerian proverb

The old believe everything; the middle aged suspect everything; the young know everything.—Oscar Wilde

Where is the Life we have lost in living?
Where is the wisdom we have lost in knowledge?
Where is the knowledge we have lost in information?—T. S. Eliot

Zeal without knowledge is fire without light.—Thomas Fuller

The essence of knowledge is, having it, to apply it; not having it, to confess your ignorance.—Confucius

Today knowledge has power. It controls access to opportunity and advancement.—Peter F. Drucker

God grant that not only the love of liberty but a thorough knowledge of the rights of man may pervade all the nations of the earth, so that a philosopher may set his foot anywhere on its surface and say: This is my country!—Benjamin Franklin

Knowledge is of two kinds: We know a subject ourselves, or we know where we can find information about it.—Samuel Johnson

The hunger and thirst for knowledge, the keen delight in the chase, the good-humored willingness to admit that the scent was false, the eager desire to get on with the work, the cheerful resolution to go back and begin again, the broad good sense, the unaffected modesty, the imperturbable temper, the gratitude for any little help that was given—all these will remain in my memory though I cannot paint them for others.—Frederic William Maitland

It is nothing for one to know something unless another knows you know it.
—Persian proverb

To know that we know what we know, and that we do not know what we do not know, that is true knowledge.—Henry David Thoreau

The trouble with the world is not that people know too little, but that they know so many things that ain't so.—Mark Twain

We live on an island surrounded by a sea of ignorance. As our island of knowledge grows, so does the shore of our ignorance.—John Archibald Wheeler

LEADERSHIP

The boss drives people; the leader coaches them. The boss depends on authority; the leader on good will. The boss inspires fear; the leader inspires enthusiasm. The boss says I; the leader says WE. The boss fixes the blame for the breakdown; the leader fixes the breakdown. The boss says GO; the leader says LET'S GO!—H. Gordon Selfridge

Leaders aren't born, they are made. And they are made just like anything else, through hard work. And that's the price we'll have to pay to achieve that goal, or any goal.—Vince Lombardi

I am personally convinced that one person can be a change catalyst, a trans-former in any situation, any organization. Such an individual is yeast that can leaven an entire loaf. It requires vision, initiative, patience, respect, persist-ence, courage, and faith to be a transforming leader.—Stephen R. Covey

A boss creates fear, a leader confidence.
A boss fixes blame, a leader corrects mistakes.
A boss knows all, a leader asks questions.
A boss makes work drudgery, a leader makes it interesting.
A boss is interested in himself or herself,
    a leader is interested in the group.—Russell H. Ewing

One of the true tests of leadership is the ability to recognize a problem be-fore it becomes an emergency.—Arnold Glasow

People ask the difference between a leader and a boss. The leader works in the open, and the boss in covert. The leader leads, and the boss drives. —Theodore Roosevelt

A leader is best
When people barely know he exists,
When his work is done, his aim fulfilled,
They will say:
We did it ourselves.—Lao-tzu

A leader takes people where they want to go. A great leader takes people where they don't necessarily want to go, but ought to be.—Rosalynn Carter

Do not follow where the path may lead. Go instead where there is no path and leave a trail.—Muriel Strode

The challenge of leadership is to be strong, but not rude; be kind, but not weak; be bold, but not bully; be thoughtful, but not lazy; be humble, but not timid; be proud, but not arrogant; have humor, but without folly.—Jim Rohn

The best executive is the one who has sense enough to pick good men to do what he wants done, and self-restraint enough to keep from meddling with them while they do it.—Theodore Roosevelt

A man who wants to lead the orchestra must turn his back on the crowd.
—James Crook

Leadership is getting someone to do what they don't want to do, to achieve what they want to achieve.—Tom Landry

Leadership is the art of getting someone else to do something you want done because he wants to do it.—Dwight D. Eisenhower

Outstanding leaders go out of their way to boost the self-esteem of their personnel. If people believe in themselves, it's amazing what they can accomplish.—Sam Walton

A true leader has the confidence to stand alone, the courage to make tough decisions, and the compassion to listen to the needs of others. He does not set out to be a leader, but becomes one by the quality of his actions and the integrity of his intent.—Douglas MacArthur

You manage things; you lead people.—Grace Murray Hopper

If I advance, follow me! If I retreat, kill me! If I die, avenge me! —Francois de la Rochefoucauld

I have three precious things which I hold fast and prize. The first is gentleness; the second is frugality; the third is humility, which keeps me from putting myself before others. Be gentle and you can be bold; be frugal and you can be liberal; avoid putting yourself before others and you can become a leader among men.—Lao-tzu

It is very comforting to believe that leaders who do terrible things are, in fact, mad. That way, all we have to do is make sure we don't put psychotics in high places and we've got the problem solved.—Thomas Wolfe

An army of deer would be more formidable commanded by a lion, than an army of lions commanded by a stag.—Viking proverb

PERFORMANCE

Performance, and performance alone, dictates the predator in any food chain.—SEAL team saying

To aim is not enough— you must hit!—German proverb

Slumps are like a soft bed. They're easy to get into and hard to get out of. —Johnny Bench

If a man or woman is born ten years sooner or later, their whole aspect and performance shall be different.—Johann Wolfgang von Goethe

I like to be against the odds. I'm not afraid to be lonely at the top. With me, it's just the satisfaction of the game. Just performance.—Barry Bonds

Great works are done when one is not calculating and thinking.—Daisetz T. Suzuki

There's no such thing as coulda, shoulda, or woulda. If you shoulda and coulda, you woulda done it.—Pat Riley

You have to perform at a consistently higher level than others. That's the mark of a true professional.—Joe Paterno

PERSEVERANCE

On the mountains of truth, you can never climb in vain: either you will reach a point higher up today, or you will be training your powers so that you will be able to climb higher tomorrow.—Friedrich Nietzsche

In the confrontation between the stream and the rock, the stream always wins—not through strength but by perseverance.—H. Jackson Brown

People of mediocre ability sometimes achieve outstanding success because they don't know when to quit. Most men succeed because they are determined to.—George E. Allen

Perseverance is more prevailing than violence; and many things which cannot be overcome when they are together, yield themselves up when taken little by little.—Plutarch

Perseverance is not a long race; it is many short races one after another. —Walter Elliott

It's not so important who starts the game, but who finishes it.—John Wooden

Most of the important things in the world have been accomplished by people who have kept on trying when there seemed to be no help at all.—Dale Carnegie

All great masters are chiefly distinguished by the power of adding a second, a third, and perhaps a fourth step in a continuous line. Many a man has taken the first step. With every additional step you enhance immensely the value of your first.—Ralph Waldo Emerson

Consider the postage stamp: its usefulness consists in the ability to stick to one thing until it gets there.—Josh Billings

Some men give up their designs when they have almost reached the goal; while others, on the contrary, obtain a victory by exerting, at the last moment, more vigorous efforts than ever before.—Herodotus

Nothing in the world can take the place of persistence. Talent will not; nothing is more common than unsuccessful men with talent. Genius will not; unrewarded genius is almost a proverb. Education will not; the world is full of educated derelicts. Persistence and determination alone are omnipotent. The slogan "press on" has solved, and always will solve, the problems of the human race.—Calvin Coolidge

I do not think there is any other quality so essential to success of any kind as the quality of perseverance. It overcomes almost everything, even nature. —John D. Rockefeller

Success is not final, failure is not fatal: it is the courage to continue that counts.—Winston Churchill

Success seems to be connected with action. Successful men keep moving. They make mistakes, but they don't quit.—Conrad Hilton

If I had to select one quality, one personal characteristic that I regard as being most highly correlated with success, whatever the field, I would pick the trait of persistence. Determination. The will to endure to the end, to get knocked down seventy times and get up off the floor saying, "Here comes number seventy-one!"—Richard M. Devos

Good ideas are not adopted automatically. They must be driven into practice with courageous patience.—Hyman Rickover

For a righteous man falls seven times, and rises again.—Bible (Proverbs 24:16)

He who asks of life nothing but the improvement of his own nature . . . is less liable than anyone else to miss and waste life.—Henri Frederic Amiel

On the plains of hesitation lie the bleached bones of countless millions who, on the threshold of victory, sat down to wait, and in waiting died.—William Moulton Marston

STRENGTH

Fire is the test of gold; adversity, of strong men.—Seneca

I love the man that can smile in trouble, that can gather strength from distress, and grow brave by reflection. 'Tis the business of little minds to shrink, but he whose heart is firm, and whose conscience approves his conduct, will pursue his principles unto death.—Thomas Paine

We acquire the strength we have overcome.—Ralph Waldo Emerson

Don't hit at all if it is honorably possible to avoid hitting, but never hit soft. —Theodore Roosevelt

Strength is a matter of a made up mind.—John Beecher

Don't expect to build up the weak by pulling down the strong.—Calvin Coolidge

Nothing is so strong as gentleness, and nothing is so gentle as true strength.—Ralph Sockman

What the lion cannot manage to do, the fox can.—German proverb

Do not pray for easy lives. Pray to be stronger men! Do not pray for tasks equal to your powers. Pray for power equal to your tasks.—Phillips Brooks

Few men during their lifetime come anywhere near exhausting the resources dwelling within them. There are deep wells of strength that are never used.—Richard E. Byrd

Greatness lies not in being strong, but in the right use of strength.—Henry Ward Beecher

The burden is equal to the horse's strength.—Talmudic saying

It is truly said: It does not take much strength to do things, but it requires great strength to decide what to do.—Chow Ching

Only actions give life strength; only moderation gives it charm.—Jean Paul Richter

Our real problem, then, is not our strength today; it is rather the vital necessity of action today to ensure our strength tomorrow.—Dwight D. Eisenhower

Life only demands from you the strength you possess. Only one feat is possible—not to have run away.—Dag Hammarskjold

Strong men can always afford to be gentle. Only the weak are intent on giving as good as they get.—Elbert Hubbard

SURVIVAL

Survival, with honor, that outmoded and all-important word, is as difficult as ever and as all-important to a writer. Those who do not last are always more beloved since no one has to see them in their long, dull, unrelenting, no-quarter-given-and-no-quarter-received fights that they make to do something as they believe it should be done before they die. Those who die or quit early and easy and with every good reason are preferred because they are understandable and human. Failure and well-disguised cowardice are more human and more beloved.—Ernest Hemingway

The more we exploit nature, the more our options are reduced, until we have only one: to fight for survival.—Morris K. Udall

Nobody is stronger, nobody is weaker than someone who came back. There is nothing you can do to such a person because whatever you could do is less than what has already been done to him. We have already paid the price. —Elie Wiesel

Once one determines that he or she has a mission in life, that it's not going to be accomplished without a great deal of pain, and that the rewards in the end may not outweigh the pain—if you recognize historically that always happens, then when it comes, you survive it.—Richard M. Nixon

The consciousness of being deemed dead, is next to the presumable unpleasantness of being so in reality. One feels like his own ghost unlawfully tenanting a defunct carcass.—Herman Melville

TEAMWORK

When two people meet, there are really six people present. There is each man as he sees himself, each man as he wants to be seen, and each man as he really is.—Michael De Saintamo

Alone we can do so little; together we can do so much.—Helen Keller

Teamwork is the ability to work together toward a common vision. The ability to direct individual accomplishments toward organizational objectives. It is the fuel that allows common people to attain uncommon results.—Andrew Carnegie

Coming together is a beginning, staying together is progress, and working together is success.—Henry Ford

The achievements of an organization are the results of the combined effort of each individual.—Vince Lombardi

The nice thing about teamwork is that you always have others on your side. —Margaret Carty

When your team is winning, be ready to be tough, because winning can make you soft. On the other hand, when your team is losing, stick by them. Keep believing.—Bo Schembechler

Individuals play the game, but teams beat the odds.—SEAL Team saying

The way a team plays as a whole determines its success. You may have the greatest bunch of individual stars in the world, but if they don't play together, the club won't be worth a dime.—Babe Ruth

If a team is to reach its potential, each player must be willing to subordinate his personal goals to the good of the team.—Bud Wilkinson

People have been known to achieve more as a result of working with others than against them.—Dr. Allan Fromme

When he took time to help the man up the mountain, lo, he scaled it himself.—Tibetan proverb

VICTORY

The softest things in the world overcome the hardest things in the world. —Lao-tzu

The ultimate victory in competition is derived from the inner satisfaction of knowing that you have done your best and that you have gotten the most out of what you had to give.—Howard Cosell

The will to conquer is the first condition of victory.—Ferdinand Foch

Men talk as if victory were something fortunate. Work is victory.—Ralph Waldo Emerson

I would rather lose in a cause that will some day win, than win in a cause that will some day lose!—Woodrow Wilson

The most dangerous moment comes with victory.—Napoleon Bonaparte

The people who remained victorious were less like conquerors than conquered.—St. Augustine

One may know how to gain a victory, and know not how to use it.—Pedro Calderon de la Barca

WILLPOWER

Strength does not come from physical capacity. It comes from an indomitable will.—Mahatma Gandhi

Willpower is to the mind like a strong blind man who carries on his shoulders a lame man who can see.—Arthur Schopenhauer

The world is full of willing people—some willing to work, the rest willing to let them.—Robert Frost

Great souls have wills; feeble ones have only wishes.—Chinese proverb

A man can do all things if he but wills them.—Leon Battista Alberti

People do not lack strength; they lack will.—Victor Hugo

What you have to do and the way you have to do it is incredibly simple. Whether you are willing to do it, that's another matter.—Peter F. Drucker

Will is character in action.—William Mcdougall

It is fatal to enter any war without the will to win it.—Douglas MacArthur

Free will and determinism are like a game of cards. The hand that is dealt you is determinism. The way you play your hand is free will.—Norman Cousins

Self-will so ardent and active that it will break a world to pieces to make a stool to sit on.—Richard Cecil

They can conquer who believe they can. He has not learned the first lesson in life who does not every day surmount a fear.—Ralph Waldo Emerson

WINNING

I count him braver who overcomes his desires than him who conquers his enemies; for the hardest victory is over self.—Aristotle

Winning is everything, to win is all there is. Only those poor souls buried beneath the battlefield understand this.—SEAL Team saying

All right, mister, let me tell you what winning means . . . you're willing to go longer, work harder, give more than anyone else.—Vince Lombardi

Winning is not everything, but the effort to win is.—Zig Ziglar

The reason most people never reach their goals is that they don't define them, learn about them, or even seriously consider them as believable or achievable. Winners can tell you where they are going, what they plan to do along the way, and who will be sharing the adventure with them.—Denis Waitley

History has demonstrated that the most notable winners usually encountered heartbreaking obstacles before they triumphed. They won because they refused to become discouraged by their defeats.—Bertie C. Forbes

You can't be a winner and be afraid to lose.—Charles Lynch

Those who know how to win are much more numerous than those who know how to make proper use of their victories.—Polybius

The harder the conflict, the more glorious the triumph.—Thomas Paine

Guts are a combination of confidence, courage, conviction, strength of character, stick-to-itiveness, pugnaciousness, backbone, and intestinal fortitude. They are mandatory for anyone who wants to get to and stay at the top.—D. A. Benton

Only a man who knows what it is like to be defeated can reach down to the bottom of his soul and come up with the extra ounce of power it takes to win when the match is even.—Muhammad Ali

The first man gets the oyster, the second man gets the shell.—Andrew Carnegie

I am not bound to win, but I am bound to be true. I am not bound to succeed, but I am bound to live by the light that I have. I must stand with anybody that stands right, and stand with him while he is right, and part with him when he goes wrong.—Abraham Lincoln

Never let defeat have the last word.—Tibetan proverb

There is no victory at bargain basement prices.—Dwight D. Eisenhower

There are many victories worse than a defeat.—George Eliot

Appendix B

RECOMMENDED READING AND ADDITIONAL SOURCES

READING LIST

Self-Discipline

Discipline: The Glad Surrender
Elisabeth Elliot, Baker Books
 Publishing, 1982
This wonderful Christian book covers
 the topics of discipline, commit-
 ment, and integrity.

The Master: Key to Riches
Napoleon Hill, Ballantine Publishing
 Group, 1965
Truly one of the greatest books of all
 time. Napoleon Hill covers self-
 discipline and successful strategies
 of the world's most noted people.

A Better Way to Live
Og Mandino, Bantam Books
 Publishing, 1990
A personal guide to developing self-
 discipline and the skills to live a ful-
 filling life.

The Tibetan Book of Living and Dying
Sogyal Rinpoche, Harper Collins
 Publishing, 1993
A comprehensive look at the philoso-
 phies and teachings of the Tibetan
 monks.

Mindscience
The Dalai Lama, Wisdom Publishing,
 1991
A direct look at ancient wisdoms and
 modern truths.

Dialogues with Scientists and Sages
Renee Weber, Routledge Publishing,
 1986
A comparison between modern scientific research and ancient philosophies.

*Personhood: The Art of Being
Fully Human*
Leo F. Buscaglia, Ballantine Books
 Publishing, 1978

A refreshing look at understanding our individual journey through life.

The Way of Zen
A. Watts, Random House, 1974
A mystical approach to understanding life.

The Crack in the Cosmic Egg
J. Pierce, Julian Press, 1971
One of the most touching books on searching for meaning in life.

Black Elk Speaks
John G. Neihardt, University of Nebraska Press, 1979
Insights from one of the greatest Native American thinkers.

How to Stop Worrying and Start Living
Dale Carnegie, Pocket Books, 1985
A masterful book for dealing with life.

The Power of Your Subconscious Mind
Dr. Joseph Murphy, Bantam Books, 1982
The most in-depth guide to understanding and using the power of the subconscious mind.

Grow Rich with Peace of Mind
Napoleon Hill, Ballantine Books, 1964
Another great book on mental discipline and success.

Zen in the Martial Arts
Joe Hyams, Bantam Books, 1982
A pocket guide to discipline.

The Tao of Leadership
John Heider, Bantam Books, 1984
Philosophies and ancient leadership styles.

Personal Achievement

How to Succeed: Dynamic Mind Principles
Brian Adams, Wilshire Book Company, 1985
An excellent book on the science of success.

Advanced Formula for Total Success
Robert Anthony, Berkley Publishing, 1988
A user-friendly guide for better living.

The 7 Habits of Highly Effective People
Steven R. Covey, Simon & Schuster, 1994
A must-read book for anyone interested in improving their life.

Your Subconscious Power
Charles M. Simmons, Wilshire Book Company, 1965
The most comprehensive book on using your subconscious for success.

The Millionaire Next Door
Thomas Stanley and William Danko, Pocket Books, 1996
A complete guide to understanding the reality behind the science of wealth.

Success Is a Choice
Rick Pitino, Broadway Books, 1998
This book examines the road to success in both the athletic arena and everyday life.

The Dynamic Laws of Prosperity
Catherine Ponder, Prentice-Hall Publishing, 1962
A great mix of Christianity and the journey toward personal success.

How High Can You Bounce?
Roger Crawford, Bantam Books,
    1998
An inspiring book to help you get over
    the hard times in life.

10,001 Ways to Energize Employees
Bob Nelson, Workman Publishing,
    1997
The complete guide of ideas for inspir-
    ing people in the workplace.

Think and Grow Rich
Napoleon Hill, Ballantine Books, 1960
Truly the greatest book ever written on
    personal achievement.

The Greatest Mystery in the World
Og Mandino, Ballantine Publishing
    Group, 1997
An inspiring tale of self-motivation and
    personal discovery.

Success through a Positive
Mental Attitude
Napoleon Hill, Pocket Books, 1960
Discover the mental science behind
    acquiring a winning attitude.

Debt-Free Living
Larry Burkett, Moody Press, 1989
A spiritual success guide for controlling
    your finances.

The Bible
The single most important book ever
    written.

Get a Financial Life
Beth Kobliner, Simon & Schuster, 1996
The complete guide to finances in the
    '90s.

The Power of Positive Thinking
Norman Vincent Peale, Prentice-Hall,
    1958
The most complete work on mental
    success in print.

The Magic of Believing
Claude M. Bristol, Prentice-Hall, 1955
A powerful lesson in personal faith.

Mind and Body
A Brief History of Time
Steven J. Hawking, Bantam Books, 1988
A unique and intelligent philosophy on
    life.

Thinking Body, Dancing Mind
Chungliang Al Huang and Jerry Lynch,
    Bantam Books, 1992
The Tao of performance in athletics
    and life.

Raja Yoga
Wallace Slater, Theosophical
    Publishing House, 1968
A complete guide to mental and physi-
    cal well-being.

Fit for Life
Harvey and Marilyn Diamond, Bantam
    Books, 1987
Sound advice for healthy living.

Dr. Whitaker's Guide to
Natural Healing
Julian Walker, Prima Publishing, 1995
An intelligent look at total health.

Muscles Alive
J. V. Basmajian, Williams & Wilkins
    Company, 1979
All you ever wanted to know about
    your body.

Seven Arrows
Hyemeyohsts Storm, Ballantine Books,
  1972
A Native Indian philosophy book for
  life.

Power Reading
Laurie Rozakis, Simon & Schuster,
  1995
A comprehensive guide to better reading skills.

12 Steps to a Better Memory
Carol Turkington, Simon & Schuster,
  1996
The science of improved memory.

Scholar Warrior
Deng Ming-Dao, Harper Collins, 1990
The development of Tao for everyday
  life.

Love, Death and Exile
Bassam K. Frangieh, Georgetown
  University Press, 1990
Poems of inspiration.

Stop Screaming at the Microwave
Mary Loverde, Simon & Schuster,
  1998
A unique guide to life-management.

The Sayings of the Viking
Bjorn Jonasson, Gudrun Publishing,
  1992
Hardy advice from the warrior society.

The Einstein Factor
Win Wenger and Richard Poe, Prima
  Publishing, 1995
A unique look at boosting your intelli-
  gence.

Psycho-Cybernetics
Maxwell Maltz, Prentice-Hall, 1960
A fascinating look at our mental possi-
  bilities.

Quotationary
Leonard Roy Frank, Random House,
  1999
More than 20,000 quotations for life.

Sports Supplement Review
Bill Phillips, Mile High Publishing,
  1999
The most complete guide to nutrition
  that you can find.

Bus 9 to Paradise
Leo F. Buscaglia, Ballantine Books,
  1977
A fascinating look at our lives in
  progress.

How to Argue and Win Every Time
Gerry Spence, St. Martin's Press, 1995
The best information on persuasion.

ORGANIZATIONS AND INFORMATION SOURCES

Special Operations Consulting
Address: 1005 Banyan Drive,
  Virginia Beach, VA 23462
Contact: Michael A. Janke
Phone: (757) 560-3701
URL: http://www.specopsconsulting.
  com
Special Operations Consulting is a pro-
  fessional consulting service that
  specializes in keynote speeches,
  presentations, books, tapes, and
  corporate consulting. Their exper-

tise covers improving personal and professional performance, leadership, teamwork, and management training. They also work hand-in-hand with meeting planners, corporations, and individuals to customize presentations and training sessions to meet any need. (Founded by the author of this book.)

C. D. Lilly, Inc.
Address: 24195 Juanita Drive, Quail Valley, CA 92587
Contact: Deborah Lilly
Phone: (800) 543-2360
URL: http://www.cdlilly.com
C. D. Lilly is a full-service speaking bureau that specializes in providing high-performance speakers for all occasions, as well as providing customized services for professional speakers.

Antion & Associates
E-mail: tomantion@aol.com
URL: http://www.antion.com

Leading Authorities, Inc.
Address: 919 18th Street, NW, Suite 500, Washington, DC 20006
Phone: (202) 783-0300

The Speakers Bureau
Address: P.O. Box 390296, Minneapolis, MN 55439-0296
Phone: (800) 397-2841
E-mail: rstrom@thespeakersbureau. com

The Jack Morton Company
Address: 1725 K Street NW, Suite 1400,Washington, DC 20006
Phone: (202) 296-1783

SELF-HELP, BUSINESS, AND MENTAL HEALTH ASSOCIATIONS

National Speakers Association
Address: 1500 South Priest Drive, Tempe, AZ 85281-6203
Phone: (602) 968-2552
Fax: (602) 968-0911
E-mail: nsamain@aol.com

Meeting Planners International, Northern California Chapter
Address: 50 First Street, San Francisco, CA 94105
Phone: (415) 896-6447

International Exhibitors Association
Address: 5501 Backlick Road, Suite 105, Arlington, VA 22219-0200
Phone: (703) 941-8275
Fax: (703) 941-3725

Professional Convention Management Association
Address: 100 Vestavia Parkway, Suite 220, Birmingham, AL 35216-3743
Phone: (205) 823-7262
Fax: (205) 822-3891

Project Management Institute
Address: 130 South State Road, Upper Darby, PA 19082
Phone: (610) 734-3330
Fax: (610) 734-3266
E-mail: pmeio@ix.netcom.com

American Diabetes Association
Address: 1660 Duke Street, P.O. Box 25757, Alexandria, VA 22314
Phone: (703) 549-1500

American Lung Association
Address: 1740 Broadway,
New York, NY 10019
Phone: (212) 315-8700
Fax: (212) 315-6498

American Osteopathic Academy of Addictionology
Address: P.O. Box 26012,
Fairview Park, OH 44126-0012
Phone: (216) 979-0211

Meeting Professionals & Associates
Address: 11021 SE 64th Street,
Renton, WA 98056
Phone: (206) 226-1727
Fax: (206) 226-0568

American Marketing Association
Address: 250 South Wacker Drive,
Suite 200, Chicago, IL 60606
Phone: (312) 648-0536
Fax: (312) 993-7542
E-mail: webmaster@ama.org
URL: http://www.ama.org

Marketing Research Association
Address: 2189 Silas Deane Hwy,
Suite 5, Rocky Hill, CT 06067-0230
Phone: (860) 257-4008
Fax: (860) 257-3990
E-mail: email@mra-net.org
URL: http://www.mra-net.org

Internet Business Alliance
Address: P.O. Box 11518,
Seattle, WA 98110
URL: http://www.alliance.org

National Association of Alcoholism and
Drug Abuse Counselors
Address: 1911 North Fort Myer Drive,
Suite 900, Arlington, VA 22209

Phone: (703) 741-7686
Fax: (703) 841-7698
E-mail: naadac@naadac.com
URL: http://www.naadac.com

National Small Business United
Address: 1155 15th Street, NW,
Suite 710, Washington, DC 20005
Phone: (202) 293-8830
Fax: (202) 872-8543
E-mail: jgalles@nsbu.org
URL: http://www.nsbu.org

National Association of Private Enterprise
Address: P.O. Box 612147,
Dallas, TX 75261-2147
Phone: (800) 223-6273
Fax: (817) 428-4235

National Association for the Self-Employed
Address: P.O. Box 612067,
DFW Airport,
Dallas, TX 75261-2067
Phone: (800) 232-6273
E-mail: kelly@nase.org
URL: http://www.nase.org

National Association of
Home Based Businesses
Address: 10451 Mill Run Circle,
Owings Mills, MD 21117
Phone: (410) 363-3698
Fax: (410) 363-3698
E-mail: nahbb@ix.netcom.com
URL: http://www.usahomebusiness.
com/expan.htm

American Society of Association Executives
Address: 1575 I Street, NW,
Washington, DC 20005-1168
Phone: (202) 626-2823
Fax: (202) 289-4049

Northern California Society of Association Executives
Address: 50 First Street, Suite 310,
San Francisco, CA 94105-2411
Phone: (415) 764-4942

National Foundation for Women Business Owners
Address: 1377 K Street, NW,
Suite 637, Washington, DC 20005
Phone: (301) 495-4975

National Women's Business Council
Address: 409 Third Street, SW,
Suite 7425, Washington, D.C.
20024
Phone: (202) 205-3850

Association for Professional Insurance Women
(APIW)
Phone: (212) 361-5880
E-mail: 754302642@compuserve.com

Leads Club
Phone: (800) 783-3761
E-mail: leadsclb@ix.netcom.com

Mothers' Home Business Network (MHBN)
Phone: (516) 997-7394
URL: http://www.homeworkingmom.
com

American Psychiatric Association
Address: 1400 K Street, NW,
Washington, DC 20005
Phone: (202) 682-6000
E-mail: webmaster@psych.org
URL: http://www.psych.org

American Psychoanalytic Association
Address: 309 East 49th Street,
New York, NY 10017
Phone: (212) 752-0450
Fax: (212) 593-0571

E-mail: central.office@apsa.org
URL: http://www.apsa.org

Center for Mental Health Services
Address: P.O. Box 42490,
Washington, DC 20015
Phone: (800) 789-2647
URL: http://www.mentalhealth.org

Families Worldwide International
Address: 75 East Fort Union Blvd.,
Salt Lake City, UT 84047
Phone: (801) 562-6185
Fax: (801) 562-6008
URL: http://www.fww.org/index.html

American Psychological Association
Address: 750 First Street, NE,
Washington, DC 20002-4242
Phone: (202) 336-5500
URL: http://www.apa.org

National Mental Health Association
Address: 1021 Prince Street,
Alexandria, VA 22314-2971
Phone: (703) 684-7722 or
(800) 969-NMHA
Fax: (703) 684-5968

Substance Abuse and Mental Health Services
Administration (SAMSHA)
Address: Room 12-105 Parklawn
Building, 5600 Fishers Lane,
Rockville, MD 20857
Phone: (301) 443-4795 or
(301) 443-0284
URL: http://www.samhsa.gov/about.htm

American Academy of Child and
Adolescent Psychiatry
Address: P.O. Box 96106,
Washington, DC 20090-6106

SelfGrowth.com
Address: 96 Linwood Plaza, Suite 264, Fort Lee, NJ 07024
Phone: (201) 945-6757
Fax: (201) 945-7441
E-mail: webmasters@selfgrowth.com
URL: http://www.selfgrowth.com

WEBSITES AND E-ZINES

Success, Self-Help, and Personal Achievement Websites
http://www.achievement.com
http://www.celestialvisions.com
http://home.hiwaay.net
http://www.anthonygalie.com
http://www.attitudeiseverything.com
http://www.au.spiritweb.org
http://www.webagency-tm.com
http://www.tracyint.com
http://www.carmine.net
http://www.dale-carnegie.com
http://www.mindtools.com/lifeplan.html
http://www.selfgrowth.com
http://www.walters-intl.com
http://www.franklincovey.com/priorities
http://www.ahandyguide.com/cat1
http://www.selfhelp.com/bootstraps.html
http://www.rockisland.com/~process/millenni
http://www.thinkright.offc.com
http://www.onlineconsulting.com
http://www.sanspareil.com
http://www.is17.com/promo/reports
http://www.success.com
http://www.geocities.com/Athens/Oracle/300
http://www.cdipage.com

http://www.mentalfitness.com
http://www.rocketreader.com
http://www.gen.com
http://www.barronspecialties.com
http://www.tiac.net
http://www.mindmedia.com
http://www.botree.com/index.htm
http://www.newage.com
http://www.newfrontier.com
http://www.inner-resources.com/success
http://www.yogajournal.com
http://www.mentalhelp.net/psyhelp
http://www.grayarea.com/gray2.htm
http://www.metamorphosis-online.com/self_improvement/self_help.htm
http://www.innercite.com
http://www.netstoreusa.com
http://www.telusplanet.net
http://www.megavision.net
http://www.tbm.org
http://www.depression.com
http://www.psych-central.com
http://www.mentalhealth.com
http://www.family.com
http://www.success-motivation.com
http://www.instant-success.com
http://www.linktosuccess.com

INTERNET RESOURCES A TO Z

Addictions
12 Step Cyber Café
www.12steps.org

3D Prevention Coalition
www.3dmonth.org

Addiction Treatment Forum
www.atforum.com

Alternatives in Treatment
www.drughelp.com

Betty Ford Center
www.bettyfordcenter.org

Join Together
www.jointogether.org

National Counseling
www.nationalcounseling.com

Nicorette
www.nicorette.com

Physicians for Prevention
www.pfprevention.com

Serenity Lane
www.serenitylane.org

Teen Challenge
www.teenchallenge.com

Advice
Dr. Paula
www.drpaula.com

Quick Advice
www.quickadvice.com

The Right Answer
www.therightanswer.com

Alternative Medicine
Alternative Therapists
www.asat.org

**American Holistic Health
Association**
www.ahha.org

Ayurveda Holistic Center
www.ayurvedahc.com

Ayurvedic Institute
www.ayurveda.com

Cosmic Breath
www.thecosmicbreath.com

Health Pyramid
www.healthpyramid.com

Holistic Internet Resources
www.hir.com

Holistic Living Magazine
www.holisticliving.org

Homeopathy
www.homeopathy.org

Natural Health
www.naturalhealth.org

Positive Pathways
www.positivepathways.com

Your Life—Your Choice
www.life-choices.com

Book Resources
21st Century Christian Bookstore
www.21stcc.com

A1 Books
www.a1books.com

Amazon
www.amazon.com

Barnes & Noble
www.barnesandnoble.com

Best Books
www.bestbooks.com

Book Buyers
www.bookbuyers.com

Book Express
www.bookexpress.com

Book of the Month
www.englishbooks.com

Book Port
www.bookport.com

Book Stacks
www.books.com

Book Watch
www.bookwatch.com

Book Wire
www.bookwire.com

Book World
www.bookworld.com

Book Zen
www.bookzen.com

Book Zone
www.bookzone.com

Books Online
www.booksonline.com

Borders
www.borders.com

Corporate Book Service
www.cidsource.com

Just Good Books
www.justgoodbooks.com

Olsson's Books
www.olssons.com

Papyrus Books
www.papyrusbooks.com

Readers Ndex
www.readersndex.com

Specialty Books
www.specialty-books.com

Super Library
www.superlibrary.com

United States Book Exchange
www.usbe.com

Business Journals
Advanstar
www.advanstar.com

Business Journals
www.amcity.com

Business Publications Association
www.bizpubs.org

Industry Week
www.industryweek.com

Electronic Commerce
All E-Commerce
www.allec.com

EC Today
www.ectoday.com

Electronic Markets
www.electronicmarkets.com

E-Marketer
www.emarketer.com

Internet Marketing Tips
www.marketingtips.com

Experts
Experts
www.experts.com

Experts Exchange
www.experts-exchange.com

Find a Professional
www.findaprofessional.com

Fitness
24 Hour Fitness
www.24hourfitness.com

Aerobics and Fitness
www.afaa.com

All About Fitness
www.allaboutfitness.com

**American Alliance for
Health, Physical Education,**

Recreation, and Dance
www.aahperd.org

Balance Fitness
www.balance.net

Cardiovascular Institute
www.cardio.com

Cybercise
www.cybercise.com

Exercise Council
www.acefitness.org

Fit @ Home
www.fitathome.com

Fit Net
www.fit-net.com

Fit Online
www.fitonline.com

Fitness Health & Weight Loss
www.landry.com

Fitness News Online
Health & Fitness Magazine
www.fitnessnews.com

Fitness Professionals
www.aahfp.com

Fitness World
www.fitnessworld.com

Forever Fit
www.fit.org

Men's Fitness
www.mensfitness.com

National Athletic Trainers
Association
www.nata.org

National Gym Association
www.nationalgym.com

Physical Fitness
www.physical.com

World Fitness
www.worldfitness.org

Health

Acupuncture
www.acupuncture.com

American Heart Association
www.amhrt.org

American Medical Association
www.ama-assn.org

America's Health Network
www.ahn.com

Ask the Doc
www.ask-the-doc.com

Better Health
www.betterhealth.com

British Medical Journal
www.bmj.com

Caregiving Newsletter
www.caregiving.com

Health A to Z
www.healthatoz.com

Health Connection
www.healthconnection.com

Health Guide
www.healthguide.com

Health Information Center
www.nhic-nt.health.org

Health Library
www.health-library.com

Health World
www.healthy.com

Lifelines
www.lifelines.com

Medical Center
www.medcenter.com

Men's Health
www.menshealth.com

Marriage
Center for Growth
www.acenter4growth.com

Marriage Alive
www.marriagealive.com

Marriage Encounter
www.encounter.org

Marriage Help
www.episcopalme.com

Marriage Toolbox
www.marriagetools.com

National Marriage Encounter
www.marriages.com

Mental Health
British Psychotherapists
www.bcp.org.uk

Counselor Link
www.counselorlink.com

Cyber Couch
www.cybercouch.com

In Stream Psychlink
www.psychlink.com

Liberation Psychotherapy
www.liberationpsych.org

Lynn Mental Health Association
www.glmh.org

Mediation
www.osho.org

Mental Health
www.mentalhealth.com

Mental Health Net
www.mentalhelp.net

Psychological Advisor
www.psynews.com

Re-evaluation Counseling
www.rc.org

Save
www.save.org

Shyness
www.shyness.com

Therapeutic Camps
www.natwc.org

Military
Air Force
www.af.mil

Air Force Association
www.afa.org

Air National Guard
www.ang.af.mil

American Legion
www.legion.org

Armed Forces Association
www.uafa.org

Army Corps of Engineers
www.usace.army.mil

Army Times
www.armytimes.com

Civil Air Patrol
www.cap.af.mil

Coast Guard R&D
www.rdc.uscg.mil

Defense News
www.defensenews.com

Department of the Navy
www.tql-navy.org

Department of Veterans Affairs
www.va.gov

Marine Corps
www.usmc.mil

Marine Corps Association
www.mca-marines.org

Militaria Magazine
www.militaria.com

Military Career Guide
www.militarycareers.com

Military City
www.militarycity.com

Military Network
www.military-network.com

National Guard Association
www.ngaus.org

Navy SEALS
www.navyseals.com

Special Forces Association
www.sfahq.org

U.S. Army Association
www.ausa.org

Veterans News
www.vnis.com

Veterans
www.vets.com

Newsletters
Bizy Moms
www.bizymoms.com

Circles of Light
www.circlesoflight.com

Global Net News
www.dalepublishing.com

Great Speaking
www.antion.com

Mind Matters
www.hypnosis.org

New Ideas
www.mgeneral.com

Parenting Toolbox
www.parentingtoolbox.com

Poor Richards
www.poorrichards.com

The Symposium
www.selfknowledge.org

Weekly Web News Clips
www.zazz.com

Women's Entrepreneur Network
www.weon.com

Parenting
Child Development Institute
www.cdipage.com

Common Sense Parenting
www.parenting.com

Cyber Mom
www.thecybermom.com

Daddys Home
www.daddyshome.com

Dads Can
www.dadscan.org

Family Network
www.familynetwork.com

Family Resource
www.familyresource.com

Father Project
www.fatherproject.com

Fatherhood Initiative
www.fatherhood.org

Fathering
www.fathering.org

Fathering Magazine
www.fatheringmag.com

Fathers Net
www.fathersnetwork.org

Fathers of America
www.ufa.org

Help for Families
www.helpforfamilies.com

Informed Parent
www.informedparent.com

Moms
www.momsonline.com

Moms Net
www.momsnetwork.com

Parent Info Net
www.npin.org

Parenting Press
www.parentingpress.com

Parents Talk
www.parents-talk.com

Positive Parenting
www.positiveparenting.com

Whole Family Center
www.wholefamily.com

Philosophy

Anthroposophic Press
www.anthropress.org

Catholic Philosophical Association
www.acpa-main.org

Confucius Publishing
www.confucius.org

Electric Minds
www.minds.com

Fellowship of Reason
www.kindreason.com

Human Condition
www.condition.org

Life Force News
www.haribol.org

Pearls of Wisdom
www.pearls.org

Veterans

American Gulf War Veterans
www.gulfwarvets.com

American Legion
www.legion.org

Catholic War Veterans
www.ocwvets.org

Families Alliance
www.nationalalliance.org

Merchant Marines
www.usmm.org

National Veterans Organization
www.nvo.org

Retired Officers Association
www.troa.org

Submarine Vets
www.ussvi.org

Veterans Observer
www.theveteransobserver.com

Veterans of Foreign Wars
www.vfw.org

Veterans Voice
www.vvoa.com

Viet Nam Veterans
www.vietvet.org

PERSONAL ACHIEVEMENT MAGAZINES AND JOURNALS

Success Magazine
Address: P.O. Box 3038,
Harlan, IA 51537
Phone: (800) 234-7324
A top-notch magazine for information about personal success and up-to-date corporate strategies.

Priorities Magazine—The Journal of Personal and Professional Success
Address: 2200 West Parkway Blvd.,
Salt Lake City, UT 84119
Phone: (800) 236-2569
One of the most interesting and informative magazines available. If you are interested in the latest information and strategies on personal achievement, this is your best bet. Published by the Franklin Covey Corporation. (Formed by well-known author and achievement guru Stephen R. Covey.)

Psychology Today
Address: 49 East 21st Street,
11th Floor, New York, NY 10010
Phone: (800) 234-8361
To stay up on the latest developments in the world of psychology and mental health, this is where the experts go. Packed full of helpful information for daily life and personal improvement.

Spare Time—The Magazine of Money-Making Opportunities
Address: 2400 S. Commerce Drive,
Suite 400, New Berlin, WI 53151
Phone: (262) 780-1070
URL: http://www.spare-time.com (one of the best small-business websites available)
A great magazine for the latest strategies and opportunities in today's business arena. Offers excellent information and resources for small to medium-size businesses.

New Man Magazine
Address: 600 Rinehart Rd.,
Lake Mary, FL 32746
Phone: (407) 333-0600
URL: http://www.newmanmag.com
For character building, achievement, and Christian-based information. A very informative magazine for all areas of life. Offers excellent personal and spiritual success resources.

Smart Money
Address: 1755 Broadway,
New York, NY 10019
Phone: (212) 765-7323
One of the best money, investment, and wealth-building information sources available. Find personal financial resources and information in every article.

Fortune
Address: Time & Life Building,
Rockefeller Center,
New York, NY 10020
Fax: (212) 522-7686
E-mail: fortune-letters@pathfinder.com
URL: http://www.fortune.com
Another personal success and finance powerhouse. This magazine covers all aspects of business, retirement, and Wall Street strategies for success.

Writers' Journal—
The Complete Writer's Magazine
Address: P.O. Box 394,
Perham, MN 56573-0394
Phone: (218) 346-7921
E-mail: writersjournal@wadena.net
URL: http://www.sowashco.com/
writersjournal
An excellent source for putting your
thoughts into words. Keep up on
the latest tools and techniques for
successful writing, publishing, and
promoting.

Entrepreneur—
The Small Business Authority
Address: 12 W. 31st Street,
Suite 1100, New York, NY 10001
Phone: (212) 563-8080
URL: http://www.entrepreneurmag.
com
This magazine is truly the small busi-
ness authority. To keep up on the
latest trends and information in the
world of small business, this is the
magazine.

INC.—The Magazine for
Growing Companies
Address: 38 Commercial Wharf,
Boston, MA 02110
Phone: (617) 248-8000
E-mail: editors@inc.com
URL: http://www.inc.com
For anyone looking to increase their
financial standing or business sense,
this magazine covers all aspects of
business and financial success.

Fast Company
Address: 77 North Washington Street,
Boston, MA 02114-1927
Phone: (800) 688-1545
E-mail: loop@fastcompany.com

URL: http://www.fastcompany.com
A hip new technological magazine for
everything you ever wanted to know
about the Internet marketplace.
Packed full of success stories and
advice from those who are making
it work on the Internet.

Bonkers?—A Magazine for Our Times
Address: 333 Royal Poinciana Plaza,
P.O. Box 189, Palm Beach, FL
33480
Phone: (800) 403-8850
E-mail: bonkers@goingbonkers.com
URL: www.goingbonkers.com
A truly unique self-help magazine.
Loaded with wonderful stories and
articles about personal develop-
ment, stress-free living, and every-
day life.

Alternative Medicine
Address: 21½ Main Street,
Tiburon, GA 94920
Phone: (604) 664-7455
E-mail: jeff@dotcom.bc.ca
URL: http://www.alternativemedicine.
com
A first-rate alternative heath magazine
that provides helpful ideas, prod-
ucts, and articles on improving your
health naturally.

Muscle and Fitness
Address: P.O. Box 37208,
Boone, IA 50037-2208
Phone: (800) 998-0731
URL: http:www.muscle-fitness.com
For the development of physical disci-
pline and health, this is the most
comprehensive magazine available.
Packed full of articles, information,
and health-related products.

Life Extension Magazine
Address: 1881 NE 26th Street,
Suite 221, Wilton Manors, FL 33305
Phone: (954) 561-8335
E-mail: lemagazine@lef.org
URL: http://www.lef.org
A very practical magazine that covers
both the traditional and alternative
medical fields. To keep up on the
latest medical and longevity infor-
mation, this is a top-notch source.

Whole Life Times
Address: P.O. Box 1187,
Malibu, CA 90265
Phone: (310) 317-4200
E-mail: wholelifex@aol.com
URL: http:www.wholelifetimes.com
Today's most comprehensive holistic

lifestyle journal. One of the most
respected magazines for content
and cutting-edge reporting. Full of
new age and holistic information.

Energy Times
Address: 2500 Grand Avenue,
Long Beach, CA 90815-1764
Phone: (516) 777-7773
E-mail: jgallo@naturesplus.com
URL: http://www.energytimes.com
Enhancing your life through proper
nutrition. This magazine is packed
full of the latest information, articles, and products dealing with diet
and nutrition. A must-read for
those interested in keeping up on
the latest health developments.

Index

About the Author

Michael Anthony Janke has over 12 years of experience as a Navy SEAL team commando, and is an internationally recognized expert on the topics of self-discipline, teamwork, and individual performance. Mike is a professional speaker, consultant, and the founder of Special Operations Consulting in Virginia Beach, Virginia. Each year, Mike helps literally thousands of people improve their lives through his books, audiotapes, and speaking presentations.

Michael Janke was born and raised on a small farm in the mountains of Northwestern Pennsylvania. It was from this humble beginning that he first came to know discipline as a force in life. After studying ancient philosophy at the University of Pittsburgh, he joined the Navy after hearing tales of adventure in a small and highly secretive unit called the SEAL teams. Having a background in survival, martial arts, and collegiate sports, the SEALs seemed like a perfect match.

In today's age of rapid change, high stress business, increasing technology, and global economies, Mike teaches people how to gain control of their hectic lives and stay focused on enjoying life. With the strong support of his loving wife Athena, Mike continues to help people from all walks of life discover a more disciplined way of living.